ISLANDS OF HEALING

A Guide to Adventure Based Counseling

◆

by
Jim Schoel
Dick Prouty
Paul Radcliffe

Project Adventure, Inc., Hamilton, MA 01936
© 1988 by Project Adventure, Inc. All rights reserved.
Printed in the United States of America.
Second Printing 1989
ISBN 0-934-38700-1

This book is dedicated to the memory of Georgia Irene Schoel
— teacher, social worker, counselor, mother —
who liked to do things with her charges,
and talk about what it all meant.

Table of Contents

Acknowledgements

To the many students, workshop participants, practitioners, community members, all the family and friends who shared in the work, to those who gave suggestions, honest feed back, enthusiasm and support, you form the essential part of the "bedrock" of Adventure Based Counseling. We extend our appreciation and gratitude to you. You know who you are.

A special thanks to those people who have had a direct impact on this book: Cindy Simpson, Bill Cuff, Tim Churchard, Joanne Maynard, Mark Murray, Dr. Dwight Webb, Rick Thomas, Beau Bassett, Rich Maizell, Barry Orms, Dr. Steven Bacon, Nicole Richon-Schoel, Doris Prouty, Herb Wostrel, Dr. Donald Nichols, John Spindler, John Elliott, John Amos, Mac Bell, Howard Richardson, Geoffrey Richon, the late Philip S. Weld, Lee and Robert Natti, and Bill Greenbaum

Credits

Illustrations
Nick Thorkeleon

Editing, Design and Production
Conrad Willeman

Foreword

Most people who pick this book up will already know that experience is the only true teacher. Even when you read something or hear it for the first time, it really only resonates with you if you can imagine it in your own experience. In that sense you already know that at some level what you are reading or hearing perhaps for the first time is both familiar and believed.

We have known for a long time that human expressions of support, caring, and encouragement build strength. These are fundamental components of how we show our love and respect for each other. We have also known for a long time that challenge and risk, in a supportive environment which values effort, create an opportunity for humans to discover and develop their potentialities.

Adventure Based Counseling (ABC) takes the best of what is known in the psychology of human behavior and makes the principles come alive. Trust does not remain just a word with an abstract definition; it becomes experience with personal meaning grounded in tested reality. ABC takes the initiative to structure psychological experience. To experience is to cope, to learn, and to integrate for future performance.

While all counseling is based on trust, ABC creates purposeful experience of trust in an environment of challenge and support. Experiences designed to be rich in responding to a wide range of human needs, such as a sense of belonging in a caring community, create a multitude of opportunities for personal challenge and growth. The essential focus throughout is the development of a sense of total self in relation to others. Responsible interaction with others and self-confrontation in a supportive environment become the means for gaining personal meaning and self-perspective.

Self-esteem is the ground from which the potential of human behavior will develop. All the daring, the freedom, and the joy of expressing aliveness are rooted in the esteem we hold for ourselves. *Islands of Healing* brings this aliveness into focus with documented and demonstrated rationale for specific interventions. Attention to quality leadership issues and clearly articulated activities and applications encourage the reader to translate and adapt these exercises and concepts into their own setting and experience.

This book synthesizes the body of knowledge from experiential learning in deliberate psychological education and provides case studies and curriculum guides in a format of vital pragmatism. The authors have distilled their considerable wisdom from experience into a useful resource book. It is an important process tool, and a landmark of healing in the sea of human experience.

Dwight Webb, Ph. D.
University of New Hampshire
Durham, New Hampshire
January, 1988

Introduction

"We do not believe in ourselves until someone reveals that deep inside us something is valuable, worth listening to, worthy of our touch, sacred to our touch. Once we believe in ourselves we can risk curiosity, wonder, spontaneous delight, or any experience that reveals the human spirit."

— E. E. Cummings

LEADING SMALL GROUPS is hard work. Make that a group of "persons in need" and it is harder still. Counselors, teachers and therapists need all the help they can get in order to bring about growth in their charges. Adventure Based Counseling can provide some of that help. Based on a mixture of experiential learning, outdoor education and group counseling techniques, it is a tool that can be adapted to almost any setting where group work is practiced.

"People are willing to support you, to show it through actions," says Debbie, a patient in a psychiatric hospital, as she describes her Project Adventure Counseling group. She made this statement during an interview following her participation in the group Initiative activity called Blindfold Square. Participants are blindfolded, then given a 40-foot rope loop (the ends are tied to form an endless piece), and asked to make a square out of it. The problem demands concentration, cooperation and communication. Support for her in this situation consisted of other people listening to her ideas, and not making her feel "alone out there with that blindfold."

Gary, a student in a high school alternative program, had this to say about trust while writing in his journal: "You must understand that I knew something change(d) but it didn't hit me until last night at about 2:00 a.m. As I was lying in bed writing in my diary about some things I had to work out and about the trip, I realized that when I was going over the lip of the cliff to start the rappel I had to TRUST people and that rope, and for the first time in my life I had come to know the real meaning of faith and trust."

What Debbie and Gary say is insightful not only because it catches an essence of Adventure Counseling. It also demonstrates how far Project Adventure concepts have reached in 16 years, with programs ranging from inside a secure treatment facility to a generic community High School. At PA's beginning the mandate was to adapt Outward Bound wilderness activities to the standard school curriculum, as an integral part of the classroom teacher's school day. In Debbie's hospital setting, PA-trained staff persons, including recreational therapists, occupational therapists, social workers, and counselors, are using Adventure activities with small, growth-oriented counseling groups. These activities are part of the overall treatment plan for groups confronting a whole series of behavioral and psychological difficulties, such as drug abuse and depression.

This is also true of Gary's school. Small groups participate in similar activities. These groups may be organized along the lines of the hospital group, or they may follow a growth-oriented curriculum for healthy and intact students who can nevertheless derive great benefit from the experiences. Adventure Based Counseling groups take patients and students through a sequence of carefully orchestrated activities. Some examples are:

- Trust exercises, leading to Trust Falls and Spotting, which develop attentiveness, risk taking, empathy, cooperation, and group spirit.
- Games, which develop a sense of fun and cooperation.
- Problem-solving exercises, which develop individual

and group initiative, spirit, independence and competence.

- Ropes course experiences which encourage trust, risk and empathy.
- Community service and learning projects , which develop a sense of caring and connectedness to the world at large.
- Expeditions (extended forays, either for several hours, days, or weeks, into "foreign" territory), which compress the above outcomes, and reinforce them in an intense mutual peak experience.

These outcomes focus on one overriding goal: **the improvement of self-concept**. Support for this overriding goal is found in the pursuit of a sense of trust and a sense of competence in the persons who participate in the Adventure "islands of healing." Trust encompasses the affective, feeling aspects of relationships, both to self and to others. Competence addresses the more cognitive, cause and effect, efficacious connections to the world. The interaction of these two elements provides for a facinating interplay of necessary components for healthy living. The Adventure group has access to both of these elements because of the ability to combine practical, physical activities with a responsible and responsive group process

Many different kinds of groups serving "persons in need" are using these activities. Learning disabled students are fully attentive while solving the problem of how to get everyone over a 20-foot area using a rope swing in order to bring blood plasma to a hypothetical dying elephant. A wheelchair-bound "physically challenged" person is pulling himself across a rope net with group members spotting and encouraging him; court-referred youth are confronting each other about their behavior during the morning activity where they all participated in a community service project helping retarded children play games; a scared, defiant and suicidal psychiatric patient is allowing a group to catch her in a trust fall; a brilliant but chronically truant and delinquent 17-year-old is raising money and providing positive leadership for a 3-day charity ski-a-thon.

These stories are coming to pass in the context of particular institutions: hospitals, schools, treatment facilities and programs supervised by the courts. Significant results in terms of enhanced self-esteem; increased ability to trust, to take risks and to care for others; and lower recidivism and higher productivity are being reported from these settings.

Groups work better together, and individuals tend to express themselves in ways they didn't think possible. As Debbie says: "Actions speak louder than words." Through the realms of physical activity, games, caring and trust exercises, goal setting and accomplishment, and perceived risk taking, new counseling dimensions are opened up.

Counseling through activities is certainly not an innovative practice. The value of activities, and of real life situations, is recognized by many theorists and practitioners. Bruno Bettelheim, for example, states in reference to hands-on crafts projects with troubled children, that "doing things is one of the best ways to counteract the feelings of worthlessness from which most of these children suffer." (p. 224, *Love is Not Enough*)

One of the losses of the mental health movement has been the closing of the "hospital farm" because of the peonage laws (interpreting the practice of patients growing their own food as a method of enslaving them). Many mental hospitals used those agricultural activities as task-oriented contact points for their patients. Through these activities, patients were able to have their own tasks, relate to the natural world, and feel a sense of worth while doing meaningful work. Certainly there were abuses to this system, but overall it was a powerful tool for the rehabilitation of patients. Small workshops in wood and art, as well as movement and drama therapy have taken the place of the activity of the hospital farm. Adventure Based Counseling has also stepped into that void.

Adventure Based Counseling is a dynamic, adaptive process. Once practitioners learn the basics, they can fine tune the techniques to their particular setting. This book is an exploration of the theory and practice of Adventure Based Counseling, designed to help readers understand those basics so that they can adapt, modify, and implement these ideas within their particular and unique workplaces.

Section 1

BACKGROUND

Adventure Based Counseling, though pragmatic in its wide ranging use of activities, tactics and approaches, nevertheless has identifiable, consistent principles that are part of a larger historical picture. In this Background section we want to outline the origins of Adventure Based Counseling, and to explore how the key elements of this counseling strategy are supported by leading theorists and practitioners.

2 Islands of Healing

Chapter 1
History

"Be ready to answer to your fellow man for the trail you leave behind. The last steps depend on the first...the first step depends on the last."

— Herman Mclville

PROJECT ADVENTURE began in 1971 through the combined efforts of the principal of Hamilton-Wenham (Masachusetts) High School, Jerry Pieh, and his staff. As the son of the founder of the Minnesota Outward Bound School (Bob Pieh, Professor Emeritus, Queen's College, Toronto, Canada), Jerry had a great deal of insight into the power of that approach to teaching. But because of the intensity, cost, and duration of the Outward Bound courses, Pieh felt that most young people were not able to participate. Jerry's remedy was to bring these ideas into the traditional school setting. It could no longer be called Outward Bound, for that is a generic term relative to specific wilderness immersion courses. Adventure seemed to be a good name because of the exciting open-ended images it creates.

Jerry sought through this Adventure program to adapt successful Outward Bound strategies and in so doing develop curriculum that could be used by trained personnel in the traditional school setting. This effort completed a circle started by Dr. Kurt Hahn, the founder of the Outward Bound movement.

Outward Bound Origins

Dr. Kurt Hahn was foremost an educator, with roots in the classical private schools of Germany and Britain. He first experimented with his Outward Bound ideas before World War ll while he was the headmaster at the Salem School in southern Germany. Because he was Jewish, he found the situation in the country to be untenable and emigrated to Britain, where he continued to develop his ideas. In essence, Dr. Hahn felt that the classical school curriculum was not enough for the development of the total child. There needed to be, in addition, places for students to express themselves in the world at large. The four steps of his Moray Badge (an award young people coveted at his Gordonstoun school in Scotland) illustrate this:

Dr. Hahn felt that the classical school curriculum was not enough for the development of the total child.

1) Perform to standards in a range of athletic events.
2) Undertake expeditions by sea or land.
3) Carry through successfully some long term project of skill, craftsmanship or research, of personal choice.
4) Demonstrate preparation for some kind of public service.

A later version became the Duke of Edinburgh's Award. (Bareton, pp.3-5)

Because there was a need, during the war, for high intensity survival training, these ideas were formed around what was to become the Outward Bound course ("outward bound" is a nautical term describing a ship leaving port). The first courses were oriented around sea training, and had an obvious practical application in the development of young seamen in the war years. Independent schools were formed to support these courses, and the present worldwide Outward Bound movement came from these beginnings. We owe the title of this book to Kurt Hahn, for he coined "Islands of Healing" as a description of what we hoped would become small Outward Bound "outposts" near major cities and international borders. (Thanks to Josh Miner, co-author of *Outward Bound U.S.A.,* and Lance Lee, Director of the Rockport, Maine Apprenticeshop, for this information.)

Adaptation to American Schools

Hahn's original impulse was, however, to work within the confines of a traditional school. Jerry Pieh sought in his Project Adventure program to bring these ideas back to the setting in which they were first practiced. This had been done before: Lincoln-Sudbury High School in Lincoln, Mass., had an Outward Bound type course in the late sixties, for example. That particular program, however, was taught by Outward Bound staff, not by public school teachers. But there were other places across the country where regular school teachers would practice Outward Bound activities, such as short expeditions, rock climbing, and ropes course. Often it was in the outing club format. Sometimes it would be part of a regular class. However, such activities tended to be isolated from the standard curriculum and were almost totally dependent on teacher interest. Pieh wanted more than that. He sought to have the Outward Bound *process* become a part of the standard high school curriculum.

The funding of a large three-year grant from the Federal Office of Education allowed Jerry to hire key staff with Outward Bound backgrounds and to begin the planning of a new curriculum approach. Many teachers were involved in the planning of this grant, and involved themselves in Outward Bound and other training experiences. Teachers, Project Adventure staff, and administrators then set to work writing and experimenting with curriculum. The largest component was focused on tenth grade physical education, but English, history, science, theatre arts, and counseling were also explored in the context of what came to be known as "Adventure Activities." In 1974 the evaluation results earned Project Adventure an award as a National Demonstration site for the Office of Education's dissemination project, the National Diffusion Network (NDN).

Bob Lentz was the first Director of Project Adventure and he stayed with PA until 1980. Bob had been a teacher, a principal and had worked at Outward Bound as director of their teacher training programs from 1969-1971. His experience with teacher education and his work with the National Diffusion Network of "teacher-to-teacher replication of model programs" was a great match for Project Adventure. Bob also had a deep understanding of the power of the experiential learning process. Here he describes one of his original insights about the effect of an

Pieh...sought to have the Outward Bound process become a part of the standard high school curriculum.

experiential/internship program on students:

> "We got back report after report on these kids about what a lively, alert, intelligent, responsible student this is. And you would visit the student on his project and my God he was alive and alert and responsible. You'd look through his records and ask teachers about him and the answer you'd get was, 'wasn't alive, was lethargic, wasn't alert, wasn't responsible.' A kid would come back off his project— for a few days he'd be alive and alert, then his old behavior would come back. That simply said to me, we're missing some vital things here."

A kid would come back off his project—for a few days he'd be alive and alert, then his old behavior would come back.

Bob found in the Project Adventure curriculum a way to bring about those changes inside schools, and to institutionalize the process. As Josh Miner and Joe Boldt say in their history of Outward Bound (p. 336), "No other innovative educational proposal spinning off from Outward Bound has enjoyed a greater success with the educational establishment than Project Adventure." The reason for this success was the willingness and ability of the Project and its staff under Bob Lentz's leadership to work with teachers and schools, empowering them to institutionalize the curriculum changes.

Origins of Adventure Based Counseling

Adventure Based Counseling in its primitive form was expressed in those early years in two ways: first was the Action Seminar at Hamilton-Wenham Regional High School, an interdisciplinary four-period class which drew on a wide mixture of students (outlined under the same title in the Project Adventure book *Teaching Through Adventure*). This class was taught by PA staff members Jim Schoel and Steve Webster. Those students participated in Adventure activities, group construction and craft projects and community service. No formal assessment of the students prior to entry was made, but quiet referrals insured that half the students were experiencing trouble in school and required an "alternative" form of instruction. The Action Seminar concept was later carried into the Gloucester Public Schools where it was incorporated as the Gloucester Museum School, and later as Project Alliance.

...half the students were experiencing trouble in school and required an "alternative" form of instruction.

The second expression of Adventure Counseling was an outpatient therapy group at the Addison Gilbert Hospital, Gloucester, Mass. Beginning in 1974, Paul Radcliffe, a PA-trained school psychologist teamed with Mary Smith, a PA staff member, and another social worker from the hospital to conduct a weekly 2-hour Adventure group. The hospital therapy group concept, with its intake and consultation process, was subsequently incorporated into the Gloucester Public School's psychological services, and was called the Learning Activities Group.

The development of the Adventure Based Counseling (ABC) process into a curriculum equivalent to the earlier interdisciplinary work at Hamilton-Wenham took place with the funding of a Massachusetts State Department of Education grant in 1980-1983. Paul Radcliffe and Bill Cuff worked with personnel from Gloucester, Hamilton-Wenham, and Manchester, Mass. to refine the process of intake, grouping, staffing, activities selection, and staff training. A formal controlled evaluation of the ABC groups at these schools is outlined in Chapter 8.

Supporting Literature

Two papers provided a practical basis for ABC: "Counseling on the Run," by Jim Schoel (a Project Adventure publication since 1974), and "Confronting Passive Behavior through Outdoor Experience," by Rick Medrick (Paul Radcliffe introduced Medrick's paper to Project Adventure in 1979). "Counseling on the Run" describes a counseling relationship that espouses *growth through action*, while exploring the strategies of listening, organizing, adjusting, following up, and being still. "Confronting Passive Behavior" introduces the concepts of *contracting* and *goal setting*.

Project Adventure, Inc.

Running parallel to the development of the ABC model had been the continued work to disseminate the original Project Adventure model curricululm. From 1974-1982, Project Adventure as a program of the Hamilton-Wenham School district, received grant monies each year from the National Diffusion Network of the U.S. Office of Education. These grants subsidized workshops for teachers and administrators from schools nationally, with the aim of replicating the original physical education and experiential academic programs. By 1982 over 5,000 education professionals had attended at least a four-day intensive curriculum workshop taught by the PA staff or their National Certified Trainers. Also by 1982 over 500 schools and other education institutions had replicated a portion of the original model. The staying power of these adoptions was also significant. A 1980 study found that 90% of all adoptions since 1974 were still in place.

In 1982, after a year and a half of planning, the PA dissemination staff started a non-profit corporation separate

...by 1982 over 500 schools and other education institutions had replicated a portion of the original model.

The fastest growing trend in PA adoptions since 1982...has been in the Special Needs or Therapeutic area.

from the Hamilton-Wenham School system. The mission of the new corporation was the same, to help others implement and run a model PA program, to "help bring the Adventure home." The main change was the acceleration of the trend to work with institutions other than schools. Camps, colleges, YMCA centers, outdoor education centers, and corporate training facilities turned increasingly to PA for help in setting up an Adventure program.

The fastest growing trend in PA adoptions since 1982, though, has been in the Special Needs or Therapeutic area. Since the first Adventure Based Counseling workshop in May of 1979, over 2000 counselors, special needs teachers or therapists, have been trained. Residential treatment centers, substance abuse clinics, state and county youth servive rehabilitation programs, school special needs departments and psychiatric hospitals have all turned to PA. Because of this trend the need for a text to help others think about and plan an effective ABC adoption became increasingly obvious. In 1985 Project Adventure received a grant from the Culpeper Foundation of New York City, to research and write this book. Other publications of Project Adventure have aided in this process. We hope *Islands of Healing* will be able to continue in that tradition.

TRUST BUILDING

GOAL SETTING

CHALLENGE/ STRESS

PEAK EXPERIENCE

Fight Gravity

HUMOR/ FUN

PROBLEM SOLVING

Chapter 2
Theoretical Perspectives

"Theory is meant to inform practice."

T HE PHYSICAL NATURE of many of the ABC activities and the real-life nature of many of the service and experiential learning activities allow practitioners of differing theoretical backgrounds to use those activities easily, and to design a curriculum appropriate for their unique setting. Counselors and clinicians with behaviorist, psychoanalytic, humanistic and religious backgrounds and support systems have all been able to use the ABC program and interpret it through their own lenses. This is a process that we have encouraged. The activities, like life itself, are by definition "holistic" and are as open to differing interpretation on what and why something is happening as any other

This openness is a strength of the program.

real event. This openness is a strength of the program and one that fits in with a trend in the helping fields. "In the clinical area, rigid adherents to particular schools have receded into a minority. Practitioners who employ a diverse range of methods and theories have replaced them." (Lazarus, p. 4) These practitioners are, in Lazarus' words, "pragmatic." We see ABC practitioners as fitting into this pragmatic mold. That is, they may have more allegiance to one theoretical school than another, but they are are also open to what works.

The very pragmatism of many ABC practitioners, however, can also be a source of weakness in the area of theory. Some leaders discount the print world of theory as being too isolated from the "real world" of experience. But without a working theory base as a guide, important decisions such as those on program design, screenings for group members, co-leadership issues, and intervention strategies are made with less skill and effect. When up against a thicket of such decisions, a good knowledge of your personal and/or program theory base can be a valuable compass.

We encourage program practitioners to define their own theoretical rationale, and to continue ongoing revisiting and study of their theoretical assumptions. Theory is intended to inform practice. The dilemmas of practice in turn will provoke the need and motivation for further study. This is a continual process and, hopefully, can be an alive and exciting one. Readings, peer discussions, professional workshops and courses can continue the process of individual growth in the field, and be a source of personal rejuvenation.

We offer the following theoretical references as our guides to understanding how and why the ABC program functions. We will first examine the theoretical underpinnings of the main goal of the ABC program, the improvement of self-concept, and then proceed to key elements of the program. A key element is an attribute of the program which is needed in program designs in order to replicate the original evaluation results.

Main Goal: Improvement of Self-Concept

Key Elements:
- **Trust Building**
- **Goal Setting**
- **Challenge/Stress**
- **Peak Experiences**
- **Humor/Fun**
- **Problem Solving**

Improvement of Self-Concept

The original evaluation of Project Adventure Curriculum (1974) that led to the award of National Demonstrator model status of the curriculum by the U.S. Office of Education found a significant increase in the self-confidence of tenth grade physical education students, as measured by the Tennessee Self-Concept Scale. (See Appendix A: Evaluations) The three-year evaluation of ABC groups in three Massachusetts school systems (1980-1983) also showed measurable and significant gain in self-concept as defined by the Tennessee. Self-concept, then, is an "umbrella concept" that has repeatedly been shown to improve as a result of a properly designed and run ABC program.

Carl Rogers defines self-concept as the way an individual perceives himself in relation to the world around him. This concept is essentially your image of who you are and what you value, both in yourself and in relationships with others. Your self-concept is acquired over the years by experiencing how other people react to you. For example, if whenever anger is expressed openly you experience a feeling of physical or emotional isolation, you might learn to deny yourself the right to express, or eventually, to feel anger. Then, when angry feelings bubbled up, you might experience both isolation and denial. This would lead to a lack of "congruence" in Rogers's view, between "self" and "organism," and lead to a loss of self-esteem and a more negative self-concept. Conversely, to the extent that a person's self-structure can become "congruent" with the real life experience of the person, then the person can grow in integrity, a sense of positive worth, and the ability to take the risks necessary to grow.

Stanley Coopersmith's work on self-esteem supports the more expansive theories of Rogers. Coopersmith found that persons with low self-esteem characteristically see themselves as inferior, and lacking in the inner resources to tolerate or reduce the anxiety readily aroused by everyday events and stress.

William Fitts originated the Tennessee Self-Concept Scale which was the original Project Adventure evaluation instrument in 1974 and was used also in the Adventure Based Counseling evaluation (1980-82). To Fitts, "the person with a clear, consistent, positive and realistic self-concept will generally behave in a healthy, confident, constructive and effective way...." From his extensive research on the Tennessee, Fitts found that "such persons are more secure, confident and self-respecting; they have less to prove to others; they are less

Self-concept, then, is an "umbrella concept" that has repeatedly been shown to improve as a result of a properly designed and run ABC program.

threatened by difficult tasks, people and situations; they relate to and work with others more comfortably and effectively; and their perceptions of the world of reality are less likely to be distorted." (Fitts, 1970, p. 15)

For Fitts, as well as for Rogers and Coopersmith, a chief cause of a negative self-concept is a series of failure experiences. These experiences, often stemming from an early age, set a pattern for a lack of confidence in entering new relationships, taking on new tasks or making difficult decisions. A basic hypothesis of the ABC program is that a series of well designed adventurous activities which focus on success experiences will help a person to break the cycles of failure and bring about an increase in that person's ability to feel good about himself. An enhanced ability to take the risks necessary for further growth will follow from this base.

The key elements that follow are present in all well designed programs and are essential, in our judgement, to replicating the results of past and on-going successful programs.

Trust Building

trust *(n)* 1. Firm reliance on the integrity, ability, or character of a person or thing. (*American Heritage Dictionary*)

One of the stronger points of the Adventure curriculum is a series of physical trust-building activities which are "required" of all participants. Whether it's spotting on the low elements or solving an Initiative problem, there is a natural rationale for all to participate. Engaging in these activities proves to the group participants that they can be trustworthy in risk situations, and that they can rely on others to be there. The physical nature of the program activities builds in the necessity of achieving a basic level of physical trust before moving on to more complex psychological and social interaction trust issues. Later activities recycle the trust themes as participants risk feeling foolish, failing or in other ways becoming vulnerable to social judgement. Appropriate trust and risk-taking judgements are intertwined necessarily.

The therapeutic value of these trust exercises is to increase the quality of group development in building a sense of community and team support. The group proceeds to move more quickly to develop emotional trust, and to be able to take emotional risks more easily in the developing climate of trust. "High group cohesion leads to sharing, openness, acceptance and support of others." (Johnson and Johnson, 1982, p. 410)

The fundamental importance of trust development is well recognized. "Faith and trust in self and the other person is such an essential ingredient in relationships that it cuts across and interacts with all other components…" of the self-concept system. (Fitts, p. 15) Erik Erikson's eight stages of human development places the establishment of trust as the first basic task of life development. Each successive "Identity Stage" of a person's life is formed on the basis of this ability to trust. Without trust there is no "glue" to hold relationships together, and indeed no identity possibility. Abraham Maslow's "hierarchy of needs" also puts trust as one of the most important "basic needs" of an individual. To the extent that these needs are not met, an individual will be set back in developing a healthy, productive life.

All therapeutic relationships obviously must work from a basis of trust. The beauty of the Adventure approach is that there is a built-in rationale for the group to "practice" trust. The trust activities are necessary for physical safety skills practice. They can be repeated throughout the year for maintenance of safety, group cohesion and individual trust development. Members begin to see the process of relying on their group as the ground for further growth through risk taking.

The physical nature of the program activities builds in the necessity of achieving a basic level of physical trust before moving on to more complex psychological and social interaction trust issues.

Without trust there is no "glue" to hold relationships together.

Goal Setting

Kurt Lewin and associates found evidence in 1944 that a person will experience psychological success if:
1. He is able to define his own goals.
2. His goals are related to central needs and values.
3. He is able to define the paths that lead to the accomplishment of these goals.
4. The goals represent a realistic level of aspiration, neither too high nor too low, but high enough to challenge. (Lewin, p. 195)

The Full Value Contract has both a physical safety rationale and a therapeutic rationale.

The experiential learning model we use places an emphasis on rewards for the learner which are intrinsic to the learning activities. The group and individual goal setting of the ABC process makes it much more likely that the intrinsic rewards of a learning activity will be on target for both the group and the individual. Each person, then, has tangible evidence that his actions make a difference.

In the ABC model, specific goals and a general guiding contract, the Full Value Contract, are both important to moving towards a better functioning group. The Full Value Contract has both a physical safety rationale and a therapeutic rationale. In the early stages of the process, members agree "not to devalue or discount themselves or other group members." This means observing the safety and spotting rules, and agreeing to speak up and confront others if they see an unsafe situation developing. It is important for all members of the group to "buy-into" this safety principle—it promotes a sense of shared responsibility for everything the group does. The transfer from physical safety to emotional safety and health follows rather easily by implication. If participants can speak up when a group member is not paying attention to correct spotting on the Tension Traverse activity, they may also soon be able to speak up when that same member needs some help figuring out how to make a general behavior goal more specific and manageable.

The experiential learning model we use places an emphasis on rewards for the learner which are intrinsic to the learning activities.

With the goal-setting process in place, members of an ongoing group know what the overall group goal is and what their individual goals are for an Adventure activity. "To the extent that members participate in their own goal setting they will be more active learners, be more invested in the process, and be less likely to scapegoat or act out." (Lewin, Lippett and White, p. 271) Goal setting is also a way to keep members focused on the present and future. It establishes the habit of planning how to meet one's needs realistically.

The use of goals and contracting for individuals and groups to begin to move toward achievement is supported by the literature of Transactional Analysis (TA). This approach emphasizes the power of the "decision to change" implicit in a contract with specific goals. Reflecting this basic optimism about change, Harris wrote "I believe that early positions can be changed. What was decided can be undecided." (Harris, p. 66) The ABC process follows also the TA practice of stressing the avoidance of global contracts such as "I want to be happy" and instead urges individuals to set specific goals which can be reached through disciplined effort.

The transfer from physical safety to emotional safety and health follows rather easily by implication.

The work of William Glasser, which has been an effective guide to many educational and therapeutic programs, also supports the importance of goal setting. Glasser defines responsibility as "the ability to fulfill one's needs and to do so in a way that does not deprive others of the ability to fulfill their needs." (Glasser, p. 13) The reality therapist teaches clients better ways to fulfill their needs, often making directive statements on specific planning options. The ABC practitioner may follow a similar approach, as the needs of the group members may call for a more directive approach in helping to set and monitor goals. This is not an either/or approach and facilitators are encouraged not to become too dogmatic. Often the discovery approach is more appropriate for goal setting, where the facilitator takes a more client-centered approach to goal setting. (Rogers, 1951)

Transferring the gains of the therapeutic intervention to the life of the participant outside of the group has been a problem for some short-term and self-contained experiential programs. The goal-setting and contracting process helps the ABC group deal with the transfer issue in a concrete way. The ongoing nature of many ABC groups—for ten weeks up to two years, with group members most often living and participating in their community—further facilitates the transfer of gains to "outside challenges" facing the members in their community lives.

Challenge/Stress

Perceived risks and "impossible tasks" that are physically demanding are important Adventure experiences. Group members' first reaction to looking at a particular Initiative or a high ropes course event is often "no way, Jose!" But if the program has been properly designed and led, the members have a good chance of rising to the challenge and experiencing success. This may be to their surprise and, for certain, to their delight.

The therapeutic value of challenging events has been addressed by Dr. Hans Selye. In an article in *Psychology Today*, "On The Real Benefits of Eustress," he outlined how dealing with stress effectively did not mean avoiding situations which evoked a "stress response." On the contrary, he suggests that finding an appropriate set of challenging activities and approaching them with the right attitudes (such as hopeful anticipation), promotes "eustress." This is a more balanced physiologic stress response which tends to promote physical and mental health. Selye thinks that much chronic negative stress of daily modern life is a result of not enough appropriate challenge, or the lack of "good" stress, or "eustress." (Selye, p. 60-70)

Youth in trouble are often caught up in the judicial system because they have done high risk activities such as provoking a fight, stealing a car, setting a fire, etc. Many of them are not unused to challenge and, in fact, often seem driven to adrenalin surge activities. However, they do not seem to know how to learn socially acceptable ways of challenging themselves and of finding rewards and meaning for doing so.

Dr. Sol Roy Rosenthal's research on risk exercise has discovered that many participants of such risk activities as horseback riding, skiing, flying, etc., experience a state of euphoria afterwards, a "natural high." Such euphoria is rarely as deeply experienced after regular repetitive physical exercise. The lack of regular risk activities, Rosenthal believes, may be a factor regarding a widespread depression in much of today's youth. This depression is caused by a lack of "norepinephrine" (a brain chemical that effects the adrenals), at the receptor sites in the brain. The "norepinephrine" is released during risk activity. This resulting depression can lead to violent acts or substance abuse as youth desperately seek to climb out of their low affect states.

The ABC program deliberately designs situations of "perceived risk" where participants will experience stress. The use of individual and group goals for participating in activities, however, removes the activities from the thrill-seeking category and puts them in a context of self-improvement and social meaning. If group members learn that they can experience and overcome difficult challenges with the support of the group, and consequently feel rewarded for achieving their goals, then a powerful success experience has been generated. In our experience this dynamic of learning to "go for it" positively rather than negatively is a prime ingredient in the ABC formula.

"The greatest of human freedoms is the freedom to choose one's attitude in a given set of circumstances, to choose one's own way." (Frankl, p. 65) With this statement Viktor Frankl summarizes the method of beating stress that he discovered in surviving Hitler's concentration camps. If one can find meaning in a situation and can choose one's attitude, then one can survive. Similarly, many ABC participants discover that "stress" can become "eustress," that the habit of self-challenge can be rewarding, that the common denominator to such transformations is a habit of mind for seeking and finding meaning in challenge.

The ABC program deliberately designs situations of 'perceived risk' where participants will experience stress.

Peak Experience

The term "peak experience," as used in the ABC curriculum refers to a challenging group or individual experience which is the culmination of a particular sequence of skill building, preparation training. Examples would be a difficult high ropes course element, a rock climbing outing, a long dory row or a service project outing with a group of Down's syndrome students.

Abraham Maslow in his research on psychologically healthy individuals, asked his subjects to describe how they felt differently in their happiest, most fulfilled moments, which he called "peak experiences" for his subjects. Among other qualities his subjects reported that they felt "most uniquely themselves," and "self-validated." He called the peak experience an acute identity experience of the most positive kind and one his subjects repeatedly learned from. Although Maslow's research was with individuals he defined as psychologically healthy, in our experience many of the "people in need" in ABC groups have had similar peak experiences during (but not confined to) those activities designed to pull it all together.

Similarly, Miholyc Csikszentmihayli, in interviewing persons who were participating and excelling in activities demanding intense involvement and challenge, found that his participants described similar characteristics of mind. He coined the term "flow state" and listed the following characteristics:

• Merging of action and awareness.
• Centering of attention on a limited stimulus field.
• Loss of self-consciousness, transcendence of individuality, or fusion with the world.

- A perception of control over self and the environment.
- Coherent, noncontradicting demands for action, and clear, unambiguous feedback concerning the person's actions.
- The absence of a need for external rewards.

Both Maslow and Csikszentmihalyi offer a similar way to conceptualize the power of the peak experience. For there are times when the "island of healing" seems to begin to shine. During a challenging task things can just "come together." Instructors use words like "jell," "good chemistry," "magic" to describe those times to themselves...a suddenly silent two minutes rowing the dory together, a time when the whole group is transfixed watching a student attempt a high climb that they all know means so much to that student.

Because they are such positive, even joyful times, the instructor and the group can use them as beacons for the group, as acute-identity experiences of the most positive kind. They then tend to become self-validating times that bond participants to the group and to a deeper understanding of the healing and growth process.

Steven Bacon offers a further explanation for the power of peak experiences and for the Adventure learning process as a whole. Bacon believes the character-change component of Outward Bound is a form of "metaphoric" education. Participants immersed in profound experiences cannot help unconsciously absorbing lessons for their lives. A young woman's behavior at important points in her life can resonate with the metaphoric lessons from her earlier peak experiences. She "knows" what to do in "similar" situations.

Bacon refers to a young woman on a Outward Bound course who was wary about assuming the responsibility for belaying another student; she would hang back and offer excuses for not proceeding. "When this woman eventually masters belaying and succeeds at catching several falls, it is likely that the experience will profoundly move her. She might or might not consciously extract the lesson that she is needed, that she has strengths, and that she can make an important difference in others' lives. However, whether or not she receives those intellectual insights, she will have absorbed that truth at some level of her psyche. Given that new learning, it is very likely that her relationship with her family will be altered when she returns home. While it is difficult to know if she will be completely different, it is safe to argue that she will be able to participate more freely in the family milieu and will be more supportive of other family

During a challenging task things can just "jell"...The whole group is transfixed watching a student attempt a high climb that they all know means so much to him.

They...become self-validating times that bond participants to the group and to a deeper understanding of the healing and growth process.

members during stressful periods." (Bacon, p.5)

Humor/Fun

People in need often have understandable reasons for being unable to laugh easily. For this very reason the intentionally humorous games and Initiatives that are integral to all Project Adventure curriculum are a key element of a functioning ABC group.

Humor as a Reliever of Tension

Norman Cousins, in *Anatomy of an Illness*, describes the curative power of laughter in the course of his recovery. Cousins documents how his personal regimen of "laughter therapy" helped him back to health from a life-threatening illness to his immune system. Cousins quotes Freud's fascination with humor as a reliever of tension. Laughter is one of the organism's intrinsic stress-fighting mechanisms, Cousins believes, and helps restore the physical and mental balance of the body necessary for health.

Group members may be familiar with the negative, often sarcastic, humor used by adolescents to put down a peer in a group. Laughing with others and with or at oneself, however, as a positive life-supporting activity is often foreign to persons in need. A successful group leader will find opportunities for a positive humorous slant as he plans activities. For some members, actually setting a goal of being able to laugh at themselves could be appropriate. For example, a patient at the Greystone Psychiatric Hospital in New Jersey felt that her learning to let go, act foolish, and laugh during the activity Samurai Warrior (played with styrofoam swords accompanied with ritual dying and plenty of noise and running around), was the most significant breakthrough she made in her group.

Problem Solving

Healthy individuals are confident of solving problems that come up in their lives. They are able, in most cases, to assess a problem, determine alternative solutions, choose the best solution and marshall the resources necessary to carry it out. Participants in ABC groups generally need to work on their problem-solving skills.

A major strength of the ABC model is that participants are

continually put in situations where they must work as a group to solve problems. In the activities known as Initiative problems, this is most clear. Participants are given a set of parameters and safety guidelines to a problem, and asked to solve the problem in the most efficient way. There is usually more than one way to solve it. This approach allows participants to experience firsthand the necessity of successful problem-solving skills. The reflections on the activities can be used to analyze the session and reinforce the learning of these skills.

There is a significant trend among behavioral group theorists to emphasize the acquiring of problem-solving skills, and other specific skills. In *Social Learning Theory* (1977a), A. Bandura stresses the importance of learning problem-solving skills and the effect of modeling, imitation and vicarious reinforcement factors in learning these skills. An experiential ABC group going from one problem-solving activity to another, is a safe place to try on and to rehearse the new skills necessary for meeting problems with confidence.

Paul Harmon and Gary Templin, in a recent paper "Conceptualizing Experiential Education," outline the work of Bandura in the 1970's as forming a strong theoretical basis for the effectiveness of experiential education in general and the standard Outward Bound course in particular. Bandura, they note, having been influenced by the developments in cognitive psychology, has developed a Theory of Self-Efficacy. This theory encompasses both the learning of performance skills and the motivation to use them. "The present theory is based on the principal assumption that psychological procedures, whatever their form, serve as means of creating and strengthening expectations of personal efficacy...an efficacy expectation is the conviction that one can successfully execute the behavior required to produce (anticipated and desired) outcomes. Expectation alone will not produce desired performance if the component capabilities are lacking. Moreover, there are many things that people can do with certainty of success that they do not perform because they have no incentives to do so. Given appropriate skills and adequate incentives, however, efficacy expectations are a major determinant of people's choice of activities, how much effort they will expend, and of how long they will sustain effort in dealing with stressful situations."

So, in addition to learning effective problem-solving skills, a therapeutic program can address the issue of strengthening motivation to persist in the face of difficult, stressful situations, then members have a greater chance of achieving "mastery of performance" or success.

The fact that the problem-solving process is experiential deepens the process of learning problem-solving skills as participants all need to be involved with their bodies, minds and emotions to succeed. The passiveness and resistance to learning new skills that many traditional groups exhibit is eased by this Initiative approach. "The resistance of group members to changes observed by other members is a typical restraining force in a problem-solving situation. One of the most successful strategies for changing the direction of this force is to involve the resisting members in diagnosing the problem situation and planning the solutions." (Johnson and Johnson, p. 410)

The learning of problem-solving skills in the playful world of Spider's Webs and Nitro Crossings (Initiative problems), pays dividends as the participants transfer these skills to their settings outside of the group. These "generalizations," to use the behaviorist term, are one of the joys of leading a successful group for the practitioner. This comment from a participant in the Quest program (a court-referred program written up in Chapter 10): "It really helped out my home life. Like, before coming, me and my mom were like at each other's necks. Since coming to this group we're getting along a lot better, talking to each other when we need to..."

Learning new problem-solving skills can be targeted for challenges encountered outside the group through the goal-setting and contracting process, further increasing the likelihood of successful transfer of learning. This transfer methodology helps answer critiques of self-concept theory (Shavelson and Marsh), which find little evidence for the idea that improvement of global self-concept will improve performance in a specific skill area (i.e., math skills). In the ABC process, specific skills are targeted as necessary, then rehearsed, and the ability to persist in applying these skills under stress is repeatedly encouraged.

The passiveness and resistance to learning new skills that many traditional groups exhibit is eased by this initiative approach.

Theoretical Overview

The conceptual framework we have referenced for the key elements of the curriculum can be regarded as covering the feeling, the thinking and the doing dimensions of human experience. The following structure is representative of the integrative and interactive structure underlying the ABC model (Thanks to Dr. Rich Maizell, school psychologist and Project Adventure certified trainer, for this triangle):

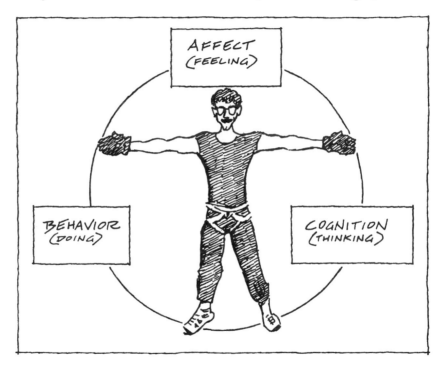

These three aspects of the human experience are addressed in a comprehensive way by the curriculum, as we shall explore throughout this book. The physical nature of the activity-based curriculum captures the doing side of experience. The trust building, challenge elements, and empathy provoking experiences address the feeling side of experience. The goal-setting and problem-solving elements of the curriculum address the thinking side of experience. In a typical ABC session of one to two hours, all three aspects will ordinarily be addressed in a planned and integrated fashion. Understanding this process on a theoretical level helps the practitioner understand the sources of power in the curriculum, and the care needed in implementing the curriculum with people in need.

The Behaviorist Perspective

If behaviorists were co-leading an ABC group, they would stress measurable change that comes as an outgrowth of experience. The activities to the behaviorist would be employed as a stimulus to provoke behavior to be reinforced positively or negatively. This behavior reinforcement comes in many forms during the Adventure group, such as peer pressure and point system rewards. Social-Learning practitioners such as Bandura or Mischel emphasize modeling, imitation and vicarious reinforcement as potent forces in the learning of new behaviors. The group as the change agent encapsulates the notion of modeling and imitation. The group arrays its cognitive, emotional and physical resources to generate novel responses to problems.

The Cognitive Psychology Perspective

Cognitive psychology is the study of how our external world is represented in our minds. People are viewed as complex beings who thoughtfully organize themselves to deal with real life situations. The ABC group is structurally representative of defining rules, making plans, and developing strategies in order to solve experimental and real life problems. It therefore offers a periscope view into the problem-solving process. It explains the structural power of the ABC model, which provides the necessary framework for positive problem solving to occur; specifically the Brief/Activity/Debrief cycle, goal setting and contracting.

The Affective Perspective

The inner Affective experience is the third consideration of this theoretical triad. The positive valuing that is the primary mission of the ABC group comes from the this affective, feeling realm. The construct of a full value, or positive self-concept, is an outcome or function of ego strength: the ability to be in touch with the external world in a healthy and fulfilling way. ABC allows clients to fulfill what Maslow calls "B" or Basic Needs. These include the need for safety, love and self-esteem. The "island of healing" is a metaphor for exploration in safety. The full value contract provides for acceptance, and the experiential process offers opportunity for achievement and the growth of self-esteem. Erikson sums up this process quite simply: "The reestablishment of a state of trust has been found to be the basic requirement for therapy." (Erikson, p. 248)

The ABC group is structurally representative of defining rules, making plans, and developing strategies in order to solve experimental and real life problems.

Conclusion

The "island of healing" is a metaphor for exploration in safety.

Because of the comprehensiveness of the ABC approach, the range of possible theoretical underpinnings is wide. We have outlined our principal theoretical guides, both to help you understand where we are coming from, and to aid you in the refinement of your approach to the theory base that makes most sense for your program and institution. There are large opportunities for further thinking and research on the interactive nature of the approach. We do feel strongly that practitioners need to pay attention to their theory base, and to the integrated and comprehensive nature of the curriculum with which they are working.

Section 2

THE ADVENTURE *WAVE*

Adventure counseling acts like a wave: peaks and valleys, turbulence, excitement, periods of calm and periods of activity. Through the action of the wave things are happening: preparing and negotiating in the valley, experiencing the activity at the crest, and analyzing and accounting on the other side. When one wave is finished, there is always another, and then another right behind. Then there are those rollers we know as "peak experiences." If one experience was particularly difficult, there are other chances in the offing. If it was satisfying, that's even better for the next one. For the counselor, all sides of the wave provide opportunities. Activities on the wave elicit behavior. Behavior in controlled situations is the bread and butter of the Adventure counselor, for the behavior can then be treated with insight, reflection, support, repetition, confrontation, or be left alone, according to group counseling skills.

28   Islands of Healing

Chapter 3

Bedrock:
The Foundation of Adventure Counseling

"...Aaaaah the shapes a bright container can contain."

— Theodore Roethke

THE ADVENTURE WAVE implies exciting and powerful activity. If that activity doesn't have strong, informed support, it may be wasted and even destructive. Foundations and parameters are therefore important, so that the activity can be prepared well, and controlled. A solid "bedrock" is the crucial first step in beginning to implement an Adventure Based Counseling program, and will go a long way toward insuring the success of first attempts.

Give everyone a break: plan early and well.

The Adventure Wave itself has three main components called Briefing, Leading and Debriefing. Each topic will be treated in depth in Chapters 5, 6 and 7. In this chapter we discuss laying the foundation, and in the next developing curriculum for a successful program.

Thus the key components of a successful ABC program are :

- **Bedrock:**
  The Foundation of Adventure Based Counseling
- **Sequencing:**
  Developing Curriculum for the Adventure Experience
- **Briefing:**
  Preparing the Group for the Adventure Experience
- **Leading:**
  Implementing the Adventure Experience
- **Debriefing:**
  Processing the Adventure Experience

The Briefing/Leading/Debriefing cycle forms a continuous wave supported by the Bedrock:

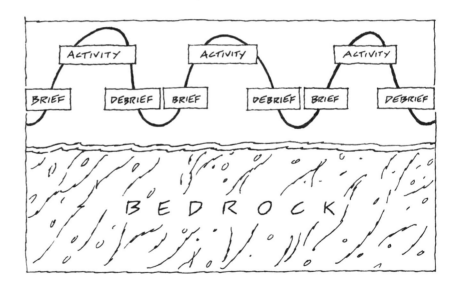

Bedrock deals with these issues:

- **Definitions**
- **Goals/The Essence of Adventure**
- **Developing a Proposal**
- **Leadership and Training**
- **Program Resources**
- **Intake Procedures**
- **Group Formation Considerations**

Definitions

The Adventure/Experiential Education field has developed a language that can at times be considered obscure. Such terms as Brief/Debrief and Initiative may not mean anything to you, at least anything special. In addition, many terms that we use in this book have their own special emphasis, or shade of meaning. Here's a list of terms that will aid you in your reading. Each will be expanded as we go along, using these definitions as a starting point.

Accessible Challenge: Adventure activities which are made accessible for persons with disability, and which serve the purposes of upgrading skills or mainstreaming (integration). The adaptations are made in the spirit of Adventure!

Acting Out Behavior: Those behaviors that occur as a result of unresolved unconscious material. This needs to be contrasted with "acting up" behavior, where an individual or group needs to blow off steam or do something foolish. Acting out behavior is issue-oriented and treatable. For example, a client may show anger toward the group by consistently talking during instruction and Debriefing times. The anger may be a result of feelings of being devalued by the group.

Adventure Base: Those activities that are available for use within the confines of a particular setting. This presupposes that the staff at that setting is properly trained in terms of both hard and soft skills to utilize those activities.

Adventure Wave: The ongoing Adventure process of Briefing/Activity/Debriefing, in operation throughout the Adventure experience.

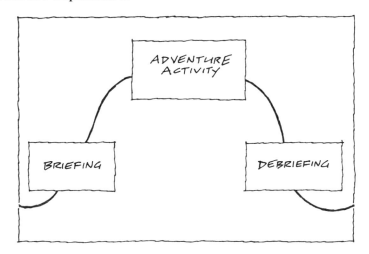

Belaying: To belay means to "tie down." It is a nautical term taken from the days of sail and incorporated into the sport of rock climbing, and now ropes course work. If a person is "on belay" in an Adventure situation, it means he is tied safely to someone else, that person being a qualified "belayer." The belaying relationship is a safe relationship. That sense of interpersonal safety is another Adventure counseling cornerstone, and every group must seek to develop it.

Briefing/Debriefing: The group discussion period. To Brief is to inform. In the briefing discussion period there are two levels of "information," 1) instructions that the leader gives the group, much of it non-negotiable safety information and 2) shared information, where there is give and take, goal setting, clarification, and framing. The use of the term connotes action: what goes on in the briefing relates directly to what goes on during the upcoming activity. To Debrief is to evaluate. Everyone gets his/her chance to have input. Some Debriefs need to be directive, where the instructor talks and the students listen. Most Debriefings, however, operate on the group process model, using the activity as the central focus of the discussion. What did we do? What does it mean? What are we going to do about it? What are we going to do next? The discussion or processing of the activity can lead to related counseling issues.

Common Ground: Taken from the idea of common or publicly owned land, available to everyone (the town "commons"). It is a result of effective Adventure Counseling, where everyone, including the leader, shares the experience. Because of the shared experience, a chemistry of closeness can develop in the group. The whole group is "grounded" in this way. The concept is useful to bring action to the here and now. It establishes boundaries, thereby reducing anxiety and allowing close examination of "observable behaviors." It corresponds to the idea of "horizontal interpretation" (the here and now or immediate past), versus "vertical interpretation" (comparing present experiences with distant, difficult to access experiences).

Confrontation: Enacted by individuals or a group at a time when it is appropriate to deal with the devaluing or discounting that is being experienced. The confrontation is positive in nature, in the sense that it comes from the locus of a trusting group, and is intended to enhance the strengths of the group's members. It is a result of a person's caring enough about himself and others to communicate what the devaluing is, and also what strategies may be helpful in effecting a change. This process carries confrontation to the next step, rather than using it just to unload on someone. Some leaders prefer the word "notify" because of its lack of negative connotation. This word can also be used in the definition of confrontation.

Contracting and the **Full Value Contract**: Much of the Adventure Counseling process utilizes contract learning, that process whereby participants agree to operate in a certain manner. The Full Value Contract is the process in which a group agrees to find positive value in the efforts of its members. This positive value is expressed in encouragement, goal setting, group discussion, a spirit of forgiveness, and confrontation.

Counseling on the Run: This is a counseling relationship which provides growth through action. It was coined in 1973 during the early years of Project Adventure out of the need for "next steps" from profound experiences which had taken place during Adventure activities. Such connections as community service, job referrals, individual and group counseling, tutoring and classroom adjustments were sorted out and provided for students. It espouses the tactics of Listening, Organizing, Adjusting, Following up, and Being Still and is the relationship of counselor to group and counselor to individuals that is kept alive all along the Adventure Wave.

Disability: A physical or mental condition which interferes with an individual's achieving his full human potential. The term does not include social attitudes (e.g., prejudice) and physical barriers (e.g., curbs) that work against such persons. In one way or another, we are all disabled. Much of the Adventure experience teaches us to recognize our disabilities, to understand them better, to adjust to them, and to accept and cope with the disabilities in others. As

Mike Stratton says, quoting Kurt Hahn, "My disability is my opportunity."

Discounting: The act of devaluing oneself or others. It is a "violation" of the Full Value Contract.

Framing: Focus time for the group where they are asked to consider the parameters of the task at hand.

Goal Setting: The conscious effort of participants to set short- and long-term accomplishable benchmarks for themselves. It implies the ability to consciously transfer this skill to life situations outside the group.

High Elements: Those activities on a ropes course requiring a belay.

Initiative: The group problem-solving process. The instructor sets up the problem, leaving it up to the group to solve it with little or no help except necessary safety considerations. The reliance on the group solving its problems with the answers that come from the group connotes a sense of power and efficacy. Initiative is the primary avenue toward that sense of group empowerment.

Intake: The initial interview with a prospective Adventure group participant. The process implies transmitting information about the group, and gathering information about the participant.

Lead-up Activities: Those activities that need to be practiced as physical and emotional training before more difficult activities are attempted. An important part of the sequential approach to Adventure programming.

Low Elements: Those activities on a ropes course that are not belayed.

Metaphorical Experience: To take the experience in one arena and apply it to another arena. It is both a conscious and unconscious process. For example, a person grows to care for a group and expresses it through becoming an active encourager and spotter. That person begins to benefit from this in the way she conducts herself in her life by being more giving and attentive at work. Unconsciously, she may be more giving and caring in all her relationships.

Modality: A discrete area of concentration regarding important personal and interpersonal operations. Using modalities to form a check list regarding the operation of the group and of its members is a helpful tool in leading groups. For example, the "affect" or feeling aspect of a group is an important modality to consider as you decide which activity the group should do, or how intense you want that activity to be.

Monitoring: Providing ongoing feedback to one another relative to working toward one's goals. It is a strategy that can be used between partners in the group within the spirit of the Full Value Contract.

Peak Experience: An activity that culminates a sequence of Adventure curriculum. It is generally a high impact or intense experience, such as a day hike or camping trip after a series of "group building" activities. It can be a summing up experience, such as a service project. It can also be an especially intense time within a regular activities sequence.

Ropes Course: A series of obstacles made of rope and cable, designed to promote group cooperation and individual achievement. These structures are built outdoors in tree settings or using telephone poles, or indoors using existing walls and beams for attachment points for the elements.

Scanning: Ongoing assessment of the group that provides material for decisions regarding activity selection, intervention, intensity, and other leadership tools.

Sequencing: Paying attention to the order of activities so that the order is appropriate to the needs of the group.

Shared Adventure: Adventure activities that are buddied up in combinations of able bodied with disabled persons. The goal is a lack of condescension and fear on the part of the able bodied, and otherwise unattainable Adventure challenge experiences for the disabled. The result is a closeness through sharing, similar to other Adventure group experiences, but also unique because of the players involved. The term Shared Adventures was coined by Ted Fay, describing his California Model State Program of the same name and philosophy.

Spotting: The same issues in belaying are at work in spotting, but without the rope. Spotting is catching, or breaking, the fall. Insistence on good spotting means an attentive, safe group. It is used on ropes course low elements, Adventure field exercises and Trust Falls. Because of the lack of "high drama" in spotting, it is easy to lose attention, so a group needs to continually monitor itself to stay on this necessary task. Spotting as an Initiative is an excellent group activity, and invites the members to become more actively involved.

Supervision: The process where Adventure leaders consult with appropriate professionals regarding the issues of individual and group problems that arise in the group and between the leaders. For example, a resource room teacher and aide that co-lead an ABC group may have periodic consultations with a School Psychologist.

Transference and **Counter-transference**: Transference is the act of taking confused and unresolved thoughts and feelings from a past experience and applying them to present situations and relationships. For example, a participant may see in the group leader a macho, insensitive taskmaster, this as a result of prior experience with a father of the same definition. This connection may touch off acting out behavior. The leader may not know where this response is coming from, but needs to be grounded in such a way as to be able to neutralize it. This can take place through relying on the present Common Ground orientation of the ABC process.

Counter-transference is the act of the leader responding to the client by acting out the part of the client's transference needs. The client may want to stimulate this response in the leader in order to resolve previous conflicts. Utilizing the above example, the leader needs to resist playing the part demanded by the client, i.e. avoid rising to the "bait" the client has set before him. The leader needs to therefore look beyond the transaction of the moment and see into the possible and positive responses that are available to the client.

The primary method of bringing about these more appropriate responses is the utilization of the group process. This will take the burden of the transference away from the group leader and diffuse it. The group will thereby provide reality testing, taking the leader out of the "helper, curer, savior" role.

Transfer Points: Those times when group members learn and internalize the relevance of lessons gained in the group to their lives both inside and outside the group. The community-based nature of most ABC groups allows members to make these connections. (Thanks to Beau Bassett, Project Adventure trainer, for this term.)

Trust Falls: Those "lead-up" activities that provide the group with tangible experiences of falling and catching in a careful, controlled setting. They begin with the act of falling back into another person's arms, proceed to falling in a circle of people, then from a height into the arms of a group. There are many variations of these activities.

Goals/The Essence of Adventure

The great danger of adaptation is losing the essence of the idea that is being transferred. Adaptation requires compromise, possible loss of specific activities, preparation of new activities, and new staff members dealing with a unique setting and population. It is therefore important to get a grip on the essence of Adventure Based Counseling. Those essentials will then act as a guide in developing your program.

The essence of Adventure Based Counseling is that the participants' **self-concept** is improved through their participation in the Adventure Counseling Group, a group that is led in a caring and responsible manner. The essential goals are **trusting** and **competent behavior.** The key elements in accomplishing these goals are:

- Trust Building
- Goal Setting
- Challenge/Stress
- Humor/Fun
- Peak Experience
- Problem Solving

Finding a form for these essentials is what adaptation is all about. That's what Peter Willauer did at the Hurricane Island Outward Bound School when he adapted an English concept to the needs of American students. Jerry Pieh did it at the Hamilton-Wenham High School with Project Adventure. Rick Thomas did it at the Institute of Pennsylvania Hospital (a private psychiatric hospital in Philadelphia) with his Adventure-based TREC program (Chapter 9, **Hospitals**). Your program design represents a form for the program essentials you want to adapt to your setting.

Your program design represents a form for the program essentials you want to adapt to your setting.

Variations in Adventure Applications

Adventure programming is used for many different purposes. How does one determine dividing lines between these applications? Is it important? Whatever the application there is a common thread which seems to carry through everywhere Adventure is practiced. This notion is expressed by the central location of the Adventure Activities in what Mike McGowan (Challenge Education Coordinator, Bradford Woods) calls the "Adventure Zen Diagram" (thanks to Dr. Gary Nussbaum, Radford University). This diagram appears on the next page.

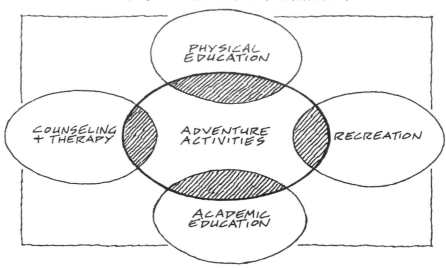

Each category utilizes the same activities. But the activities and the Debriefing strategies are practiced differently by each one. That is the reason for the interlocking circles. They all share the same "base," but have unique qualities as well. Here are some definitions that highlight the differences:

Physical Education is used to foster group cooperation, problem solving, individual challenge and physical well being. It can be used with small or large groups. Group discussions center on the activity and the lessons that the activity presents.

Counseling and Therapy focus on the need for participants to consider their behavior, and to change or modify it where there is a mutually agreed-upon need to do so. This behavior focus is accomplished through (1) Adventure Based Counseling strategies organized by the leader through "reading" or "scanning" the participants and the group as a whole, and (2) goal setting and monitoring, relative to the Adventure activity as well as to other areas of the participant's life.

Recreation can be one short session of experiences and skills instruction, or a longer period of the same, with goals ranging from the acquisition of leisure time activities to personal and interpersonal growth.

Academic Education utilizes the process of Adventure to promote a more active and involving academic curriculum for school programs. Team building for the purpose of small groups solving real life problems is an example of this strategy. The Alternative Program or Alternative School is an example of Adventure Education, as is the use of Adventure in the teaching of traditional science, English, history, etc., classes.

These activities are mutually interactive. The fact that Adventure curriculum is growth-oriented makes it a natural setting for counseling. However, a growth orientation in a physical education class touches part but not all of the counseling circle where the participant's behavior is being carefully monitored. Realistically, all of the categories deal with behavior. In this regard, these definitions do not mean that Physical Education cannot use counseling strategies. However, as an overall approach the two categories emphasize different things and therefore have different program requirements. The decision between these strategies gives you guidance regarding staffing, and other program design issues.

Section 3, **Applications of Adventure Based Counseling** gives a good cross section of groups that utilize Adventure counseling techniques. ABC applied to schools, the courts and hospitals is explored there. Accompanying this is a discussion of such issues as intensity of experiences, types of experiences, staff training, Intake, and unique activities.

Developing a Proposal

Many good ideas for an ABC group do not materialize because of lack of a good proposal and an effective implementation plan. The realities of the institution one works in must be realistically considered and addressed, a process we call "assuring institutional congruence." A principal way to make sure you will be congruent with your institution is to do a needs assessment.

Needs Assessment

A needs assessment can be as rigorous and as formal as an outside study of your institution's needs and possibilities. In some cases Project Adventure consultants have been called in to conduct formal assessments for start-up programs. Assessment tools include interviews with key people, questionnaires, and time for observation. In most instances, though, a needs assessment can develop from discussions with key supervisors, administrators, teachers, and other service delivery people. These discussions identify the unmet needs of the populations under consideration. Outside program audits or accreditation visits often provoke a discussion of unmet needs, and are useful to refer to in these discussions. Other regular evaluation sessions, core team meetings, or department meetings can be useful sources of input for your needs assessment.

There is a great deal you can accomplish in any institution, if you are willing to share the credit.

Often input from key people within your institution at the planning stage is crucial to the later survival of your program. A key person "on board" with your developing proposal can help overcome an unforeseen hurdle. Also, sharing the planning process provides a way to later share the credit for your program's success. There is a great deal you can accomplish in any institution, if you are willing to share the credit.

Creating a Written Plan

Once you have a good fix on the needs of the institution you can then develop a proposal, and make some choices. Even if not required by your institution, a written plan is a good idea because of the clarity it forces. A summary outline of a proposal should cover the following areas:

- **Rationale.** Do you have a clear and convincing rationale that addresses the needs of your assessment?
- **Objectives.** Are you clear about what objectives you want for your program and ABC groups? Is it realistic to expect the objectives to be obtained? Can they be measured?
- **Practical considerations.** What is the schedule, length of sessions, and duration of specific groups? Is the budget and resource planning adequate? Does the proposal have ongoing planned input from groups necessary for its health and support?
- **Leadership and training plan.** Have you planned and budgeted for proper staff training? Do staff have appropriate backgrounds for the groups being planned? Is ongoing supervision properly planned and budgeted?
- **Evaluation.** Does your proposal have realistic and practical strategies for evaluating program objectives?

Once you have a draft of your proposal, you need to work on the continued task of building support and working within the system. Try to answer questions before final approval meetings with directors, superintendents, or boards. Use support material from other programs. For example Project Adventure has slide tapes, videos and a network of other programs that could be of help.

The Importance of Institutional Congruence

The work of building support and maintaining institutional congruence should be ongoing. Think of it as belaying: to insure program safety, you must be tied in. This works both ways. No institution needs another idea that is a rewash of old techniques. If it is being represented as an improvement, then it should be just that. Work hard at communicating the congruence. This doesn't mean you cannot do things differently than other groups within your setting, but what you do needs to tie-in with the overall needs of the institution. A strong connection depends on good communication. If you are perceived as off there "doing your own thing," just knowing in your mind that you are connected to the institution is not enough. Adventure Counseling has been translated into nearly every setting imaginable. Successful translations have been attended to by people willing to take the time to form solid relationships with their parent institutions.

If you are perceived as off there "doing your own thing," just knowing in your mind that you are connected to the institution is not enough.

Leadership and Training

Regardless of what activities you have assembled, and what kind of program you have chosen, without good leadership the program will not be effective. Evaluations have shown that the effectiveness of Adventure programs depend on leader interest and competence. Competence comes in four areas:

Area 1: Adventure Activities Skills
Area 2: Adventure Activities Experience
Area 3: Group Counseling Skills
Area 4: Group Counseling Experience

Co-leadership can ease the pressure on one leader to be competent in all areas. For example, some hospitals team a recreational therapist with a clinical therapist. Together, they are able to address these four issues. At Manchester High School (Mass.), a school counselor teams with a physical education teacher.

Skills Different from Experience

Let's discuss Adventure Skills and Experience. The two are separate issues. Spotting techniques are Adventure skills, for example. They are taught the same as any technique: instruction, repetition, "let's see if you've got it." All technical skills of spotting, climbing, ropes course/Initiative activities, and expedition techniques need to be learned in a qualified setting.

Experience isn't taught, it is accumulated. Adventure experience means that you've been there yourself, having "gone through" a range of activities. Mastering the skill does not presuppose the experience, and the opposite is also true. Finally, having experience does not imply that you know how to lead groups or instruct others. Project Adventure and other organizations have skill-building workshops and training programs. The Project Adventure Accreditation process is described in Appendix C. Liberties should not be taken in this area.

...technical skills of spotting, climbing, ropes course/Initiative activities, and expedition techniques need to be learned in a qualified setting.

Additionally, Adventure Experience provides an opportunity for *Common Grounding*. It is one of our key elements, and with good reason. If you've been there yourself, then you've had a range of personal experiences that are the same as or similar to the ones that your students will have. You have become part of a group that has grappled with problems, obstacles, successes, and the behavior implied by those issues.

For example, the Adventure skills of Spotting, and Low and High Ropes are essential to the conduct of certain Adventure programs, but Common Grounding in terms of actual Adventure experience is important also. Glasser states, "…closeness is necessary to help a person fulfill his needs so that no teacher need be afraid of closeness." (Glasser, p. 158) Common Grounding is a step toward closeness because the leader, who has been there himself, can identify with the feelings of the student.

Most Adventure leaders come from a teaching background, where they have already been in a leadership role. Going through their own Adventure experience requires them to give up this "position" and become part of a group of other adults. And giving up "position" is one of the most important experiences for any participant in an Adventure group. The positive nature of the group frees one from the need to feel on guard all the time. This permits the "leader" to let down his hair and get involved, free from the concerns of managing and controlling a group. He can let go and have fun. Also let go and examine personal issues, look at them from a different light, with the support of the group as a foundation. The experience of "opening up" and "letting go" produces a vital interpersonal chemistry within the group. That experience can become a source of positive energy for the new "leader" taking on his own Adventure group.

Finally, it is important for Adventure leaders to continually seek new experiences, not only for upgrading their skills, but also for maintaining a positive connection to their group work "back at the ranch". Many experienced Adventure leaders fight "burnout" in this way—by giving themselves a vital experience, they get back in touch with the basics they are teaching to their students.

In the areas of Counseling Skills and Experience, there is a similar overtone, but it is, realistically, a more difficult one to identify and integrate. Making oneself vulnerable while doing Adventure activities differs from the vulnerability experienced in a group counseling situation. Yet again, we are asking our clients, when participating in an Adventure counseling session, to do just that: Make themselves vulnerable. Added to this equation is the fact that there are certain counseling skills that can only be gleaned from personal experience.

Counseling as Learning

Many effective Adventure leaders have never participated in group or individual counseling. Yet because of the kinds of persons they are, they intuitively provide powerful growth experiences and counseling insights for their clients. But untrained intuition can lead to hunches, projection, or even cultural bias. (Johnson and Johnson, p. 390) What conclusions can we draw from this, then? How can we help improve the counseling skills of Adventure group leaders?

We recommend that practitioners gain experience as participants in counseling or therapy groups. That experience can help with group processing techniques, such as how to deal with silence, acting out behavior, resistance, and body language. It also extends the concept of Common Grounding, for if the leader has "been there" she is more likely able to understand what the participants are experiencing.

Resistance to this direct experience can be overcome by viewing the counseling group as a time for learning, rather than "head-shrinking." This learning process has to do with emotions, and how those emotions relate to other people. For many people it is difficult to subject themselves to such a process of self-examination. They can be open when learning to speak a foreign language, or belay on a Ropes Course, but when it comes to interpersonal skills, the trail becomes more difficult. In addition to important practical skills that can aid in leading a group—what to do when a participant is pushing our buttons and getting us to respond in irrational ways—for that "irrationality" can lead us into transference and counter-transference issues. Self-knowledge in this area can help stave off difficult power struggles, and turn potentially unworkable situations into successful experiences. Therefore, if we define our own counseling as *acquiring skills that will aid us in our work*, perhaps we can strip away the stigma of "head-shrinking" that has been attached to it.

...if we define our own counseling as acquiring skills that will aid us in our work, perhaps we can strip away the stigma of "head-shrinking" that has been attached to it.

The Need for Supervision

We strongly recommend that leaders and co-leaders use strategies of consultation and support. This strategy of group leaders and co-leaders participating in regular and on-going dialogue with credentialed and competent practitioners allows for a greater assurance that groups are being managed effectively and safely. For example, too often group leaders have the "Robin Hood" complex of feeling that they should be able to help anyone who comes along. In addition, leaders are often left to their own devices regarding appropriateness for the group, and how to deal with specific behaviors or "crises." The person in the depth of the problem is often not able to see the larger picture. The third voice provided by the supervisor-consultant relieves the tension that group leaders experience, giving them a sounding board. It also provides a place to discuss appropriate intervention strategies, both inside the group as well as outside (for example, outside referrals for individual counseling can be processed during the supervision session). This is one of the most effective and necessary institutional "belay" techniques that is practiced.

Code of Ethics

Finally, a code of ethics needs to be considered for this field of Adventure Counseling. Responsible professional organizations have ethical codes that provide broad guiding principles for their memberships. As practitioners, we are obligated to know the ethical codes in our areas and practice our trade in a responsible manner. Because ethical codes are not sufficiently explicit to deal with each and every situation, the Adventure counselor is not always able to rely on standardized prescriptions. The most accurate measure of professionalism is the design and development of a personalized code of conduct. This does not imply that there is total freedom regarding what you are able to do. If the fundamental consideration is the protection and respect of the client, you must exhibit evidence that you have covered those important bases.

The process of defining your own personal code of ethics will be an ongoing task. Your willingness to be open to change, to reflect upon and reexamine your values and positions can only serve to make you a more expert and mature leader. Your thoughtful deliberations and discussions with others can form the basis for sound judgments, careful decision making and responsible action in the best interests of your clients. Our goal in presenting these guidelines is to stimulate you into further thinking on the issues so that you will clarify your own values and be encouraged to work toward professional maturity as a group leader.

As practitioners, we are obligated to know the ethical codes in our areas and practice our trade in a responsible manner.

- Leaders must have the ethical standards of their profession and accept the responsibility to find appropriate answers in cases where there are no obvious answers.
- Leaders should have training and experience necessary to lead each specific group and should not lead a group that is beyond their scope of training and experience.
- Leaders need to be aware of the boundaries of their professional competence and follow suitable strategies for appropriate supervision, and ongoing education.
- Leaders need to develop accurate Intake and screening procedures to differentiate between appropriate and inappropriate clients for a specific group.

The most accurate measure of professionalism is the design and development of a personalized code of conduct.

- Leaders need to inform clients about the focus, goals, techniques and activities that are used in the group and clearly point out the psychological and physical risks involved.
- Leaders must always be alert to symptoms of psychological and physical debilitation in clients and be prepared to refer clients who need further assistance to other professionals.
- Leaders should have a theoretical framework of behavior change and be able to relate their practice to that theory.
- Leaders should clearly convey to clients what is expected of them as participants in a group. Examples of these expectations are: making appropriate confrontations and self-disclosures, trying new behaviors, developing trusting and open relationships with others, expressing feelings and thoughts openly and honestly, and trying new behaviors outside the group.
- Leaders need to be aware of their own needs, values, beliefs, behaviors, and personal identity and to understand how these factors can impact group participants. Leaders need to avoid imposing their personal beliefs upon their clients.

Program Resources

Program resources (funding, staffing, facilities, and time) are often limited, so you must be willing to take the road that helps you get started the easiest and best way. Once you are underway with a functioning program, opportunities begin to appear. A teacher at a large suburban high school tried and failed for five years to get a full Adventure program accepted by the school committee. The committee always seemed to find a way to lop off the expenditure at the last minute. If he had asked for a much smaller "starter" sum, he would probably have had his full program implemented over that time period.

Doing Better With Less

If you fail to deal with program limits by trying to do too much too soon, you will be setting yourself up for frustration. In the first years of the action seminar, (written up in the Project Adventure book *Teaching Through Adventure*), we adhered religiously to an outdoor curriculum that included a "solo" (a three-day period where students are placed outdoors by themselves with minimal equipment). It was a popular activity, but it drew too much of the staff's energy away from other activities. We finally decided to eliminate the "solo," and, although we experienced the loss of a great activity, the overall program became easier to implement. In any program there must be trade-offs—you can't do it all. Find out what you can do, and do that well, gradually adding activities where appropriate. It is easy to get caught up with the activity itself, and miss the process that goes on around it. Students can get lost when this occurs.

The pragmatic approach of Charles Gardner, a shop and Adventure teacher at the Hunterdon Learning Center, Califon, New Jersey (an alternative school for Emotionally Disturbed students), illustrates this issue. He sees the ropes course curriculum as offering a "greater payback per staff and student hour than the canoeing trips we have traditionally run. We'd have to truck the kids to the river, then truck them home …in order to get to the same student objectives we can get to in 2 hours on the ropes course." They now use canoeing as a "peak experience."

It is often possible to scale down an activity and still derive significant outcomes. For example, don't be locked the 3-day format for a "solo." Try offering it as a 2-hour component during an action day, or even as a 15-minute exercise, right after a morning reading when the day is clear and the students are in a thoughtful mood. You won't get the full impact of the 3 days, but you are able to get some of it. This is adaptability, molding Adventure curricular ideas to the needs of a particular institution. The fact that these ideas are in operation from inside that institution makes all the difference. The program must be tailored to what is possible, with the knowledge that group process is what makes the difference.

Building an Adventure Base

Now let's say you have a class of ten learning disabled kids who also have emotional difficulties. You have an aide. You have a gym period once a day. "Group counseling" is written into the program. You have no ropes course facilities, and no budget. The Adventure process can work here! Group formation, Briefing, goal setting, Adventure activities, Debriefing—all these can be practiced. Start with trust activities. They don't have to be connected to a preparation for high ropes or low elements. High ropes can in fact get in the way of the profound lessons that come out of trust activities, for too often there is a tendency to rush through the trust elements,

If you fail to deal with program limits by trying to do too much too soon, you will be setting yourself up for frustration.

without looking at their deeper meaning. Include games, and if they get too silly, center the group with some Initiatives. Constantly talk with them, making connections, encouraging, building excitement. Connect these activities to a possible field trip. (Hiking and map/compass exercises can take place most anywhere, and are wonderfully gratifying in terms of accomplishment. Community service is another powerful tool.) Learning Disabled students leading younger students in Adventure games or other activities, or tutoring them in skill areas is an example of this.

As you go along, gradually build your unique Adventure Base. It is an exciting, innovative process, adapting Adventure to your workplace and generating program activities. Perhaps there will be enough budget money for a rope, carabiners, a climbing helmet, and some slings. Find some rocks, or a climbing wall or a place to rappel. Blend it in as one more activity (make certain you have appropriate training, of course).

Networking

Sharing resources with other groups is another technique. Successful networking may save you from acquiring something that you seldom use, and could save the other group the same. This could be in the form of cross country skis as a trade-off for a ropes course experience; a camp site for canoes; a gym for a theater. Not only are the resources shared, but the students get a chance to meet other people doing the same things, in different settings. Urban/suburban strategies are a rich source of this kind of sharing, each giving the other something unique.

Building community support is also important. Many school programs have been saved, and enriched, because the staff took the time to let community people know what they were doing, and what effect it is having. Effort at communication in this arena can come back at you in terms of material and activities support, too.

The following is a list of possible Adventure Experiences to illustrate the range of activities you can build into your Adventure Base:

Trust Falls
Games
Initiatives
Low ropes
High ropes
Rock climbing
Caving
Canoes/boats/rafts
Camping
City Search
Hiking/map and compass
Urban planning
Interviewing
First Aid and rescue
Outdoor academic curriculum
(nature studies, local history)
Construction/repair projects
Photography
Solo (individual and group)
Journal writing (individual and group)
Community Service
Theater
Art
Journal, story and journalistic writing

As you slowly expand your Adventure Base, continue planning ahead. This applies particularly to budgeting. You can't list an item on the budget without communicating the need for it. Bring in supervisors—have them observe, and even participate with the students. The students will want to help sell a successful program. Encourage them to ask, *"What can we do to insure that we are able to continue doing this, and more of it?"* Again, remember that communicating is an essential ingredient to being congruent, or "in synch" with the institution.

As the Adventure activity base interacts with the needs of the Adventure group, the goals you have set can act as a guide. The dual goals of trust and competence should be considered. We will spend more time on this when we explore curriculum planning in Chapter 4, **Sequencing**. Avoid the tendency to plough ahead with a sequence of activities that are not necessarily tailored to the particular situation or to the overall nature of the group.

Intake Procedures

"There is no therapy as long as the patient only asks for advice. There is no therapy when the therapist decides for the client what he ought to do." (Corliss and Rabe, 1966)

As the initial diagnostic and introductory session, Intake tends to be kept separate from the actual therapy. It can, therefore, be a dry, merely factual exercise. "Let's fill out the sheet, answer the questions, and get on to the next person."

...the counseling session begins when the client walks through the door.

Bill Perry (past Head of the Bureau of Study Council, Harvard University) looks at it differently. To him, "the counseling session begins when the client walks through the door." The "door" can be the secretary who receives a call for help, the counselor who fills out the form, or the group sessions themselves. The client who needs help views the process as a whole, unable to discriminate between these stages. For him, it's all a head-shrinking experience, no matter who is doing it. First impressions are therefore extremely important. The "work" takes place all along the line.

Joint Ventures: Engaging the Client

Some thoughts may help this process. First, the Intake counselor must see the first session as being vital to the future relationship, and act accordingly. Second, try to have the person who will handle the counseling participate in the Intake, either directly, or in a secondary screening process, so that there is a connection to that first session. Third, let the client take the lead as much as possible. Call it "joint venture" counseling, where everyone's input is valued. Goal setting, as an initial activity, can aid in this process. It not only helps in the assessment—the ability and desire to change can be measured to some degree by a person's ability to express what needs to change. It also helps set the tone for the overall counseling. The client experiences an important aspect of what the group offers. Goal setting rarely occurs without the help of the counselor, however. Hence, the joint venture nomenclature.

It is not uncommon for clients to be vague and confused as to what they expect from counseling, and what they must do to get help. They may simply want "answers" and "solutions" to their problems. In many cases, they may have no goals whatsoever, and are present only as a result of authority figure coercion. All they really want is to be left alone, and get it over with. The counselor must weed through this cluttered framework, keeping in mind that the Intake procedure should do the following:

- Communicate to the client that she will have a safe, meaningful place to work on her issues.
- Communicate to the client that she will not change without her own effort.
- Communicate to the client that goal setting will be an ongoing activity of the group.
- Communicate to the counselor the "workability" of the client.
- Communicate to the client that since the group will become very important in her dealing with issues, she should seek answers from her interaction with the group, not just from the counselor.
- Communicate to the counselor particular issues that need to be addressed.

Throughout the Intake process there must be a balance between what you would ideally like to do and what the present capabilities really are. Here are some realistic issues to address:

- *What can the group handle?*
- *Will this person really be able to function with these other people?*
- *Is this a group that can handle risks?*

And here are some unrealistic or egotistical ideas to be wary of:

- *I know I can help any person that comes my way.*
- *Won't we look good if we're able to turn this person around?*

It can help to tell participants that their first sessions constitute a trial period, subject to review, thereby giving everyone a way out of potentially untenable situations. Groups feel bad enough when a member leaves. They need to have understandable structures for departures, or that "badness" will permeate and get in the way of the counseling. The trial period also allows time for more accurate assessment. The Initiative and game sequences are significant tools for this, for they provide immediate behavioral information.

It can help to tell participants that their first sessions constitute a trial period, subject to review, thereby giving everyone a way out of potentially untenable situations.

The Intake Interview

Intake questions can adhere to the same format used during discussion on Debriefing (Chapter 7, the "What?", the "So what?", and the "Now what?"). First, find out what brought the person to you rather than starting out with qualitative or interpretive issues which can be threatening. Here are some sample "What?" questions:

- *What have you heard about the Adventure group?*
- *What happened to you, or what did you do, or what do you do that makes these people think that you need to be in this group?*
- *What is it that makes you want to participate in this group?*
- *What strengths do you have?*
- *How do you see your world?*

Next, the "So what?"

- *Why are you seeing a counselor?*
- *Why are you in this predicament?*
- *Why are you having trouble in school?*
- *Who is it that you have the hardest time relating to?*
- *What is it that you have the most difficult time with?*
- *Are you satisfied with yourself?*
- *What is keeping you from being happy?*

The "Now what?" moves us into goal setting. It needs to be upbeat, and full of hope.

- *What do you expect from counseling?*
- *What kinds of activities do you want to do?*
- *What do other people want you to change?*
- *What do you want to change?*
- *What do you want your life to be like in two years? Five? Ten?*
- *What would you like your family life to be like?*

Using these "What?", "So what?", and "Now what?" questions (Rhoades, p. 104), helps us make decisions regarding sequencing the Intake interview. It also addresses the tendency to be random in our selection of group members, in our ongoing assessment of those members, and of the group as a whole. Instinctive "seat of the pants" or "seat of the Swiss seat" (a climbing harness) decisions probably work more times than not. Making thoughtful, informed decisions can help us do a lot better, however. As Lazarus says: "...*Task readiness: how do you assess it? That is a crucial thing. There are no easy answers for task readiness. When you see a great deal of resistance, a BASIC ID scan* [Lazarus, "Modality Profile," 1981] *would pick up just where the barrier is for you more quickly than most other inquiries. Then you can work on that particular barrier.*" (Lazarus interview, Spring 1986). Please note that we have developed our own "Modality" profile that is appropriate to our needs. It is entitled GRABBS, and is explored in Chapter 4.)

Finally, if the counselor is full of spirit during the Intake, when it comes to planning for the future and talking about the activities and their potential, the client will for a time try on different clothing. The different person that comes alive (whether a flicker or a flame) is the client's potential, reflecting hidden desires and capabilities.

Group Formation Considerations

Adventure Counseling has been applied to a broad range of groups. Criteria for participation in each of these group types cannot be addressed here because of the immensity of the task. However, there are general formation principles that need to be kept in mind for each grouping. Attention to this issue can avert "group long" problems. However, you can form a more diverse group than you may think.

To help assure the success of the "island of healing," the following key issues must be considered when determining the composition of a group:
- Common Issues
- Group Balance
- Abuse Potential
- Cognitive and Physical Ability
- Degree of Intensity/Group size

Common Issues

Within the range of needs that are addressed in a group there must be potential that some of these issues will become common issues. You must be able to judge whether the group will be able to "jell" around them, so that it can move from a jumble of separate personalities with competing needs to a group of people who have devised a common purpose from their experience together. This is the avenue through which Kurt Hahn's "island of healing" can become operative.

Common issues can be artfully brought to the surface and dealt with within the context of common goal setting. For example, a group comprised of academically unsuccessful students made success in their classes a prerequisite for participation in the planned expedition. They began to monitor each other's class work. Only those who earned the trip were able to go. Those who went became the elite, the standard of excellence. There was pride and accomplishment.

Staying out of prison is also a significant common goal.

The common issue becomes a wedge in the long, hard struggle to split the shells of resistance surrounding the clients' abilities to change.

The struggle to deal with behaviors that lead to incarceration can be effectively orchestrated with a joint venture of peer and counselor pressure. The group gains identity as it works towards its goals: the members share a reason for being there. The common issue becomes a wedge in the long, hard struggle to split the shells of resistance surrounding the clients' abilities to change.

Group Balance

Balancing weakness with strength can be helpful in settings where there is great diversity of individuals, such as in schools. A group dominated by difficult clients may not join readily in planned activities, but adding one or two "ringers"—those you can count on to have a positive attitude—can provide a valuable counterweight for such a group.

Mixing Regular Education with Special Needs Students

Bring an interested regular education student into a special needs grouping. Everyone can benefit from this, and motivated students will find students with problems "aren't so bad after all." Often motivated students are packed away in a competitive cocoon where they have no opportunity to look at relationship issues that are important to a successful life. Although they function very well, they still have needs that can be addressed by the group.

The stigma of special needs can be a hard cross to bear.

One motivated student who experienced this change of emphasis in the Gloucester Alternative Program said, "I was getting dizzy and depressed that semester. All I could think about was studying. Getting involved in Project Adventure really saved me." What it also did was to give the other students a unique and rewarding experience. She formed new relationships and eagerly participated in activities. Her enthusiasm was infectious. Her presence not only helped us do the activities, it also made everyone feel more "normal." The stigma of special needs can be a hard cross to bear. This kind of mixed grouping alleviates that stigma, and puts the group on a plane it would otherwise have a difficult time achieving.

Recycling Participants from Previous Groups

Having a successful participant repeat the group can also work. No two groups are alike, so there is little problem repeating the activities. Just make certain that this person is given a new set of challenges. These can be discussed in the group goal setting. Some of the goals can be:
  • Become a trusting group member who is aware of the needs of others.

- Be a good listener.
- Challenge yourself to participate in a controlled manner so that you don't have to blurt out an answer.
- Develop sensitivities for others' limitations: blindfolded while others have their sight, operate out of a wheelchair, or be a student leader, doing tasks ranging from "go-for" to belayer's assistant.
- Establish a leadership "sherpa" program where there is official, earned status.

Having a successful participant repeat the group can also work.

These twists can change the experience for everyone. Because you know this person, and trust that he will be a good influence, you are providing the group with predictably positive input, as well as reinforcing the things learned in the first group experience for that person.

Identifying Natural Leaders in Homogeneous Groupings

When dealing with homogeneous groupings, there is still room for some of the above strength/weakness "rigging." Every group will have its leaders. Attempt to use that leadership power to your advantage. When dealing with groups of the same "stripe," you have less latitude, especially with certain abusive groupings (acting out and drug abuse, for example). These groups are generally fully of con-men and women. Group balance may be helped by developing, from the start, a tight goal/rule structure and a system whereby the group can bring pressure on its members (refer to the court-referred program "Project Challenge," summarized in Chapter 10). This goal/rule structure helps leaders emerge: they know the expectations, the boundaries, and will respond accordingly. Any variance will have strict consequences. Too many exceptions regarding the goal/rule structure will result in loss of control and ensuing chaos.

Passive homogeneous groupings can be the most difficult of all. A New York City streetworker/counselor, Bill Milliken (author of *Tough Love*, 1968) reported that he'd much rather work with gangs than with addicts. *"At least they (the gangs) have some fire and motivation."* (Discussion, Winter 1966) A subsequent discussion with Milliken underscores the current dilemma: present day gangs are involved not only in violence, but drugs as well. The passive group can be especially vulnerable to the "unworkable" participant, so an extraordinary degree of care in composing the group must be taken. Passivity is a discount in which you have to dig for movement and signs of life. If any group can use the "ringer' technique, it is this type.

A saving grace in group work is the fact that groups naturally look for a peer leader. You must be on the lookout for this leadership to emerge. We have had experiences where the most negative group member has become the most respected leader. You have to use every method you can dream up to get such a person to participate, and then even more to get him to accept his own success.

Besides your observation of group interaction, you can use a "sociogram" to identify potential leaders within the group. Have the group members write down the three persons they'd most like to "tent with" or invite to their birthday party. You can see which members are looked up to and which members are avoided. (Thanks to Andrew Mente from Project RAP, Beverly, Mass., for this technique.)

A final point: the more severe the difficulties within the group, the more time it takes to deal with the Wave cycle—Briefing/Activity/Debriefing. This is why group balance is so important. You may not be able to deal with a certain group "type" in your setting, or if you can, there may be need for some modifications. That doesn't mean that there won't be tough sledding, but at least you will have a good chance for success.

Abuse Potential

Adventure groups can address many types of abuse, ranging from anger toward others all the way to sociopathic behavior and anger towards oneself, as well as low achievement problems, drugs, and suicide. The severity of the abuse, however, needs to be measured against the composition of the group. You must consider whether the potential participant will so dominate the group that it is forced to dwell solely on that person's issues.

When mixed with a confronting population, certain "abusers" can be handled, but if group members are a passive lot, or on a different developmental plane, or simply are not strong enough to deal with the issues, then the active abuser will not fit. Tactics for inclusion may presuppose assigning a staff member solely to the person in question, giving versatility in terms of defusing a volatile situation, but this should be done only as a special arrangement, with a hope that eventually the added personnel would not be necessary. In addition, certain personality types are not appropriate for group work, most notably those who show no remorse, or have illustrated no ability or desire to work with a group.

At the Institute of Pennsylvania Hospital there is a three-level system. Potential group members must progress beyond a "parallel" level to a level where they are able to relate to others, thereby determining that they have a chance of success, before they are allowed to participate in an Adventure group.

Abusive Behavior

The following is an example of a successful "mix/match" of an abusive boy with an alternative school group. Learning and socially disabled, he was obsessed with cars and car engines, and could talk of little else. Classmates made fun of him. He acted strangely, made the girls nervous, couldn't stay on task or follow directions, and had low impulse control. Out of his frustration, he would verbally assault the other students.

Given the overall strength of the group, however, we felt we could handle him. He also had some definite strengths: he came to school every day, willing to try; he was a talented artist, and was not malicious. His abusing was a result of frustration, of never feeling a part of things, of an overall sense of defeat. He was also likeable, although he would push everyone's tolerance level.

His year in the alternative program helped him in numerous ways—he made it through his 10th grade year in high school (something that had him terrified); he felt accepted at school, and felt that there was a place for him to blow off steam; he actually completed tasks in the wood shop "projects" component of the program, and was able to say that he was a participant in the building of a small boat; he was able to accomplish one of his original goals—to participate with other group members in all the Adventure activities and all the group discussions.

This is no magical success story. Everything has come with tremendous difficulty for him. He left the program after one year, attending a nearby vocational school and studying auto mechanics. He had difficulties there, being asked to leave the program (but finish the school year), because of his lack of impulse control. He hung in there, though, and came back to the high school to graduate. All during his senior year he would drop by the alternative program just to check in. He

For the student, the hard work he did in the group provided him with a base to begin to hear people when they talked to him, and to accept the areas where he was irrational, angry and impulsive.

then went on to a post-graduate course, completed that, and now has a good job in his field.

This boy pushed the group to its limits, but the group was still able to function, and in fact gained insight into its own issues as a result of dealing with him. For the student, the hard work he did in the group provided him with a base to begin to hear people when they talked to him, and to accept the areas where he was irrational, angry and impulsive.

In another case, accepting a student without having thoroughly screened him led to a near disaster. It soon became clear that he had no interest in the group, and felt ripped off that he had been taken out of the junior high school where he could socialize, sell drugs and get into fights. He immediately began to distract other students from group discussions, devalue the activities, and generally maintain a "no connection" attitude with the leaders. He also kept the other students on edge, because they didn't feel safe around him.

The situation peaked when he took a wooden Don Quixote figure from the desk of a teacher, broke the arms and legs off, leaving the body on the desk, and spread the rest of it around the school.

In dealing with this student, the staff began to piece together the mistake they had made: they had taken a student who clearly wanted to be elsewhere, who had expressed violence toward many school officials up to that point, who was a suspect in a serious arson charge, and a person with whom no one had formed a bond in the early screening (note the warning regarding sociopathic behavior). When the problem arose, there was no commitment or fledgling relationship to fall back upon. A favor had been done for some school officials.

Adventure groups must have as their priority helping the individual group members, not finding a place for problem students.

Adventure groups must have as their priority helping the individual group members, not finding a place for problem students. Protection for the other students, whether physical or emotional, must also be the priority over serving any one individual. The group must have the capability of becoming a safe, trusting place, or it will result in a bunch of people who are simply doing activities together. A somewhat humorous postscript: climbing ropes were stolen in a break-in at the alternative program. This boy was later caught rappelling into a warehouse where he and his friends had plans to steal some coats....We had at least taught him some practical skills!

Risks are often taken in group formation, so know as much as you can about those risks. Remember that a desire to be a participant and an ability to at least buy into some group goals are two essential beginning points.

Passive behavior can dominate a group as powerfully as acting-out behavior. The student who refuses to participate, who is constantly late, and who misses school for the Adventure action day is saying that she doesn't want to get involved, that the activities are threatening, or that she doesn't want to expend the energy. On the other hand, the Adventure group is an ideal place to confront passive behavior. The Intake procedure must determine whether the passivity can be dealt with in the particular group that is being formed.

Substance Abuse

Substance abuse is one of the great passive responses to the challenge of putting together a successful life. What kind of group is best able to deal with substance abuse is one of the great questions of our age. There are so many variables. Here are two possible options for dealing with substance abuse in an ABC group:

Option 1: Substance-involved persons can participate in groups that are not specifically tailored for substance abuse if they are getting help in another setting, but you shouldn't pretend to deal with a problem of this magnitude without being able to confront it head on. Walking the line with a person who is trying to stay clean can be very effective, for the Adventure group can be a place of success, and a mini "half-way house" between the substance abuse group and the world at large. Counseling On the Run strategies need to be employed: organizing, adjusting, following up. Make the outside group part of the counseling. Make sure the other students know that a struggle is going on, that this issue is not going undetected. It is complicated because of the potential destruction that abusers can bring to a group.

It is possible for just one abuser to initiate a drug culture in the group. Accepting such a person is a real risk, but it *can* bear fruit. A student who was a chronic abuser accepted this combination treatment, and was able to pull himself together in order to bring his grades up and become a group leader. (He had been the butt of jokes because he was always so spaced-out). His production in school had been so poor that we decided to test him. He achieved an above average rank in all academic areas. There were no more excuses. We told him he couldn't work up to his potential if he continued to be stoned all the time.

He was willing to accept that and work within the confines of the dual program.

In this case, the Intake and initial monitoring during the trial period gave enough evidence that this person was workable, and would not destroy the group by his presence. (This underscores a rule of group formation: the issue is not whether this or that person will create problems in a group, but whether the group can manage those problems. In essence, the group is there to create problems that can then be managed.)

Option 2: Substance abuse Adventure groups are easier to construct, for in the treatment of that symptom there is an immediate common purpose. The same issues apply regarding willingness to try, etc., but abusers will trick everyone in the Intake, telling them just what they want to hear.

Residential situations where substance intake is not allowed is the optimum situation, of course. "Clean" periods lead to good feelings about self. Mix that with positive group experience, parental involvement, goal setting, outside jobs, and ongoing Narcotics Anonymous or Alcoholics Anonymous follow-up, and there is hope for success.

Getting [substance abusers] in touch with their bodies is an essential avenue out of that deep pit.

The nature of the disease of alcoholism and drug dependency is very body-oriented. Getting these people in touch with their bodies is an essential avenue out of that deep pit. In addition, the endorphins released through exercise and through challenging activities are comparable to some drug experiences. This is an addiction we can encourage. Mixing in Adventure activities with intense counseling work forms a compatible scenario.

Other forms of passivity that are being confronted by Adventure counseling include low involvement, unwillingness to try, poor hygiene, tardiness, inability to get out of bed, eating disorders, etc.

Cognitive and Physical Ability

Diversity in these areas can contribute significantly to the group process, but you must proceed thoughtfully to minimize the potential for discounting. Selected group members must be strong enough to be able to see the lessons that a diverse group can offer. If it is a priority to place several acting-out participants, beware of setting up a low cognitive student as an easy target. If you are confident it can be controlled, then do it. Examine priorities and visualize outcomes.

A student with low academic achievement (2nd grade reading level in the 11th grade) became an important group leader. He became invested in the group because of the success he experienced in activities removed from the classroom, where he had always experienced defeat. Originally diagnosed as "retarded," he was engaged by a counselor at the middle school, who placed him in an Adventure group. This move kept him in school and gave him a positive community of friends. He was and is severely learning disabled, but not in any way retarded. The mixture of the Adventure group and the learning disabled classes proved ideal: he graduated from high school, was named the outstanding Adventure student, and now manages a sandwich shop. The whole process took 5 years.

When dealing with low cognition, keep in mind the participant's ability to "hear" the other group members. A participant lacking that ability can negatively dominate a group as much as an abuser. Low cognitive or mentally retarded groups can have separate Adventure groups, and still pair up from time to time with regular Adventure groups for shared Adventures. Such sharing provides diversity experience without having the two groups become one. They operate separately, but have a very real and alive relationship. There is a give and take throughout the activities, everyone gaining respect and trust for each other according to his degree of participation.

Physical disabilities can be addressed through accessible challenge courses and low-level Adventure activities. Shared Adventures (mixing disabled and able-bodied students), in this context are very effective, for physical disability does not presuppose mental disability. Social interactions can provide challenges equal to the physical activities.

Buddying up with an epileptic boy during rock climbing and other Adventure activities (ropes course, camping, rowing) was extremely successful. In this case, two students stayed with him during the experiences, ready to spot him if he had a seizure. Ms. Judith Hoyt of the Association for the Support of Human Services, Westfield, Mass., and Dr. Chris Roland of Roland Associates, Hancock, N. H., have spent many years developing activities for disabled persons, building on the shared Adventures approach and working with the dynamics of the whole family unit as it engages

Low cognitive or mentally retarded groups can...pair up from time to time with regular Adventure groups for shared adventures.

the issues presented by their disabled relatives.

John Doberman, Adaptive Physical Education teacher in Gloucester, contrasts Adventure activities with his disabled students with their participation in regular Physical Education:

> *Adventure is a varied amount of things, not just sports related. You can do all kinds of things, and you do them as a group. It is non-competitive. Everyone does it. It's exciting. You can make anything into a challenge....bumps, tunnels, and obstacles. They are forced to work together.* (Interview Fall 1985, expanded in Chapter 8)

Degree of Intensity and Group Size

Intensity can mean deciding whether it is an Adventure education experience or an Adventure counseling group. Intensity is also defined by how challenging the activities are and/or how much time is spent on them. For example, a student who was appropriate for an Adventure counseling group that met once a week was inappropriately placed in a week-long residential camp that was not equipped to deal with his problems. It was too much of what might have been a good thing. There was no escape, time to reflect, or take it in smaller doses. Respect a student's barriers, noting that it takes time to change, and that change needs to be enhanced with doses of other successful experiences.

Some students need strong confrontations, where there is no escape. But there need to be "lead up" activities for group formation, and to allow the participants time to buy into the "heavier" experiences where those confrontations take place. Peak experiences built into groups that are able to engage them are good to plan. Implementing a winter camping trip can be an excellent focus for a group that is ready for more challenge. The additional intensity gives them an experience of deprivation, where they are forced to cope with discomfort and long term difficult tasks. There is no option for escape, either.

At Project RAP in Beverly, Mass., a community-based counseling center, they use camping experiences early on in their group building process, though they make certain that the stress is not too extreme for what the group can handle. They feel that the issues emerge more quickly with this format. At the Pennsylvania Hospital, substance abuse patients are given the option of a four-day Adventure intensive in the Pocono Mountains after completion of their earlier group work. The idea is to put the cards on the table: live life outside the hospital, within the same group, dealing with all

Intensity is also defined by how challenging the activities are and/or how much time is spent on them.

the same issues, in a controlled, intense, natural atmosphere.

Intensity also relates to how you choose to lead each activity. Woven into the fabric of this book is the concept of "Challenge by Choice" (explored in Chapter 6). This can mean that you only do what the participants choose at any time during the activity. It may also mean that if the participant has chosen to climb to the top of a pole and jump for a trapeze, then that person must be held to her commitment and is not allowed to change it in mid-stream. The basis for these decisions will continue to be explored.

Finally, group size relates to the standard counseling group size; 8–15 members, depending on the goals of the group, with one group leader or two co-leaders (co-leadership is also recommended).

At the Pennsylvania Hospital, substance abuse patients are given the option of a four-day Adventure "intensive" in the Pocono Mountains after completion of their earlier group work.

Conclusion

Adventure Based Counseling demands that we be aware of certain key elements: definitions (the language of Adventure), goals, institutional tie-ins, training issues (including co-leadership and supervision), program resources (the Adventue Base), initial interviewing (the Intake), and the ability to form a balanced, potentially healthy group. The program rests on this Bedrock. On this solid footing a responsible sequence of activities can be planned, relevant to the needs of your specific group.

64   Islands of Healing

Chapter 4

Sequencing:
Developing Curriculum for the Adventure Experience

What Are We Going To Do Today?

— title of the first
Project Adventure
publication

DURING THE FIRST YEARS of Project Adventure the staff often came to work after dreaming up a new idea in the night or having an inspiration come to them in the shower. Many times we'd field test those ideas the same morning. Sound familiar? Many new activities were invented with that necessity hanging over us. It sure was exciting! Thankfully, we've got a lot of experience under our belts now, though we know that if we stop dreaming up new ideas, the pizazz of Adventure will have left us. Our experience leading Adventure activities provides us with some predictability and order to the game plans that we form. There's no way around it, we've got to make choices:

What should go first?
How does the activity relate to program goals?
What if the group won't do what I give them?
What "stage" is the group at now?
How hard should I push the group?
What about the individuals in the group, are they getting what they need?

Practitioners new to the field often ask veteran leaders about which activities should be used at what times. The reply is often "My gut told me that we needed to do that" or, "The more you do this stuff, the better you'll be at making choices." Certainly there is no substitute for experience in leading Adventure activities. But as we attempt to "do" something with the experiences of our participants (help them carry it over into other aspects of their lives), so too we should "do" something with our experiences, so that we can present the best possible activity at any given time. Hopefully, the following thoughts on curriculum development will aid not only the novice, but the veteran as well.

Sequencing (making the order of activities appropriate to the needs of the group) involves the following:
- **Components of the Adventure Wave Plan**
- **Forming the Adventure Wave Plan** based on both the overall goals and objectives of the program and the information gathered during the Intake. This plan (or curriculum) is established before the group has had its first meeting.
- **Adjusting the Adventure Wave Plan** relative to ongoing individual and group needs and goals that are manifested during the life of the group.

Components of the Adventure Wave Plan

The use of "lead-up" activities is a key to Sequencing. Without appropriate lead-up, you can jump into activities that the group is not ready for. For example, use of the Trust Fall/Spotting Sequence before any ropes course activities is a must for most groups. The lead up activities provide you with time to assess, to establish rapport, to have fun, and to deal with the basic group process. You establish the fact that ultimately, the group is the issue, not whether the group is able to accomplish the activities. The group will make the experiences successful, in a counseling sense.

The lead-up activities provide you with time to assess, to establish rapport, to have fun, and to deal with the basic group process.

Sequencing also relates to the necessary adjustments that are made when one leads Adventure activities. Because the activities elicit a range of behaviors, feelings, and attitudes, your own observations of what is going on with a specific group is an equally important key to Sequencing. No two groups are the same. Just because there are similar overall characteristics does not mean that each group shouldn't be treated individually.

The initial Wave Plan is written as a base "guide" for the ongoing activities of the group. It is set up through the utilization of all the data that is available to you before the group has started. This data has its sources in: (1) overall program goals and objectives and (2) the assessment of individuals during the Intake procedure.

Program Goals

First define the general goals of the program in terms of the major anticipated learner outcomes (including those things the institution dictates). Keep in mind that as you define your program goals you should think of them as ideals.

Example: Program Goals for LD Groups
Say you have a middle school counseling group that is built into a learning disabled classroom. A primary focus of this group is "behavior management." Here are some program goals that would address their needs:
- Participants will develop more responsible behavior in their interpersonal and intrapersonal relationships.
- Participants will increase confidence and self-esteem by developing and implementing more appropriate behaviors.
- Participants will challenge old behaviors and approaches to life and experiment with realistic alternative behaviors.

Program Objectives

Program Objectives, on the other hand, stem from the more general goals (ideals). They are much more specific, and are defined as the major program/learner outcomes written in terms of measurable performance objectives. Whereas well-defined goals provide a focus and framework regarding what the group experience is and is not about, program objectives specifically detail the skills and competencies that you are hopeful of having group members achieve. In the ABC evaluation presented in this book, it is the Program Objectives that are evaluated.

Example: A Program Objective for LD Groups

Here is a Program Objective that would be useful for learning disabled groups:

- By the end of four group sessions dealing with learning to give and receive feedback (communication skills), participants will have demonstrated a significantly greater ability to convey intentions of helping, to establish trust, to understand intentions of helping, and to reciprocate trust as measured by data provided by group peers, self-assessments, and scales 6, 9, and 10 of the Platt Affective Behavior Scales.

Next, think about any special issues that emerge from the Intake process. For example, a group member may be extremely overweight. The participant is not able to talk about it, but you take a note of the fact that the eating/exercise/body-image problems can and should be addressed. This kind of information may only go so far as to be instructive regarding

how the activity is led. It may, however, cause you to eliminate specific activities in the beginning.

Another Intake issue might involve members who exhibit abusive behavior towards others. These participants may not be able to handle the full Trust Fall/Spotting Sequence. Low-level Trust Falls may need to be practiced and repeated over and over before you are able to move through the more intense falls.

Then make a list of activities available to you. An activity is not available if you haven't the resources to practice it. One of those resources of course is familiarity and expertise. This realistic approach helps you establish your Adventure Base.

With your Adventure Base in place, you can then consult the **Activities Selection Chart** (see **Appendix B**). You can then choose specific activities from your Adventure Base that will tend to address your objectives. Complete instruction regarding the conduct of these activities can be found in the *New Games Books* and the Project Adventure books *Cows-Tails and Cobras II, Teaching Through Adventure,* and *Silver Bullets.* The categories on this chart are:

- Ice Breaker/Acquaintance
- De-Inhibitizer
- Trust and Empathy
- Communication
- Decision-making/Problem-solving
- Social Responsibility
- Personal Responsibility

The following is a definition of these categories, including some sample activities:

Ice Breaker/Acquaintance Activities
Objective:
> To provide opportunties for group members to get to know each other and to begin feeling comfortable with each other through activities, Initiatives and games that are primarily fun, non-threatening and group-based.

Features:
> - Fun is a major component.
> - Group members interact in a non-threatening manner.
> - Success-oriented; tasks can be easily accomplished with minimal amount of frustration.
> - Requires minimal verbal interaction and decision-making skills.

Examples:
> Duo Sit, Add on Tag, Soccer Frisbee, Cobra, Impulse, Rope Push, Name Game with tennis balls or blanket.

De-Inhibitizer Activities
Objective:
> To provide a setting wherein group participants are able to take some risks as well as make improvement in commitment and a willingness to appear inept in front of others.

Features:
- Activities involve some emotional and physical risk which may arouse some discomfort and frustration.
- Success and failure are less important than trying and making a good effort.
- Fun activities allow participants to view themselves as more capable and confident in front of others.
- A cooperative and supportive atmosphere tends to encourage participation and increase confidence for all members in the group.

Examples:
Dog Shake, Hog Call, Yells, Python Pentathlon, Samurai, Inch Worm, Prui, Funny Face.

Trust and Empathy Activities

Objective:
To provide an opportunity for group members to trust their physical and emotional safety with others by attempting a graduated series of activities which involve taking some physical and/or emotional risks.

Features:
- Involves group interaction both physically and verbally.
- Generally involves fun, but some fear as well.
- Involves the support and cooperation of group members to care for the safety of others.
- Risk taking occurs at many levels in most of the trust activities.
- The development of trust occurs within the group gradually.
- Trust activities are chosen with the intent of building trust; basic trust activities are initially chosen and can be performed repeatedly to reinforce and insure the safety of group members.

Examples:
Yurt Circle, Trust Falls, Trust Pass, Hickory Jump, Blindfold Compass Walk, and Blindfold Soccer.

Communication Activities

Objective:
To provide an opportunity for group members to enhance their ability and skill to communicate thoughts, feelings, and behaviors more appropriately through activities which emphasize listening, verbal, and physical skills in the group decision-making process.

Features:
- Physical activity, verbal interaction and discussion are major components in the sharing of ideas.
- The solving of the problem is the established goal.
- Some frustration is generally evident in the solving of the problem.
- Leadership abilities and skills usually evolve from participants within the group.
- Most activities require at least five members.

Examples:
Traffic Jam, Trolley, Blindfold Polygon, Porcupine Progression, Tangle, Journal Writing, Lost in Maine, Bridge It.

Decision-Making/Problem-Solving Activities

Objective:
To provide an opportunity for group members to effectively communicate, cooperate, and compromise with each other through trial-and-error participation in a graduated series of problem-solving activities which range from the more simply solved to the more complex.

Features:

- Physical activity and verbal communication are involved in order to solve stated problems.
- Arousing a higher level of frustration teaches that patience is a virtue.
- Activities demand that group members can demonstrate an ability to listen, cooperate and compromise.
- Leadership roles evolve in the attempt to solve the stated problem or reach the stated goal.
- Trial-and-error approach to learning is most often employed by the group in the problem-solving/decision-making process.

Examples:
Wall, Amazon, Nitro-Crossing, Tin Shoe, Jelly Roll, The Great Egg Drop, Spider's Web, Interviewing, Team-Oriented Community Study Projects.

Social Responsibility Activities

Objective:

To provide a setting wherein group participants can build upon previous gains in areas of acquaintance, trust, communications, and decision making, to develop skill in assessing and working effectively with the strengths and weaknesses of individuals in a group.

Features:

- Success in these activities is somewhat dependent upon individuals being able to learn how to support and encourage each other's efforts.
- Activities tend to help participants learn the value of thinking and planning ahead rather than reacting in an impulsive and random manner.
- Activities tend to emphasize that participants in the group communicate and cooperate verbally and physically.
- Activities help participants develop skills in assessing problems and formulating solutions.
- Activities help relate the group to the world "outside" in an empathetic and concerned manner.
- Activities tend to help individuals and the group identify and develop leadership in the group.

Examples:

Spotting, Belaying, "Sherpa" Leadership, Litter (for rescue purposes) Construction, Community Service Projects (Environmental Repair, Social Service).

Personal Responsibility Activities

Objective:

To provide activities and Initiatives of a somewhat more individualistic nature which challenge participants to develop persistence and resistance to frustration in attempting to reach a desired goal.

Features:

- Most activities are "classic" ropes course events that are both the most difficult and trying and the most exciting.
- Activities help group members acknowledge individual and common reactions to fear, stress, and physical limitation.
- Participation in these activities encourages group support for individual efforts.
- Participation helps group members extend the limits of their self-perceived competence and builds self-

confidence by successful completion of a difficult task.

- Activities help group members to act on what they have learned about working together, supporting one another, and taking responsibility for one another's safety.
- Many activities require some special equipment and construction and expert advice and training.

Examples:

High Ropes Course Elements, Construction and Craft Projects, Journal Writing, Photography, Knot Tying and Splicing, Equipment Repair.

The **Activities Selection Chart** (see **Appendix B**) has evolved from consultation with elementary, middle and high school counselors and teachers who have practiced Adventure Based Counseling for a number of years. It was compiled by Paul Radcliffe and Bill Cuff. These categories do overlap, with each activity capable of achieving several outcomes. They have been so placed because of an overall tendency to achieve a certain outcome. You may use a given activity to elicit an outcome that does not "line up" up on the chart. And then there must always be room for unexpected outcomes, and the concomitant need for us to respond to them. The chart is a guide, a starting point, to be used as an ongoing reference. The more familiar you become with the Adventure process, the more you will rewrite this chart so that it is responsive to your own needs. The chart is a place to start in your programming, and a guide for ongoing planning.

Forming the Adventure Wave Plan

The next step is to use the above information and, in concert with your co-leader, form your Adventure Wave Plan. To briefly reiterate, that information is:

- Establish goals and objectives from information provided by your needs assessment.
- Make a list of available activities from your Adventure Base, and relate them to the "activities selection chart."

Then mark on a calendar the available days you will have for your group. For each day, consider the categories of:

- Briefing
- Activity
- Debriefing

For the initial group, write in what you plan to cover in the Briefing. Then sketch in the beginning activities, always adding some extras to cover yourself timewise, and to have a "plan B" available. In this way you can be prepared for unexpected successes, early completion, and "What if" scenarios. Be certain to explore the roles you and your co-leader will take, and plan for set up time, materials, and transportation. (Use of an additional check list entitled "Micro-Planning" will be presented later on to aid you with those details.) List an ideal sequence of activities you would like to present to your group over the time period you have, knowing there will be many changes to the "ideal" sequence as you respond to the group needs. Here is a sample 10–week Wave Plan that could be used with the above mentioned Adventure Based Counseling group.

Sample Adventure Wave Plan

A 10–week Adventure curriculum for a middle school counseling group which meets once a week. This is a minimal curriculum for the listed program goals and objectives. An additional 26 weeks of curriculum can be planned using the same format, so that the class is able to benefit from one year of Adventure Counseling.

The Sequencing of activities in the Wave Plan means that you want to achieve some specific things from each session. These specifics are then focused on in the Debrief.

Week 1
> *Brief:* Discuss the activity. Talk about the need to work together as a group, and how we shouldn't devalue or put anyone down.
> *Activity:* Warm-ups. Name Game with tennis balls; Duo Sit; Gold Line Joust; Group Juggling; Moon Ball
> *Debrief:* "What?, So What?, Now What?" Focus on group work, finding those areas where they worked well and praise them for it.

Week 2
> *Brief:* Introduce concept of the Full Value Contract.
> *Activity:* Warmups. Toe Tag, repeat Duo Sit; Group Get Up; Clock. Initiative: Blindfold line-up by height.
> *Debrief:* Focus on how they related to the Full Value Contract, using it as a time to reinforce the concept and continue to build the sense of group.

Week 3

> *Brief:* Review Full Value Contract; discuss activity; generate group and individual goals.
>
> *Activity:* Warmups. Add-On Tag; Yurt Circle; Trust sequence to Circle Pass (two-person Trust Catch, three-person Trust Catch, Circle Pass).
>
> *Debrief:* Focus on goals: definitions of their goals, initial goal monitoring.

Week 4

> *Brief:* Discuss activity; generate goals
>
> *Activity:* Warmups. Impulse; Carabiner Walk; Trust Fall from height.
>
> *Debrief:* Focus on trust, and monitor goals.

Week 5

> *Brief:* Review Full Value Contract in terms of trust, how this relates to last week's Trust Fall, and how it will relate to this week's activity.
>
> *Activity:* Warmups. Rattail; Trust Dive; Hickory Jump.
>
> *Debrief:* Focus on trust again, and how it relates to the ability to take risks. Introduce idea of a day hike.

Week 6

    Brief: Talk more about the day hike, and focus on group tasks: food, equipment, how the Full Value Contract will help them have a good experience. Set goals for the hike.

    Activity: Warmups. Tangle; Trolley; Disc Jockey.

    Debrief: Focus on the concept of Initiative, how the group has power, and that no one does it unless everyone does it. Touch on disabilities: how you can do more than you think you can.

Week 7

    Brief: Review the discussion on disabilities, and use it as an introduction to the compass (how the compass is an aid to help you when you are "blind" in the woods). Relate this instruction to the day hike.

    Activity: Warmups: Rowboat Stretch. Blindfold Compass Walk; introduce Map and Compass.

    Debrief: Tie in the Compass activity to the upcoming day hike. Focus on the need for the group to stay together on the hike, and to help each other out.

Week 8

    Brief: Introduce the concepts of "orienteering" and "orientation," and how we are all "blind in the woods" in some way, and need to find tools to guide us. Brainstorm what some of those tools are that help us live our lives.

    Activity: Warmups. Review map and compass; prepare for hike (food, logistics, money, permission slips, clothing).

    Debrief: Review Full Value Contract; set group and personal goals for the day hike.

Week 9

    Brief: Review activity, review Full Value Contract, review group and individual goals.

    Activity: Peak experience: Day hike. Hike to an objective using map and compass. Prepare a meal. Do an Initiative. Give them a half-hour solo, where they must be completely separate from the other group members. Hike to a third objective, with new members figuring out the course. Then hike back to the starting point, and go home. Save time for the Debrief.

    Debrief: Focus on the issues that came out on the hike. (Example: Perhaps the group took on a community service goal to pick up litter during the hike, as a response to the positive nature of the Full Value Contract; certain members may have shown willingness to be helpful, to take initiative, to carry the load, to control themselves, to figure out the route, to carry the First Aid kit, etc.).

Week 10

Brief: Focus on the hike, and what their thoughts about it are after a week has passed. Discuss the activity for the day.

Activity: Games: Inchworm, Add On Tag.

Debrief: Review the ten weeks in terms of their goals, connecting the issues to what they do in their class (provide plenty of time for the Debrief). Awards, pictures, celebrate! If there is to be another ten week sequence, talk about what that will be like. If the Adventure unit is over, then treat it as a termination.

Adjusting the Adventure Wave Plan

A rigid sequence will not serve an Adventure Based Counseling group. There are a variety of reasons for this, but the most important one is that each group must be respected for what is going on inside that group at any given time. The members may not be ready to do an activity. Their group goals may need to be met. They might require something more intense than what you have originally planned. Their resistance may be too severe for particular activities. Particular individuals may require attention. Adjustment of the activity may require only small changes in how you lead the activity. It may, however, require a radical revamping of the Adventure Wave Plan.

A rigid sequence will not serve an Adventure Based Counseling group.

A good sequence for one group may not work for another. There is no exact formula. The game plan that has been organized before the group starts acts as a guide. But there has to be room for adjustments. This is emphasized by the Counseling on the Run strategy of "adjusting on the run." This adjustment may come during careful consultation with your co-leader, or team leader, supervisor. It can also occur during or after an activity, where you need to quickly put your adjusted plan into effect.

For example, leaders of that middle school counseling group may observe a need to get away from the school building, take a walk to a park or up into a wooded area, and do their activities in that location rather than in the area of the school. This decision comes from observing the interaction of the kids: An unwillingness to do the activities, their insistence that what they are doing is "dumb." What they may really be saying is that they don't want the other kids to see them doing these things, that they need privacy.

"Adjusting on the Run"

Another example would be a decision to go directly to a problem-solving activity, in place of some of the games or trust activities. This decision would be based on your assessment that the group is not ready to relax, let go, have fun, and touch each other. If a group is initially resistive to the games, perhaps you should substitute the Trust Fall/Spotting Sequence, moving it from Week 3 to Week 2. The group may just not be able to loosen up enough to play. There is more seriousness to the trust sequence. You can come back and do games at a later time, if it is appropriate, perhaps in this case, during the day hike. Please note that certain trust activities are prerequisites for activities that require spotting, and are in fact a determinant as to whether a group is ready to move on to the more intense activities.

We cannot say enough how all the activities provide excellent material for ongoing assessment, both for the group and for the individuals. You will find your favorites for initial assessment. Some leaders like Trolley. Others use Group Juggling or Poison Peanut Butter Pit. If, after your scanning, you think you need a change, don't hesitate to make it.

Adjusting for Intensity

Adjusting the activity also relates to how intense you want the activity to be. Just how far do you want to go with a particular activity, or how complicated do you want to get? Group Juggling can be played where no balls are allowed to touch the ground. Or it can be played in a much more loose manner, where the balls do touch the ground, and even a little "cheating" is tolerated. Same with Spider's Web, or Rebirth, or Prouty's Landing. You can play it tight by disallowing any touching of the perimeters (if one person touches, the whole group goes back). Or you can play it loose (if a person touches, that person goes back). Or looser still (you are allowed two touches per person). Part of the artistry of leading the activities is being able to scan the group for intensity decisions such as these.

An interesting adjustment was made by a leader who saw a group getting complacent. She split them into two groups, and introduced a competitive game (Italian Golf: go around a "course" throwing a rubber ring that you have to catch in a certain way. Each group must keep score regarding numbers of tosses). She then put them in a situation where the two groups were forced to work together (T.P. Shuffle: two groups on a log must pass each other without falling off). The collision of competition and cooperation provided some good discussion material, to say the least! That material related a group goal that focused on the ability to work together as a group.

Any changes in the Wave Plan can be made by either moving activities up or down, or substituting new activities, or simply focusing on new issues within the already constructed Wave Plan. If you look at the whole picture each time you make a change, you can keep a rhythm to your planning. It also gives you an easier mind regarding "what am I going to do today?" Relieving that pressure is no small task, and can be a welcome ancillary benefit.

What is the process one should follow in order to adjust the activity sequence? First, you need to scan, or read, the group in order to gather information that will help you make your decision. Here are some general issues that may be helpful:
- Are there any resistive members?
- Are they comfortable touching others?
- Are there any leaders?
- Are they passive and reluctant?
- Are they particularly self-conscious?
- Do they like to have fun, to let go of "being cool?"
- Is the group beginning to "jell?"
- Are there common feelings and issues?
- Are they active, chomping at the bit?
- Do they listen, to you and to each other?
- Is the Full Value Contract coming clear to them?

Another helpful scanning device is GRABBS, the name for our modality check list. A modality is a discrete area of concentration regarding important personal and interpersonal operations. As you observe your group, look for the following areas in which the group can be defined. These modes are Goals, Readiness, Affect, Behavior, Body and Stage of Development. (More information on Modality Therapy can be gathered from Arnold Lazarus, *The Practice of Multimodal Therapy,* 1981.)

GRABBS Modality Check List

Goals — How does the activity relate to the group and individual goals that have been set?

Readiness — This regards levels of instruction (skills) and safety capabilities. Is the group ready to do the activity? Will they endanger themselves and others? Do they have the ability to attempt or complete? What will you have to do to change the event to compensate for lack of readiness?

Affect — What is the feeling of the group? What kinds of sensations are they having? What is the level of empathy or caring in the group?

Behavior — How is the group acting? Are they resistive? Disruptive? Agreeable? Are they more self involved, or group involved? Are there any interactions that are affecting the group, both positive and negative? How cooperative are they?

Body — What kind of physical shape are they in? How tired are they? Do they substance abuse? Are they on medication? How do they see their own bodies?

Stage — Which developmental stage is the group at? Groups will go through levels of functioning. Having a schema to describe these levels will provide you with another means of assessment.

Stages of Development

The final modality of GRABBS, the "Stage of Development," merits a thorough discussion. There are many developmental systems. We have chosen one that Richard Weber discusses in his paper, "The Group: A Cycle from Birth to Death." He explores developmental issues in a way that allows for continual change. This is consistent with our view that activities elicit behavior. Since the group is continually experiencing activities, the potential for new behaviors is always present. The group may leap forward to an advanced stage. They also may go back to an earlier stage. He states:

> "Groups may proceed through the three stages quickly or slowly; they may fixate at a given stage; or they may move quickly through some and slowly through others. If they do indeed complete all three stages, however, and have sufficient time left in their life together, they will again recycle through the stages. This additional development will lead to deeper insight, accomplishment, and closer relationships. "

We would add that a group will generally grow to a stage that can be somewhat relied upon, though it will revert depending on how it responds to significant challenges. Those challenges can be called "pinch points" or "crunch points" (discussed in Chapter 6 under Conflict Resolution), the pinch growing to a crunch if the group fails to deal with the challenges. Weber uses the stages developed by Tuckman (1965), Schutz (1971) and Bion (1961). Those stages are: Forming, Storming, Norming, and Transforming.

Forming. When groups form, members are scrambling for leadership and whom to follow. There is confusion, anxiety, willingness to please, along with solid glimpses into what the group will be like. This is an important time for the group to achieve something, for they may be more willing to please each other and the leaders at this stage than they will be during the Storming stage. Those solid immediate first achievements will be important building blocks: "But look, you did these things before, and you had a good time doing it. You can do them again."

Storming. Others call this the control stage. Weber describes it as "possibly the most difficult stage to tolerate in either persons or groups." (p.3) Alliances between members have formed sufficiently to generate negative behavior. Real testing of the co-leaders begins. It is truly an all-out get-to-know-you time. Group members are asking through their behavior: *Is this group safe? Am I going to like what*

I am doing? Can these leaders handle us? They are essentially reacting to the situation, with very little initiative or independence being exhibited. It is important to continue to deal with the uses of achievement and negotiation, giving them the solid experiences that will help them move on to the next stage.

Norming. The group is beginning to operate as a unit, taking pride in what it is doing, and using its own strengths. The group is also moving away from its dependency on the co-leaders, taking initiative and experiencing pride in group accomplishments. They are more able to confront each other in terms of goals and behavior.

Transforming. Others call it "termination." It's what a group must do when it has accomplished its goal, or has run out of time. According to Weber, there are two choices. One is to Redefine, or start again with a new agenda and time period. The other is to Disengage. "The group must decide on its future or it will proceed down a frustrating, unfulfilling path…."(p.4).

These developmental stages can help you decide on intensity decisions and on specific tasks. Tasks that require a high degree of initiative and responsibility should be reserved for the Norming stage. Tasks that must be watched closely through narrow parameters should be slotted into Forming and Storming.

It is important to remind yourself that groups will recycle back through the process. This is another way to talk about "two steps forward, one step back." A group will move to a general level. But it will also run into difficulties, and these may force them to go back to another level. If the difficulties are addressed, the group will grow in a normal "zig-zag" kind of way. If they are not addressed, the group may very well fall apart. This will be addressed further in Chapter 6, **Leading**, under the heading of Conflict Resolution.

The next step is to take the information you have gathered and decide what the dominant issues are. Make a list of them, then decide which issue or issues you want to focus on. A most important aspect of this decision is a safety one: Can the group handle what you are prescribing? Psychological safety is just as important as physical safety. When in doubt, take the less dangerous route. If it doesn't produce the effect you want, you will have at least been able to learn from a not-so-good experience rather than from a damaging one.

Micro-Planning Sheet

A Micro-Planning sheet can help you determine those dominant issues and then frame them in an effective manner. These are the categories of the Micro-Planning sheet:

Client: (Name and description of the group)

Wave Plan Activities: What activity the group should be doing according to the pre-ordained sequence (including focus objectives).

Scanning Information: What is happening with the group at the present time (use of GRABBS).

Focus Issues: What are the primary issues that can be abstracted from the scanning information?

Activity Adjustment: What is the activity that best lines up with your focus issue or issues, and what are the practical considerations around leading it (logistics, time limitations, and what you want to achieve). This includes:
- Briefing: (How you plan to frame it)
- Activity: (Leadership roles)
- Debriefing: (What you would like to focus on)

On the following page is an example of how a Micro-Planning sheet would be used in a typical activities adjustment.

Sample Micro-Planning Sheet

Client: Junior high school Adventure Counseling group in an L.D. classroom.

Wave Plan Activities: (refer to program objectives, and the week #4 sequence): Warmups: Impulse. Carabiner Walk; Trust Fall from height

Scanning Information: GRABBS check list:

Goals The group has set goals of working together and having fun. The Full Value Contract has been explained and accepted. Individual goals could be: participate, be with the group, "control my mouth," don't wander off, get involved.

Ready They have had spotting training through the Trust Fall/Spotting Sequence up to Circle Pass.

Affect They are low energy, and show little emotion.

Behavior They are resistive and self-involved. They don't want to play any "stupid games."

Body They seem tired, but it relates to depression. There is no substance abuse. They see themselves as somewhat capable.

Stage Storming/Forming.

Focus Issues: Low energy, resistance, toying with the Storming stage, goals of working together and having fun. The group needs to loosen up, get some exercise, laugh a little bit, and get rid of the depressive "heavies." They also need to accomplish something.

Activity Adjustment: Review the spotting exercises they have already learned, relating them to the upcoming Initiative. Then do the Tire Traverse Initiative (Social Responsibility), using a bucket of blood plasma (water) that needs to be transported to the aid of a dying elephant.

Logistics: (Set up time/Consequences/Variation/Intensity: 5 minutes for Briefing, 10 minutes for tag game, 30 minutes for Tire Traverse, 15 minutes for Debrief. Total: 1 hour. Need a bucket with a wire handle (#10 tin can). Need extra water in two used milk jugs. Need to carry the tires out (allow ten minutes for this). If one person falls off the tires, that person needs to go back to the beginning. The whole group will not be penalized. It is not intended as an extremely challenging exercise; let them know that if they do not finish within the time limit, they will be able to come back the next week and complete it.

Briefing: Frame the spotting with the reality of the Tire Traverse Initiative: The dying elephant needs everyone there to help, for it must be turned over in just the correct manner to have the plasma I.V. put in place. The elephant is also very group-oriented, and will not cooperate unless it knows everyone is expressing his/her concern by being there. This activity requires spotting for certain transfers. Ask what their group and individual goals are. Be able to state them if they happen to forget.

Leading the activity: One leader will stress the spotting, and will monitor the rules. The other leader will focus more on the group interaction, looking for cooperation issues in particular.

Debriefing: The leader that observed the interaction will lead the Debrief. That person will confer with the co-leader about what issues to look for, knowing that every issue cannot be covered.

Conclusion

As your experience confirms or attacks your conclusions, you will be able to build up your own information regarding what works where, when and why. This process appears laborious, and we are realistic enough to know that it will not be followed every time an adjustment to the sequential Wave Plan is made. We also know that there is no substitute for experience. However, we have outlined many of the issues that one should consider when planning the curriculum, and provided a rationale for adjusting it. By polling many veteran leaders we have found that they instinctively think of most of these points when they make their decisions regarding which activities to choose. Use of the check lists can be done in your head once you have mastered the process, without a lot of hated paperwork.

If you can keep in mind that the group is affected by different modalities of preparedness, that it does move through stages, and that you need to work with your co-leader regarding roles, intensity decisions, and management of the Adventure Wave Plan Brief/Activity/Debrief cycle, then you should have some informed ground to stand on regarding your decisions.

Chapter 5

Briefing:
Preparing for the
Adventure Experience

*"If we only knew what we were about perhaps
we could get about it better."*

— Abe Lincoln

THE NEXT CONSIDERATION is, how do we Brief the group? We have done the Intake, and formed the group. We have sketched out an appropriate Adventure Wave Plan, and have in place the criteria for adjusting that plan. But we haven't actually engaged the group as a whole. The initial Briefing session is the beginning of group action. Whatever happens during that initial session, and each succeeding one, will be stored in the collective history of the group.

The discipline of Briefing establishes a thoughtful, controlled tone. Though most everyone wants to get on with the activities, the dynamics incorporated by successful Briefing time provides a framework within which the group can function safely and productively.

As we look at Briefing, the following issues will be considered:

- **Authority**
- **Framing the Experience**
- **The Full Value Contract**
- **Goal Setting**

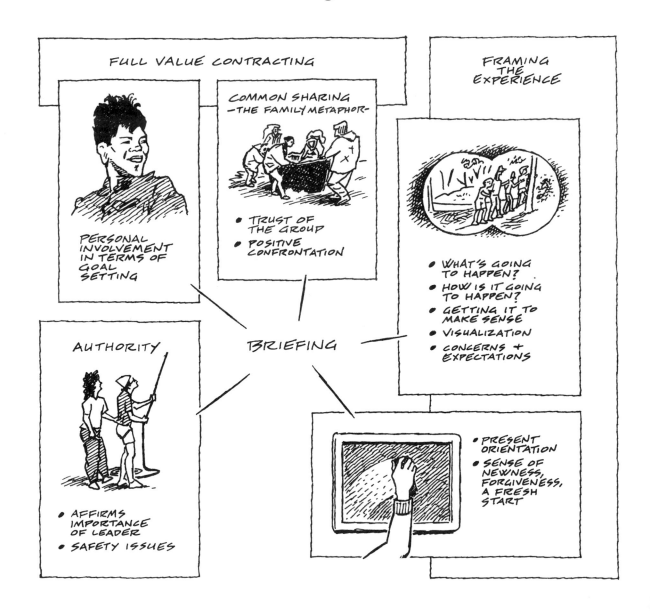

Authority

Since Initiative plays such an important role in group development, there may be confusion about who actually is in control. Let there be no confusion: Adventure Based Counseling is centered on the leader, who has ultimate authority and responsibility for the group. In practice the group controls many aspects of the experience, because a major part of its reason for being is learning to make responsible choices. But the final authority, the bottom line is always the leader.

Preparation: The Key to Effortless Leading

Experienced leaders learn to conceal their ultimate authority through exhaustive preparation. That preparation includes Activities selection, logistics, a "pace through" reconnaissance where necessary, and planning appropriate alternatives for those times when one or more things don't work out. It also includes adequate Briefing, where the group understands clearly what it is getting into, what is expected of it, and how it will measure its success. If these issues have been dealt with, the Activity tends to take care of itself. Uninformed outsiders will say that "Wow, and you call this work?" when they observe Adventure leaders with their groups. What they see is a bunch of kids doing all the sweating, and you standing around. What they don't see is all the work that went into setting up the Activity. Nor do they see the work involved in being with a group while it struggles with an Initiative (listening, scanning, recording, empathizing, spotting and reading body-language).

Safety

Finally, safety issues make leader-centeredness even more important. Adventure Activities include elements of risk. You must be able to keep control in this area. There are also times for straightforward safety instruction. There is no room for latitude here. It must be done correctly. If the group is unresponsive to it, you may have to decide against doing the Activity. In fact, instruction periods offer ideal times to assess the strengths and weaknesses of the group.

Safety also applies to emotional areas: You simply cannot let a group run roughshod over itself. Structures must be in place to maintain control, and constant vigilance needs to be applied to the maintenance of those structures. It's just as important as tying knots correctly.

Framing the Experience

Framing the experience attempts to answer the questions, "What is going to happen?", "How is it going to happen?", and "What is expected?" For the student, it begins in the Intake, as a result of comments from referring personnel and out of scuttlebutt that comes from previous participants. The instructor uses Framing to clarify these hazy impressions, and draw a common picture for the group, so that the experience is not entered into in a random manner. Focus is another word for framing: Directed, narrowed, clear. For example, a participant may have heard that the Adventure group is all about climbing high ropes and pushing oneself to the limit. Those may be some of the objectives of the Adventure group, but the instructor would need to frame them in such a way that the *group* is involved in decision making and mutual support.

There are times when things need to be "reframed." That's when confusion has erupted, and things must be slowed down so that the task can be looked at from a new perspective. The same language of the original framing may be used, which is another important consideration: just because you've said it once doesn't mean that it shouldn't be repeated. Framing and reframing may appear laborious, but repetition of important concepts is essential.

Here are some of the key elements of Framing:
- Description and expectation
- Here-and-now orientation
- Sense of newness, forgiveness, a fresh start
- New use of language
- Building momentum and providing lead time

Description and Expectation

Part of the framing deals with the nuts and bolts of the experience: What is going to happen, and what the details are (where, what time, what clothes to wear, who is going to do what). How these details are presented goes a long way toward building a quality of expectation. The military origins of the term briefing implies excitement (with the violence excluded): bomber pilots clustered in a room with a chalk board looking at target areas. Briefing connects that scene to kids in a grove of trees talking about the Hickory Jump, or high school students standing outside a nursing home getting ready to play games and converse with old folks. There is excitement and expectation mixed in with a few butterflies, underscored by the fact that the students are not alone (*we are all going to do this together*).

How these details are presented goes a long way toward building a quality of expectation.

Here-and-Now Orientation

Framing also gets across the idea of the present, or here-and-now, orientation of ABC. It is a group intent on dealing with personal issues, but with a focus on the interactions experienced by the group rather than on the interactions outside the group. Certainly issues outside the group are appropriate to discuss, but we are referring to the overall emphasis. It is in light of those growth-oriented, controlled experiences that outside issues are considered.

Sense of Newness, Forgiveness, a Fresh Start

Group members have a history that they bring. And a group itself develops its own history. This history can bog the group down. That is why its important that the leader carries an implied "newness", a forgiveness, a fresh wave to ride. (*Yeah, what we did last week is important, but only for the learning it gave us. This week is a new week. Let's treat it that way!*)

Visualization

Framing can be used to help the members visualize what they are going to do, to pace it through beforehand. This can be done through the overall structural presentation, where the description is visually oriented.

Thinking about the experience and preparing for it is a large part of the counseling/learning process. This ties in with a statement made by family therapist Claudia Schweitzer, M.S.W.:

> "A great deal of the therapy is accomplished before the counseling session just through the act of the family getting into the car and coming—together—to the session. They are doing something together, and have a common goal, an experience which is lacking in their family system." (Interview, Fall 1985)

The fact that the group agreed to participate shows that they first envisioned a result they wanted. Visualizing, or "seeing," the result brought about an activity that was not even part of the therapy group. This "seeing" is a giant step, and shouldn't be minimized. Often the later action that is accomplished is anticlimactic, albeit necessary to complete the experience.

You can also use a present tense Gestalt visualization technique. For example:

> "You have climbed up to the Hickory Jump. You see the trapeze. You see the arms of the group held out to catch you. You feel butterflies in your stomach. You are focused

on the trapeze. You are coiling your legs to jump. You are jumping out with all your effort. You feel your hands get hold of that bar. You are feeling the group congratulate you, hold you, and let you down."

New use of Language

Much of framing deals with definitions, and cuts right to the heart of language and communication. For the Adventure leader is introducing new language. Though the concepts are part of our overall social upbringing, they probably have not been discussed in the context of this type of group doing these activities. This newness is an advantage, for it can catch people off guard, and thereby provide a fresh voice. "Spotting" becomes another word for "caring," "Debriefing" another word for "discussion." Words that have been used as clubs by myriads of caretakers over the years can be redefined in the Adventure setting by the use of this "other" language.

Careful leaders can weave in language from the culture they are dealing with, creating new levels of translation. For example, New York City youthworker Barry Orms feels that the action of Adventure provides an important bridge for kids who are tied up in a basketball- and street-oriented framework. This world gives them a sense of power, but does not relate sufficiently to the "outside," or larger world. He first relates the Full Value Contract to how they operate as a group, then applies it to their Adventure experience, and finally cross-applies it to the way they tend to play basketball. (*One-on-one does not win games.*) He then carries it further into goal setting with their schooling and street issues. Valuing the street and ethnic culture and its language enables him to form this bridge.

Building Momentum and Providing Lead Time

Briefing takes place wherever it is appropriate to discuss the next Activity. It can be at the end of an Activity, or be a part of a Debriefing (the process of discussing what went on during a specific Activity) as the "Now what?" stage. And it can take place just at the beginning of the next Activity.

Brainstorming for the next Activity while one is in progress is also effective, because it takes the energy from that experience and pushes it ahead, like riding a pogo stick (or a wave). "Hey, let's do some more of these Initiatives, what do you think?" If students are having a successful time doing an Activity, they'll often want more. Those are valuable opportunities. Passive students who have needed persuading to do Adventure tend to see it all differently once they are inside the

Brainstorming for the next activity while one is in progress...takes the energy from that experience and pushes it ahead, like riding a pogo stick (or a wave).

experience. Seize the moment! Get them talking and dreaming. Even if they change their tune in a day or two when the old depressive habits set back in, they have verbalized something. You can support that something, treating it like an Olympic flame being passed along at night during a rain storm. Having the students "buy off" on the Activities by actually helping select them is an empowering experience. Certainly it needs to be controlled (perceived selection where the group appears to be making the choice, but the boundaries for choosing have been set by the leaders is an effective tactic). All this is accomplished with the accompaniment of your scanning and assessment antennae.

If you can provide the group with lead time before the next Activity, participants will have time to think about it and prepare for it. But often this is not possible, for the leaders need to consult with each other, and utilize their planning time. You may need to build part of the Briefing into the one session per week that you have with the group. The Briefing can be split up: part of it at the end on one session, part of it at the beginning of the next session. And they don't have to be long! Just because we are spending a great deal of time talking about Briefing in this chapter doesn't mean that you need to cover all of the issues in each session. You take the time you have, figure out priorities, and go ahead.

Whatever lead time you have, it is important to assemble the group just before the experience and repeat the basics.

Whatever lead time you have, it is important to assemble the group just before the experience and repeat the basics. We assume that our groups understand what they are going to do, and this may be so. But repetition, however quick, is helpful. Here is a sample checklist:

- *Who is in charge of the water jug?*
- *Who has the rope for the Blindfold Square?*
- *Tom, do you remember your goals?*
- *It's your turn to carry the First Aid belt, right Mary?*
- *Do you remember the Full Value Contract? Let's all agree to it.*

The Full Value Contract

Undergirding the Briefing process is the concept of contracting. It is the group's first line of defense as it goes into the Activity.

Like love we don't know where or why
Like love we can't compel or fly
Like love we often weep
Like love we seldom keep.
— W.H. Auden
from the poem "Law Like Love"

We would add, "But we try." That is what Adventure contracting is all about. The essential "law" of Adventure counseling takes the form of a social contract, both personal and interpersonal. It is a law built on value for each person and for the group as a whole. It is a first line of defense when it comes to the group's having a safe place to be.

Some practitioners prefer to call it a "no-discount" contract rather than a Full Value Contract. In fact, we used the no-discount terminology for many years at Project Adventure. We changed to Full Value because of the positive aspects of the expression. Other leaders refer to Full Value only at the beginning of the group, finding other means to express the same point. The important thing is maintaining the idea, in whatever form it is expressed.

"Full Valuing" is a handy way to discuss the social contract. (*"In order for us to honor our contracts, we must support one another. If we don't support one another, we are* discounting *each other."*) This also relates to the practice of goal setting, where a group has spent time coming to an agreement about what they are going to do, both individually and as a group. Whether from an educational or therapeutic point of view, effective learning occurs in an environment where what is learned can immediatly be put into practice and the learner can receive accurate feedback and reinforcement. Through the use of goal-oriented Personal Action Plans (p.114), group members are helped to define what they want to achieve, how they are going to accomplish this, and what evidence will serve to demonstrate that they have achieved a specific goal.

True "jelling" of a group comes about when there is a realization and enactment of common values and common goals. The result is an expression of the Full Value Contract. Rowing a 20-foot dory with four rowers, a coxswain-"scuttler" (person who steers), and a lookout, is a case in point. The six crew members can work as a series of frustrated individuals, or they can come together, complement each other's strength, hit the water in unison, make a smooth entry with their oars, steer a straight course, and move without hesitation or frustration to the destination. There are plenty of chances to violate or discount the law of the boat: inattention, quitting, not speaking up, anger at others, disrespect for the equipment. But the crew has a goal of pulling together. That's something tangible to work for, the ideal. When they do jell, there is a lifting up, where things become easier, more connected, less fragmented. Those are some of the most powerful healing times.

Jelling happens during intense spotting situations, where everyone is focused on one individual's effort. Quiet sets in; involvement pervades. Achievement brings immediate joy and satisfaction for everyone. And the focus isn't only on the achievement, but also on the effort involved in trying. You often see it during a game of Moon Ball where a group tries to keep hitting a beach ball in the air as long as possible. Everyone scrambles for the ball, falling and tripping and laughing and running into each other, having good, solid fun.

That's the ideal. The Full Value Contract is an avenue to those close, healing experiences. Realistically, achieving that dynamic in a group takes a lot of work. You may see only an occasional glimmer. It's always a building process. The sequencing process helps us go in a step-by-step, sensitive manner toward it. Contracting, and its implied goal setting, helps us form a conceptual bond around how we "do" the Activities.

Groups take to contracts, but not all at once. They need to be explained and studied and negotiated again and again. Briefing/Debriefing provides an ideal place for this necessary repetition. Basically, this contract is a statement, written or oral, made by each group member concerning what she is willing to do during the group experience or outside the group experience.

[Contracts] need to be explained and studied and negotiated again and again.

The following three commitments form the backbone of the Full Value Contract:
- Agreement to work together as a group and to work toward individual and group goals
- Agreement to adhere to certain safety and group behavior guidelines
- Agreement to give and receive feedback, both positive and negative, and to work toward changing behavior when it is appropriate.

Commitment Number One:
Agreement to work together as a group and to work toward individual and group goals

The simple agreement to work together is a goal in and of itself, and may be the maximum expectation that can be presented at the start of a group. This agreement to work together, however, implies giving 100% effort and making use of ongoing goal setting. These goals are developed throughout the life of the group. Goal setting provides a framework where individuals can measure what they have achieved, and set new goals from the locus of that achievement. This goal setting will be explored further later in this chapter.

The Family Metaphor

A way to introduce the emotional side of the Full Value Contract (for it offers rich ground for exploring and establishing practical values), is to use the metaphor of the family. It is effective because there is universal experience here. Everyone stands on Common Ground! We might say:

"We need to act like an ideal family. We're doing these Activities together. We need to be able to relate to each other positively, supporting each other, and allowing ourselves to trust each other. It's in your self interest! If you are doing something that takes a great deal of difficulty, you want to be able to trust the person next to you. The ideal family provides that. I'm not talking about a family that's always ripping each other apart. I'm talking about a positive family. And you can't tell me that a supportive family is not a good thing! We all want that!"

Family is a powerful symbol for everyone. Either you have a family, or you wish you had one. Either your family is intact or it is at odds with itself. Either it fosters goodness or it encourages confusion and tragedy. Or multiple shades of the above. Because of this universality of experience, everyone can relate to the metaphor. Because of the importance and seriousness of establishing a social contract, everyone in the group must understand it. The family metaphor provides this.

The healthy family becomes the main point of reference for the chief group goal. The reality-based experiences provide ample groundwork for getting into family emotions. The group becomes a place to contact the positive emotions, and a place to work out some of those issues that result from bad experiences, such as loss of trust. This journal quote from an Adventure student underlines the family-like system that can be developed:

The healthy family becomes the main point of reference for the chief group goal.

> "I learned that you can trust a lot more, and you guys I know I can talk to about just about everything; anything I wanted to. This experience, you know, going down mountains. At first I wasn't going to let anybody put me down this hill, except maybe Rich or Gary, but I realized that you guys are just as much capable of doing that as anybody else. I just want you to know that you are all like sisters and brothers."
>
> (Project Quest student, see Chap. 11)

When presenting the family metaphor to the group, you can also ask "What are some family contracts you can think of?" Look at marriage vows, care for kids, physical violence, no excessive alcohol, drugs, or stealing, the need to stand up for each other. Without these agreements, families fall apart. They succumb to affairs, alcohol, abuse, rage. Participants don't have to divulge personal experiences in order to understand the metaphor. That kind of probing isn't necessary in an introduction.

But as we frame the contracting process, the family metaphor gives us a reference point for later, more in-depth counseling work. Discuss the ideal family. The family as a "team." The family as a place to be accepted. To be able to relax. To have your needs met. That feels good to be a part of. That loves you. That you love. The connection to the group can then take place. "We need to operate like a family. Like a positive family. That's why we need to make a contract with each other. Without the contract, we won't get anything done. Or what we get done will happen only by chance. We need to have some rules to live by. We need to have ways to encourage each other, and bring out the best in each other. Like an ideal family."

Implied in this is the fact that each group member, as part of the group "family," has value. Value, in the healthy family, must be encouraged. If it is not encouraged, then the family unit breaks down. Because the group "family" can't be allowed to break down (what are we here for, anyway?), anything that devalues individuals, or the group as a whole, takes away from the positive family.

The group family becomes the expression of "law like love." That's the law. Or the rule we must live by. We will violate it. When we do, we're going to talk about it, and mend our fences. Then we'll go on. For without the contract, it would be just like what happens on the street, or in the hallway, or in many living rooms. Because of the Adventure Wave, where there are always more experiences in the offing, there are more chances to adhere to the contract, to encourage each other, and yourself, when discounting does take place. Family contract items become goals to work on. Goals are not achieved all at once. But they are important signposts in a confusing world. As the contract becomes more clear to the group, goal setting emerges as the understandable items to work for. And everyone has goals, including the leaders. "Like love, we seldom keep." But we try.

Some groups are too fragile to handle the family metaphor.

Some groups are too fragile to handle the family metaphor. Their family relations may be too raw and volatile. They may need another metaphor, like the importance of one's word, or about such legal contracts as lease arrangements, wills, a title to a car, sports teams, any image that is familiar. You can introduce the image of family later on. Often it will just emerge. Participants will be the ones who bring it up.

Give examples of valuing and devaluing. Going back to Moon Ball, what if one student is making fun of another student's repeated failure to keep the ball in the air? Is that helping the group, or helping that person do better at the game? The contract that underscores the need not to discount anyone else should be enforced. If discounting is allowed to go on, the value of the Activity is drained. It becomes only an activity that is controlled by the rules of the street. The Full Value Contract allows the leader to say something other than "Stop that! Don't you see that you are hurting him? What's the matter with you?" That's the judgement/lecture cycle that doesn't work with most people, especially those in need. The Full Value Contract is a positive approach to limit setting.

Commitment Number Two:
Agreement to adhere to certain safety and group behavior guidelines

There is a tried-and-true way of introducing the Full Value Contract. In this approach (and this is universal for any kind of Adventure group or Activity), the instructor says "We are going to ask everyone here to enter into a contract to listen to the safety rules, to follow certain group behavior guidelines, and to help enforce them. Everyone needs to agree that if he sees any of the rules being violated, he will speak up. And everyone needs to agree that if he is forgetting a rule, he will allow himself to be reminded by other members of the group. To the extent that we follow this, we will be able to carry the experience to a safe and satisfying conclusion. Does everyone agree?"

You may simply make the contract clear to the group by explaining it to them. Some leaders make every group member say "I hear what you are saying, and I agree," or "I agree to honor the Full Value Contract." You can use a written contract, also. That contract may include goals that the participants wish to achieve. Without it, our experience will be unsafe. Having started with this essential physical, safety-oriented conceptual base, we can talk about the emotional safety of the group. "We also don't want to put anyone down, or exclude anyone. We therefore want the group to agree not to devalue anyone."

Without these limits, a group will run itself, and its leader, right over the cliff. No one in a group wants to operate without limits. Lack of control is scary, and counterproductive. Groups that can't be managed with reasonable controls should be discontinued, with new tactics of composition, leadership and approach applied.

Although participants don't want to operate without limits, they will constantly test them, pushing against authority, order, and discipline. This is the contradiction of group work. It is reasonable when one thinks about it, for they are testing whether the group will actually succeed for them. Those who don't need to test tend to be those whose gear is well organized, and not sliding all around the deck. Those who test the most tend to be those whose gear is loose. They are asking for help in tightening it up. "Will this group work, and will it help me where I haven't been able to get help before?" Practitioners who are surprised by this acting out and testing should look again at what the the overall group goals are. Yet staff rooms are filled with surprised complaints regarding the behavior of "persons in need."

By using the Full Value Contract, an activity that is out of control can be stopped, and the question "How does this relate to our Full Value Contract?" can be asked.

By using the Full Value Contract, an Activity that is out of control can be stopped, and the question "How does this relate to our Full Value Contract?" can be asked. "How does this tie in to what we set out to do? To our agreement?" A group striving to be a "family" will recognize the discounting, and say something about it. An essential part of the contract is the agreement to confront and be confronted.

Commitment Number Three:
Agreement to give and receive feedback both positive and negative, and to work toward changing behavior when it is appropriate.

Honest feedback from a group is an important learning tool. The perceptions of fellow group members regarding goal accomplishment and behavior can be extremely helpful. Yet it is also one of the most difficult to structure. That is a reason why trust is one of our overall goals, for with a trusting atmosphere, members are more able to participate in a feedback agreement. With trust of the group as a basis, participants are asked to enter into an agreement that will allow for this feedback. This feedback takes the shape of what we call appropriate or positive confrontation. We use the term confrontation because of the strength it implies. Some leaders prefer to use the less abrasive term of feedback because of the possible misunderstanding that can be created by the use of the term confrontation.

Positive Confrontation

Confrontation means to speak up when devaluing is going on. Each person agrees to be confronted when their behavior does not match the behavior they identified as a goal. Similarly, each person agrees to confront others when their behavior does not match the behavior they had identified as goals. Positive confrontation precludes negative collisions between group members—that would be devaluing and discounting—ranging from negative behavior, to not working on one's goals.

Confrontation is one of the most difficult things to nurture in a group, for people are reluctant to speak up, have a verbal and even a physical battle, and end up with only hurt feelings to show for it. Or worse! That's why positive confrontation must be discussed and agreed to *in the Briefing* so that it is not a surprise when it is utilized during the Activity, or in the Debriefing. Group members must learn to confront each other in an open and responsible manner. Essentially, confrontation is a challenge from one's own self or from another to look at one's own behavior, or to look at the discrepancy between what one says and what one does, or to view the degree to which we are being honest with ourselves and/or others. And then to do something about it.

We are not asking group members to become "goodie two shoes," lording it over each other. But we are asking them to speak up when something is not going right in relation to the agreement that has been made by the entire group. In this way, the group begins to have the power to monitor itself. This doesn't happen all at once, but with repetition, nudging, and a continual pursuit of the group strengths, always asking their opinions. That self-monitoring power is an important weapon in the healing process.

No longer is the leader the only person who sets limits, encourages, plans, or has all the answers. Members of the group are able to make decisions, and within that decision making they become able to take care of each other. Because the group doesn't just monitor itself for rule infractions, it will confront its members for not trying hard, not sticking to goals, and other issues that emerge.

Take the Tension Traverse (a low ropes event where a participant balances and traverses a cable that is 2 feet off the ground, utilizing a rope attached at one end for support). In order to finish it, maximum effort is needed. You must go to the "end of your rope." Trying is an elusive quality. It can be easy to pretend to try. Say a participant sets a goal of doing the traverse all the way to the end. Group members want to help out, to varying degrees. If the traverser is thrashing about, and decides to give up, there's an opportunity to confront. How do we do it? By reminding the traverser of her goal, not by calling her "chicken" or some other descriptives! By being gentle, but still present with our observation. (*"Perhaps you should try it by depending a little more on us to hold you up." "You can do it by yourself after you've done it this way."* Or, *"Take a break, and come back to it."*)

Self-Confrontation

We also need to teach our groups the ability to self-confront. This can be done by removing the specter of success at any cost. (*If the ref didn't see me cheat, then I didn't cheat!*) When an honest atmosphere is encouraged, group members will be exceedingly straightforward about their participation, breaking the experience down into the minutest detail. (*I really didn't try that hard. I could have made it.*) This can become grounds for another goal. (*Next week I'm going to really put out.*)

The person on the wire is not the only one being considered in the Activity. The spotters play an essential role. The family is hard at work here! Without good spotting, maximum effort from the "traverser" would be foolish. The spotters need to keep good attention, or they are discounting. This is grounds for discussion between the spotter and the traverser! Since the spotter and the traverser will soon be changing places, it is in the self-interest of the spotter to do a good job, a fact that shouldn't be missed.

Nurturing Confrontation in the Group

The combination of nurturing empathy and the fact that confrontation must be a two-way street aids in the realization of the commitment to confront and be confronted. This includes an agreement to increase awareness of when we are devaluing ourselves or others, and to make a direct, conscious effort to confront and work toward changing this behavior. Again, the agreement to change behavior is a challenge to look at the discrepancy between what we say and what we do, or to view the degree to which we are being honest. This agreement includes the construction of goal-oriented action plans to change that behavior in response to this self-appraisal.

Confrontation needs to take place in an empathetic environment, as much as possible.

Important counseling strategies need to be operated around this concept, not allowing the confrontation to become hurtful or out of bounds. You need to make intensity decisions, as you manage the group. How much confrontation can this group handle? Confrontation needs to take place in an empathetic environment, as much as possible. Without a developing sense of empathy, and "group feeling," confrontation becomes abusive.

As the group forms a sense of trust, the members begin to feel safer. Confrontations become ways to encourage, to bring out the best. Confrontation from a base of trust insures the safety of the group members. Trust takes time to develop. The Activities imply trust, both physical and emotional. They are there, ready to be used, in that building process as we ride the Adventure Wave. As the group experiences the gradual increments of trust and is able to relax in the knowledge that it is being managed well (the instructor maintaining the bottom line spotting position), more and more behavior issues can be dealt with.

Goal Setting

It is difficult to support and confront each other without having an idea of what someone wants to do and why she is part of the group. That's why we practice goal setting, that process by which a person is encouraged to analyze and specify what she wants to achieve, according to her ability.

Some effective goal-setting guidelines are found in the definitions of the following goal categories:

- *Conceivable:* Conceptualize the goal and make it understandable.
- *Believable:* The goal must be believable. You need to carefully monitor this one, or participants may set themselves up for substantial failure. Understandable or manageable failure can be beneficial, however.
- *Controllable:* What are the factors that might make the goal out of your reach (things you have no control over, for example).
- *Measurable:* You need to have some means of reporting back to yourself whether you accomplished your goal or not.
- *Desirable:* Your goal should be something you really want to do. This can include things that you have decided to do because they are necessary though you are reluctant. The "really want to do" goals should, on balance, relate more to what you personally want than to a duty-obligation matrix.
- *Stated with no Alternative:* Set one goal at a time, without a bail-out plan. If you qualify your goal, there's a tendency to go easy on yourself. You can change your goal at any time. This keeps things clear and uncompromised.
- *Growth-Facilitating:* Goals should be positive, so that you can build on them in a healthy way. Negative goals have no place in this process.

(Billy B. Sharp, with Claire Cox, 1970)

There are two kinds of goals:

- *Activity Goals:* Goals that are expressed within the context of the group Activities.
- *Spiral Goals:* Goals that are expressed outside the group "in the world."

Here is a diagram of Activity and Spiral goals, when placed on the Adventure Wave:

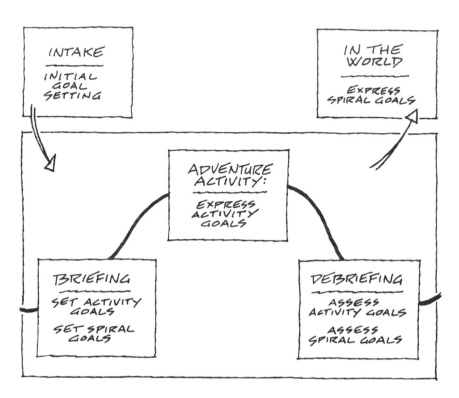

When the "inside" and the "outside" issues are too mixed up, it can be hard to focus on either.

Differentiation between the two kinds of goals helps the participant focus first on behavior within the group, and second, on behavior outside the group. When the "inside" and the "outside" issues are too mixed up, it can be hard to focus on either. Since the group and what the group does together is of primary importance, what occurs in the group can act as a basis for what goes on outside. And by implication, what goes on inside the group can influence what goes on outside.

If changed behavior feels good enough, it is worthy of testing in other areas. This testing does not have to take place in terms of goal setting. Improved behavior will unconsciously carry over. The goal setting should be seen as one avenue for this carry-over. Addressing outside issues too soon, however, can have a negative, sometimes punitive impact, giving the message that all you care about is that the person doesn't get in trouble. Also, outside behavior, though certainly not just hearsay, is nevertheless something that does not take place where all group members either observe or experience it. There is no Common Ground. And Common Ground is critical in the formation of the islands of healing.

So we begin by addressing those goals that can operate inside the group. There is a natural spiralling effect that takes place when a participant is ready to consider his or her behavior in the world. It may happen immediately. It may take much longer. When and where to encourage spiralling comes from our sensitivity to the readiness of the participants. That readiness is not in our control. But what goes on during group time is in our charge, and that's where we must begin.

Activity Goals

Activity goals encompass both individual goals and group goals. At all times both concerns must be kept in mind:

What can I do as an individual?
What can our group work toward?

The group is an organism, and members are asked to look out and care for that organism. But the individuals must not be absorbed by the group. Asking these two questions side by side helps keep them separate. The goals co-mingle. The essence of the counseling is based on that. The group represents relationships, and those relationships present opportunities for members to untangle some of the issues that are keeping them in a negative place. The Full Value Contract is a social contract, as well as an individual's contract with himself or herself. Individual goals and group goals are worked on jointly, under the auspices of the overall Full Value Contract.

Goal setting begins during the Intake. One of the ways the instructor can decide whether a person is appropriate for a particular group is by the manner in which he responds to the initial goal-setting questions. Intake goal setting should address the issue of behavior, and the fact that there is a need for a behavior change. Assessment of this commitment by the counselor comes from observing what the participant is able to communicate regarding his potential involvement in the group. Realistically, this may produce nothing more than a commitment to participate in the group on a trial basis. It may mean a commitment to show up and watch. It may mean an agreement to participate in several sessions. It may mean that the group is to become the avenue on which the participant must travel in order to stay in school, or out of jail. It may focus on a plan to "try everything," or "become a part of the group," or to "control myself."

Whatever they are, the initial Intake goals need to be

Individual goals and group goals are worked on jointly, under the auspices of the overall Full Value Contract.

stated as clearly as possible and understood by the negotiators. Relations with the group is the focus. Participants need to feel they will not be going into the experience alone.

Clarity at the beginning sets the stage for ongoing goal monitoring.

Clarity at the beginning sets the stage for ongoing goal monitoring. It's hard to monitor something that is fuzzy, undefined, confusing, and not agreed to. We don't want to clobber the person with her agreement, but we need to be ready to use it in an effective way. That's why the Intake session is so important. Since the potential participant generally has a desire to get what the group has to offer, she will have a tendency to be open to thinking about what she needs to do in order to change. Resistance, which is a natural antecedent of familiarity (note the family analogy), will tend to not be as severe as it will become after the group is in operation. And it is the changing that we are about.

Factors for Psychological Success
Kurt Lewin and his associates (1944) came up with four factors that suggest a person will experience psychological success as opposed to psychological failure. Presented in the Theory Chapter, these factors bear repeating in this context. A person will experience success if:

1) That person is able to define his own goals.
2) These goals are related to that person's central needs and values.
3) That person is able to define the paths that lead to the accomplishment of the goals.
4) The goals represent a realistic level of aspiration for that person: neither too high nor too low, but high enough to challenge his/her capabilities.

As we work with our participants in the initial sessions, keep these four issues in mind. They go from personal responsibility to realistic aspiration to identifying the paths that will lead to goal accomplishment. All four of Lewin's issues can be discussed in the initial interview, albeit couched in the language and intensity relative to the needs of the participant.

By involving the therapeutic Full Value Contract with Lewin's goal setting, we have a vehicle to activate his "four factors of psychological success." The Full Value Contract specifies:
  • That each person is engaging in the Activity.
  • What each person wants to get out of the Activity.
  • How each person is going to accomplish this.
  • What support will be needed in order to accomplish this

- That each person will not devalue himself or others while they seek to achieve their goal.
- What evidence will demonstrate that each person has achieved the goal.

Ongoing goal-monitoring involves continuous negotiation and the formation of new goals. This is a dynamic process, based on the presupposition that strength begets strength. Through the positive experience, the participant begins to gain confidence. This is groundwork for new goals. Your repetition of the goal-setting process helps it become a habit. As the habit becomes ingrained, the carry-over through spiralling is a natural outcome.

Ongoing goal monitoring involves continuous negotiation and the formation of new goals.

Warm-up Questions
Here are some warm-up questions to ask:
- What are your expectations for this adventure?
- What will be the hardest thing you will do?
- What will be the easiest thing you will do?
- What do you look forward to the most?
- What are you risking in going on this adventure?
- How well do get along with others?
- What types of people do you like best?

Goal-Setting Activities
Here are some examples of goal setting activities.

• Fantasy Activity for a Younger Group
Young kids (ages 5–9 or so) often can't address their issues directly, but will respond productively to opportunities to use their imagination. For example, say a youngster wants to conquer his fear. You can help him visualize his fear as a dragon, a bad animal, or the devil. Then figure out what he will need (tools, or weapons, or attributes) to confront this opponent. A tool might be other people as protectors or fellow warriors; attributes might be trust, strength, or the physical ability to do it. In this "Dungeons and Dragons" manner, the child is able to break the experience down into its elements. It must be noted here that you need to keep absolute control over this "role playing." Otherwise youngsters can get locked into it, and the element of play is lost. Keep it fun, balancing on the edge of fantasy, but not becoming absorbed by it. (Thanks to the staff of Elmcrest Psychiatric Institute, Portland, Conn.)

This use of fantasy can fit into other Activities: The Spider's Web has Charlotte hanging from the top strand. Prouty's Landing goes out over a Poison Pit of Boiling Yogurt.

If you fall in you will turn into a blueberry. In this way, you can take the fantasy characters, and "see" them during the Activity. (*Look, there's your dragon. Let's all get him. You don't need to kill him by yourself.*) It helps to know the culture of your population when you concoct these situational fantasies. You can ease a lot of tensions by making things familiar, and adding a twist of humor.

• *How Do I Feel About Myself?*
This self-describing activity can open the door for goal setting around the rating scale attributes:

How do I feel about myself?

This is an activity to help you become aware of your unique resources. Each statement below describes a feeling you may have about yourself. Circle one number for each statement that is best for you.

	Never	Not Often	Sometimes	Most Times	All the Time
I am friendly	1	2	3	4	5
I am happy	1	2	3	4	5
I am kind	1	2	3	4	5
I am brave	1	2	3	4	5
I am honest	1	2	3	4	5
I am likeable	1	2	3	4	5
I am trusted	1	2	3	4	5
I am good	1	2	3	4	5
I am proud	1	2	3	4	5
I am lazy	1	2	3	4	5
I am loyal	1	2	3	4	5
I am cooperative	1	2	3	4	5
I am cheerful	1	2	3	4	5
I am thoughtful	1	2	3	4	5
I am popular	1	2	3	4	5
I am courteous	1	2	3	4	5
I am jealous	1	2	3	4	5
I am helpful	1	2	3	4	5

You can easily adjust this for your setting. You may want to have the group consider only a few of these attributes, for the sake of simplicity. You may want to add colloquial attributes, or attributes that relate to the things you want to achieve.

• *Looking At My Strengths*

This Activity asks a person to look at an experience in her life where she has utilized her strengths in order to "get through it" or "deal with it." It is used to set the stage for goal setting, assuming that if a person focuses on her strengths, she will be willing to ride those strengths into the next experience. It is a "framing" or "stage-setting" exercise (Thanks to Dr. Arthur Underwood, Counselor, North Shore Community College for this Activity.)

Looking At My Strengths

All of us, from time to time, have times of conflict during our lives. Times when we were troubled, confused, upset and felt sad and despairing. Even times when we may have thought that there was no solution or way to solve the conflict or problem. Think of a time or times when you were involved in such a conflict or problem during your life...then circle the strengths or abilities which you had that helped you get through.

My self-confidence	My creativity
My faith and trust in others	My physical endurance
My sense of humor	My commitment to my values
My hard work	My stability
My courage	My independence
My honesty	My loyalty to others
My commitment to others	My flexibility
My acceptance of others	My assertiveness
My empathy with others	My inner security
My self-discipline	My open-mindedness
My acceptance of events	

Add any others that you can think about in the space below:

Sample Goals
Individual:
> I will ask for help when I need it.
> I will participate without horsing around.
> I will speak up if I feel uncomfortable with the exercise.
> I will try to control my tendency to put other people down.
> I will help Cynthia do the Tension Traverse.
> I will attempt one Activity.
> I will be responsible for the First Aid kit.
> I will call and make an appointment for the group at the nursing home.
> I will get to know other group members better.
> I will be less afraid to try new things.
> I will be willing to express my thoughts and feelings.
> I will feel better about myself...learn to accept myself better than I do.
> I will learn to accept criticism better.
> I will learn to listen to others.

Group:
> We will honor the Full Value Contract.
> We will not bring any drugs or alcohol.
> We will not devalue anyone in the group.
> We will confront each other if anyone is messing around.
> We will attempt to row around the Cape, keeping the boats together and wearing life jackets.
> We will support each other by spotting carefully.
> We will all write thank-you notes to the person we interviewed.

Examples of Personal Goal Setting

Group-centered goals

Wayne was asked to participate in an elementary school counseling group because of his "fist first" habits. He had no friends because of his fighting. He acknowledged this as a problem during the Intake. One of his initial goals was to work on this impulse to fight first and talk later. He was to try and find other ways to relate to his peers. This goal was "group-centered"...which is the definition of the Activities contract. We were not trying to get Wayne to change his behavior on the "outside" at that point. Certainly outside situations where appropriate were discussed. But the emphasis was to deal with Wayne in the group. Because of the Common Ground everyone stands on, the issues can be seen by everyone: his behavior, good and bad.

This Activities-centeredness keeps us from generalizing too soon. Persons in need know they have problems. It's the solutions to the problems that hang them up. As Wayne began to accomplish his goals in the group, he was reality testing in a "new" environment, which was a carefully controlled one as well. Planning success-oriented experiences, seeing to it that he gets through the session without blowups by the judicious use of time-outs, encouraging and reminding him of his goals, all are a great help to him during the Activity time.

Staff-training sessions

Goal setting has a significant impact on staff-training sessions. Phil Ritchie at Elmcrest Psychiatric Institute noticed a dramatic difference between the productivity he saw in his first session, where there was no goal setting, and the second session, where time was spent early on in figuring out what each staff member in the training wanted to accomplish. There was much less nervous horsing around in the second group. And the subsequent feedback regarding the success of the training was both more specific and more positive.

The non-verbal participant

Susan was a non-verbal group member, but she always showed for the sessions. Her non-verbal, symbolic "action" communicated a great deal. She demonstrated her contracting by always being there and by volunteering for anything that came up. She was goal setting in her own way. Should we have required her to establish goals to overcome her silence? If she had been forced into the verbal realm too soon, it wouldn't have worked. The important thing is that she was communicating through her actions. Our "reading" of those actions and adjusting to her needs were critical to her success in the group. Gradually we "fed" her goals. She let us know if she didn't like them. It went back and forth that way for a year and a half before she began to open up verbally. Interpreting her was a struggle, but once we understood how she was wired, it became easy and a pleasure, for she was so willing!

Bettelheim (1950) supports this interaction with non-verbal participants when he states:

"In interpreting the school to the new child we rely more on the actual daily Activities he can watch or take part in, and less on what we may think his acute problems are, or his major anxieties or delusions. Even if we knew for a fact what they were, it could only seem presumptuous on our part to show such superior knowledge instead of waiting until the child in his own good time should take us into his confidence. If we were to talk about his anxieties without waiting, we might only intimidate him into feeling we think him inadequate. Actually, we aim at eventually giving the child the feeling that we believe that neither he alone nor we alone can solve his basic problems, but that he will be able to solve them with our help in a process of daily living together." (p.51)

Note that Bettelheim is referring to his work with an autistic children's school.

Limiting anxiety about goals

For our purposes, forcing one's goals into conscious awareness can create anxiety. Some participants can and should handle the process, but others will be unable to. One must be able to read ability levels in this area, and act accordingly. Symbolic behavior can carry a long way. The Activities and

the group should be attractive enough for these persons. We must work more at helping them be comfortable, and in reading their symbolic behavior. Because of our pragmatic multi-modal approach, we should be flexible enough to adjust. Developing these instincts, and others like it, so that we know when to push and when to back off, is clearly one of the most important Adventure Counseling skills.

The example of Susan suggests an important question: does goal setting, and the emphasis on talk time in general, take away from the impact of the Adventure experience? The response is twofold: persons in need often lack the ability to a) understand and assimilate their experience, and b) apply behavior in one theatre to behavior in another. Good talk aids in both of these areas. But we shouldn't be tigers ready to pounce on openings, for either goal-setting or interpretive opportunities. A friend relates this story:

Our three-year-old son hadn't yet said one word. He had raised our anxiety level to a frenzy. One day in the car he said "Tree" while pointing to one. I slammed on the brakes and shouted,

"You said something! What was that? Say it again!" He didn't say another word for six months.

When we inevitably make mistakes like these, we can rely on the continual opportunities that an intact family has to rectify misdeeds. The late-talking child went on to become a healthy adult, so the damage wasn't all that great. In ABC, we have the continual motion of the wave to help process mistakes. And, we have the family metaphor to lean on. As we set goals and discuss our Activities we provide a model for dealing with experience. That model presupposes that the cognitive realm can aid us in taking control of our lives and helping us negotiate situations without giving in to impotent and destructive impulses. More simply stated, families sit down and plan what they are going to do, do what they plan, and talk about what they did. Healthy ones, anyway. It is not the whole answer, for an overemphasis on cognition has its own pitfalls, as stated above. But through combining Activities with reflection, by breaking down experience into its elements, and by mixing in the focusing power of intention as it relates to goal setting, we can begin to gain mastery over ourselves. That includes controling impulses, forming relationships, understanding cause and effect, and planning.

...through combining activities with reflection, by breaking down experience into its elements, and by mixing in the focusing power of intention as it relates to goal setting, we can begin to gain mastery over ourselves.

Overlap of Personal Goals and Group Goals

Activities goal setting goes on for the life of the group. Early in the year, Nancy was doing Criss Crotch, a low element, while the others spotted.When the bus arrived to pick up the group, her spotters left her. She was forced to get off the element before she completed it. She voiced her displeasure at their discounting. "I hadn't finished yet." Spotting involves trust. Her spotters proved to be untrustworthy by leaving her. They weren't too receptive to her criticism, arguing that the bus had come and they had to leave.

Six months later she repeated her observation about that instance, this time in the context of the improvement the group had made. They understood her better then, and showed that they had actually heard her the first time. They simply echoed what she had said, both times, then left it. The group was receptive because of those improvements. The specific incident hadn't been hammered into them over the six months, but it had slipped into the consciousness of the group, without a lot of folderol. The issue of trust kept cropping up in other forms through the myriad experiences they had together. The theme was the same, but the shape of the theme was continually changing. In this situation trust became a group goal because of Nancy's experience and the subsequent Activities which gave everyone the opportunity to practice it.

Aids to Goal Setting

The following exercise to aid in goal setting is based on the buddy system. Everyone buddies up (triples up, if necessary) with a person he trusts. Partner A then relates his individual and group goals to his buddy (partner B). Partner B writes these goals down in partner A's journal, or simply remembers them. Sharing with the group is the next step, with partner B doing the talking. (*Joe wants to be more positive. He also wants to take a leadership role in the Initiative.*) If anything was missed, partner A can embellish. The written goals can be collected by the leader, which will aid in the Debriefing.

The group can aid in goal setting, too. ("*Can you guys think of anything that Joe needs to work on?" "Yeah, he needs to get in there and spot better. He's always walking off." "Does this fit in with your goal of being more positive, Joe?"*) The agreement to confront positively can be exercised to great advantage in this way. Also, the group is helping the individual get specific about how she is going to accomplish the Activity. It's too easy to be general about goals, and thereby miss the nuts and bolts of what it means to actually accomplish them.

The next step refers to what support Joe will need from the group in order to accomplish this. (*Will it be OK with you that the group calls you back in order to spot when you wander off?*) Finally, what is needed as evidence that the goal has been worked on or achieved or avoided must be made clear. In this case, the evidence is seen in whether Joe spotted, and attempted to be a leader. Did he or didn't he? That is reviewed in the Debrief.

The therapeutic Full Value Contract can act as a checklist:
- What you want.
- How you are going to get it.
- What support you will need.
- Agreement not to discount.
- Show the evidence regarding achievement.

This checklist organized into a Personal Action Plan would look like this:

Personal Action Plan
- What do I want to accomplish (my goals)?
- What do I need to do to accomplish it (what actions am I willing to take)?
- What resources will help me? (People, information, other resources) What support do I need from the group?

- How will I know if I accomplished it? (How do I know if I am reaching my goals? What will be my criteria for measurement?)
- How can I help others in my group achieve their goals? (How can my strengths be used to help others?…How do I relate to the Full Value Contract?)

Spiral Goals

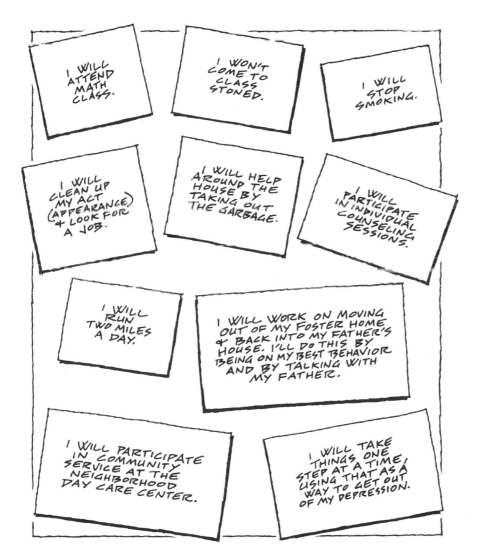

Once individuals have begun to meet goals articulated within the group, they are encouraged to set and monitor goals that are to be enacted outside the group. We call these

We call these "spiral" goals, to convey the sense of a process that does not repeat and that shows growth.

"spiral" goals, to convey the sense of a process that does not repeat and that shows growth. Because change is slow, it can appear to go in a circle. Because of the strength of the group experience the spiral goal setter is not making these goals in a vacuum. He can rely on the group to support him. The spiral emanates from the group, is slow and appears repetitious, but in fact is always new, always growing, moving out into the "world."

Here are some case studies illustrating the use of personal Spiral Goals:

Wendy, a high school senior, needed to get out of her mother's house. Her mother showed more care for her own boyfriend, and for going out to the bars, than she showed for Wendy. But Wendy didn't want to leave her sister. An option was discussed and agreed upon. Wendy would move in with the neighbors. That way, she could stay close to her sister without having to continue on in a situation that was overwhelming to her. This proved to be the first of many Spiral Goals: job, tutoring, counseling, Outward Bound, college. Each goal had its own sub-goals, reminding us of the process.

Matt was an alternative school student. At the end of his junior year, he set a series of goals for his senior year. We had been setting goals all year for his Adventure Activities, and for other issues. The next fall he was eager to see the written copy of the goals he had set three months before. He had been thinking about them all summer!

Lori-Ann had expressed an interest in jewelry making. We got her a job with a local silversmith. This gave her a success "in the world"….She began, through this experience, to control her depression. She was doing something she liked, and she was good at it!

Spiral Goals [must] make connections to the outside world...or they will be just a wish-list.

Larry never completed his school work, though he had excellent abilities. Because of his participation in the group he began to feel valued by his peers. He was good at the Activities, and was super attentive to the campcraft: make the fire, pack the gear, all done with incredible thoroughness. He gave to the group, and they in turn put up with his individualistic idiosyncrasies. He was asked to do a lot of volunteer work for the program beyond that asked of other group members, such as fixing boats, vans, and our camping area. All this activity was discussed in the group. Larry later responded by becoming our youngest camp counselor, and has gone on to graduate with honors from a two year college. When he got into legal difficulties, he came to us for help in sorting it out. Because of the kind of "accounting" we had been doing, he was better able to hear what he needed to learn regarding the incident, and not try to cover it up, as had been his tendency.

These Spiral Goals make connections to the outside world. They must be administered carefully, or they will be just a wish-list. They need to be monitored, as well. Forgotten, they are another of a long line of unrealized dreams referred to in a poem by Langston Hughes: *"What happens to a dream deferred? ...It dries up, like a raisin in the sun."* Like the Activities, they must be "doable," or defeat will be the end result. But because of the connection to the group, "defeats" (lost jobs, failed reunions), can also be dealt with. There's a context, a home to come back to.

An element of risk is necessary in "spiralling out." We can't be overly protective. It's a real world out there. That's why we need to know when the participants are ready to spiral out, to try on their new attitude and behavior. (*What if the jewelry maker doesn't like me, or I'm no good at it?*) That can be discussed in the Debrief, while a new spiral is being hatched. There's always another chance on the Adventure Wave!

All Adventure experiences lead to Spiral Goal setting. The sense of trust and of competency gained in the Adventure group is a basis for being able to function in the world. The following activities focus specifically on preparing for Spiralling:

The sense of trust and of competency gained in the Adventure group is a basis for being able to function in the world.

• *Interviewing*

Interview another person. Start with "safe" subjects, like the group leader! Or other group members. Or a staff person from another part of the institution, a person the participants choose (with your help). Group interviews work well because there is little focus on individual members...unless your goal is to have one person doing the interviewing. That's an intensity decision.

• *Role Playing*

Role play a job application or family situation. Involve the other group members. Include players like the secretary, receptionist, security guard at the door, personnel manager, the president of the corporation. Or father, mother and siblings.

Be careful with role playing, for it can get very serious very quickly. Participants can go too deeply into their roles. Role playing allows important defenses to come down, which can open up potentially hurtful situations. Work on making it meaningful, but fun at the same time. Participants will take the roles and make them very believable. You must be prepared to intervene. Emphasize the "play" aspect of role playing. Do this by interrupting with comments and humor, getting them to go in and out of their roles.

• *Brainstorming*

Brainstorm all the contingencies of spiralling out. Make a list, and discuss it. This can be excellent material for papers, journals, and ongoing discussions. It can help everyone understand the cause and effect factors in the dilemmas we face. The lead-up process to spiralling gives participants practice, and acquaints them with and consequently demythologizes the situations. It not only helps those who are going out. The other group members benefit from what they are going through. Soon it will be their turn.

• *Community service*

Community service is an important spiral activity. Relationships at the service site, because of the giving and relationship elements, have a feeling and quality to them similar to those experienced in the ABC group. Adult leaders at these service sites tend to have a protective and instructive instinct for volunteer helpers. Communication with them about the strengths, weaknesses and goals of the volunteer can enhance those relationships. If an essential goal of ABC is to develop trust, then it is important to provide trusting experiences in the community. This also encourages a positive transfer point for the "out there." Students will have choices. (*Do I want to spend my time in abusive relationships, or do I want to relate to positive Islands?*)

The habit of realistic goal setting needs to become a life-long tool.

If contracting is made part of the group, the carry-over after termination from the group is made easier. It's not such a jolt. The process of setting goals and then careful monitoring to ensure success helps develop a habit (*If I want this, I need to do that*). The habit of realistic goal setting needs to become a life-long tool. The group is teaching them that tool, and reinforcing the lessons with continual use.

Secondly, Adventure Counseling experiences themselves provide an unconscious model for dealing with the outside world. Steven Bacon refers to this relating process as the "transderivational search:"

> "Effective generalization essentially requires that the course experiences be highly isomorphic [means 'having the same structure'] with student's real life experiences. If they are, and if the course Activities have provided successful resolutions to formerly unproductive strategies, then there will be positive changes in real life. Isomorphism, new endings to stereotypical strategies, and success experiences are the critical requirements for generalization." (Bacon, 1983)

Constantly striving to make connections to the structures the students are familiar with (isomorphism) is essential to nailing down the concept. The community-based presence of Adventure Counseling aids greatly in this transfer process. Participants generally begin their group experience "at home" on familiar ground. They may go away for certain Activities, but that home locus keeps them connected.

Finally, remember that many participants don't see the real lessons of a group until some time later. They may show no change at all during the time of the group. But take heart. The strategies, the Activities, the structures you are giving them are not being met by deaf ears. It takes time to change. Like a spiral, slowly, at times reluctantly, with bright lights and dark spots. It's the long haul we're concerned with.

> "If you're in trouble, get help!"
>
> "You are a good person. Look at what you've done here."
>
> "You are able to do things, to have ideas, to take meaningful risks."
>
> "Things can work out for you."

These are the messages we want our group members to carry with them into the world. And they are heard much more than we know.

Here are some examples of what former participants are doing with the things they learned in the Adventure Counseling group:

> Jolene was a good student/athlete, but with home problems that forced her to live in a tent for most of her senior year. She had no relationship with her family for that period of time. Her involvement in the group was total, although mostly non-verbal. She was one of those students one could always count upon to pitch in: finishing her projects, going on trips, cleaning the gear. In speaking to her five years later, she wanted us to say this: *"Remember the long distance rowing trip? The one where we stayed up all night,*

...remember that many participants don't see the real lessons of a group until some time later.

going down the back side of Plum Island? I keep thinking about that trip while I'm doing my school work (she was a senior in college)...that I can do more than I ever thought I could."

Another student, who had drug and attendance problems in high school, found in his Adventure group a place to focus his energies and experience success. He did a post graduate internship with us, building a climbing wall and leading small groups of younger students. He came back to the group ten years later as a successful broker of security systems. His advice to the current Adventure group: *"Take it one step at a time; don't say you can't do it; demand the best for yourself; don't put things off; be honest with your clientele."* These statements indicate that he had internalized the contracting process, and made it work for himself in his professional life.

Mike was a severely depressed man who had participated in an Adventure group in a mental hospital. After termination, he had returned home, and had gone back to bed, where he had been virtually immobilized before hospitalization. He decided to get back out of bed and go back to the hospital in order to talk to former group members and his counselors. He was seeking help and association, something he had not been able to do before he had been admitted by his parents. The ability to seek help by himself can be seen as a response to the goal setting he had done in group. *"When you need help, ask for it. Don't discount yourself by staying away from help."*

"When you need help, ask for it. Don't discount yourself by staying away from help."

Conclusion

Framing the experience is what we are concerned about in the Briefing process. The basic principles of hopefulness and newness, and the positive nature of the Full Value Contract provide the group with a kind of power that would not be available if we were to introduce the activities as simply "this is what we are going to do today, gang." Certainly it is more complicated and takes more time to go through this Briefing scenario, but the result is a group that knows better what it is doing and why it is doing it. What would at first appear to be a fistful of controlling by the leader turns out to be the avenue whereby the group members gain real control over what they are doing.

The next chapter, **Leading: Implementing the Adventure Experience**, explores leadership strategies. Keep the goal setting in mind as we go through it. It will emerge again, both in Leading and in Debriefing, as we follow along the Adventure Wave.

Chapter 6

Leading:
Implementing the Adventure Experience

"In the midst of winter I finally learned that there was in me an invincible summer."

— Albert Camus

A$_{}$S WE GO OUT TO LEAD the Activity, let's just remind ourselves that the original impulse of Counseling on the Run was to extend the view that counseling takes place all along the Adventure Wave. This means that counseling is not limited to the sit-down-and-let's-talk-about-it mode. Conversations, contracts, ideas, experiences, confrontations and plans that transpire before, during and after the Activity, in the van, hallway, in small groups while doing projects, all present natural and beneficial counseling situations.

The counseling takes place with the whole group. It takes place with small sub-groups. It takes place with individuals. The Adventure Counselor maintains a core of concern and connectedness to the individuals and to the group.

Participants in response to that growth atmosphere begin to relax, to try new things, to trust, to grow. They also act out and rebel, fighting the things that they are seeing and feeling. Their behavior, all of it and at all times, is material for counseling. You may selectively choose not to use some of it. You may wait for the right moment. You may pounce right down upon it. You may test, then draw back.

Adventure Counseling is pragmatic: If it works, use it. Certainly different groups require different approaches. Court adjudicated youth need a tight, iron fist in relation to their behavior. They can laugh and have fun, but they cannot be allowed to step out of line. School counseling groups need the intimacy and attention provided to them by a small group, along with appropriate limit setting. Personal growth classes need to explore their own decision processes, and their own personal power and experience.

We as counselors have decisions to make, also. The sequencing process which acknowledges the change that every group is continually undergoing helps us keep track of what is happening, and how to make appropriate decisions. This chapter is devoted to further explanation of our framework for making those decisions, so that we can come up with an effective leadership style.

Here are some skills that can aid you in leading the Adventure group:
- **Leadership Voice**
- **Common Ground**
- **Challenge**
- **Instruction**
- **Intervention**
- **Empathy**
- **Readings, Fantasy, and Journals**
- **Competition**
- **Centering**
- **Co-leadership**
- **Conflict Resolution**

Leadership Voice

In order to become effective Adventure counselors we must start with addressing our own personal style. Our lives are dotted with many examples of leaders, and it is easy to incorporate the approach others use into our own approach. This is O.K. Modeling and experimenting is one way to learn. But in the midst of that we need to come to our own "voice," for without that voice, we are merely acting like someone else. A colleague said that for years he tried to use the humor patterns of a co-worker. It wasn't until he decided "that just wasn't me" that he began to feel comfortable with what he was able to offer.

How do we find our voice?

- Experience is the most obvious resource: Put in the time leading groups, doing the activities, training, preparing, reading, slugging it out with the issues presented by the Adventure field. This will produce an ease with the activities to a point where they become friends.
- Be open to new ideas and approaches, not locking yourself into one leadership pattern, hardening up to a point where you are unapproachable. That's a voice all right, but a negative one. The pragmatic approach applies here. After all, we are asking our group members to be able to hear input from others. Adventure leaders need to be able to do the same. This means letting yourself be vulnerable, to your participants, and to your peers. If you aren't comfortable with something you are doing, ask a peer or supervisor. Also, realize that there are many ways to lead without compromising safety. Being open to them can bring a vigor to your style.
- Be able to operate from a "gut feeling level." *This is how I feel about it!* Adventure work is emotional. We are dealing with feelings, and we need to be in touch with our feelings. It is a primary source of our voice.
- Accept yourself. You may not be some things, but you are other things. Think through what you are, not dwelling so much on what you are not. If you want to change, be sure that you can find a way to be increasingly clear about it, not just blindly pursuing it. Then you can break it down into goals, and it can be achievable and measurable. Often when we get specific about these things we become more aware of what we really want.

...realize that there are many ways to lead without compromising safety. Being open to them can bring a vigor to your style.

You also need to be aware of what impact you have on the group. Adventure Counseling is group-centered, but it is also leader-centered. The leader's presence is always felt:

- The group learns to monitor itself, but groups do need leaders to provide focus and boundaries. You must keep group issues "in bounds."
- Your participation in the activities puts you in a special, connected place.
- Role modeling is an important part of Adventure Counseling. Participants are learning how to approach situations, and function in the world with the lessons that they learn. The group will emulate you, as the closest responsible adult. This role modeling is natural and appropriate.

Adventure Counseling is group centered, but it is also leader centered. The leader's presence is always felt.

Be realistic. You may set up an Initiative, and try to retreat to the background. But you are always in the consciousness of the group. It has to be that way. It is a serious position to be in, for participants are asked to open themselves up, to stretch and trust and relate in new ways while they are in your care.

This leader-centeredness underscores the need to develop that voice. Lazarus, as he defines what it means to be a successful therapist, speaks to this point:

"I have been impressed by the fact that skillful therapists, especially great psychotherapeutic artists, share certain features regardless of their background, school affiliations, or professional identifications. They are responsible and flexible individuals with a high degree of respect for people. They are essentially non-judgmental and firmly committed to the view that infringement on the rights and satisfactions of others is to be strongly discouraged. They will not compromise human interests, values, and dignity. They bring warmth, wit, and wisdom to the therapeutic situation, and, when appropriate, they introduce humor and fun. They seem to have an endless store of relevant anecdotes and narratives. They are good role models (they practice what they preach), and are authentic, congruent, and willing to self-disclose.

"Why am I bringing these issues into a chapter on the selection of techniques? Mainly to stress that the final orchestration of successful therapy depends on what techniques are selected, how they are implemented, and by whom they are delivered. As surgeons are apt to point out, it is the person behind the scalpel who can wield it as an instrument of destruction or of healing. In psychotherapy, it is even more difficult to separate the specific technique from the person who administers it." (Lazarus, pp.155-56)

This quote comes from Ted Woodward, an Adventure practitioner at the Friend's Seminary, New York City:

"I went on a search to become a leader. I searched high and low. I spoke with authority, people listened. But at last there was one who was wiser than I and they followed him. I sought to inspire confidence but the crowd responded 'why should we trust you?' I postured and I assumed the look of leadership with a countenance that glowed with confidence and pride. But the crowd passed by and never noticed my air of elegance. I ran ahead of the others, pointing new ways to new heights. I demonstrated that I know the route to greatness. And then I looked back and I was alone.

"What shall I do, I queried? I've tried hard and used all that I know. And then I listened to the voices around me. And I heard what the group was trying to accomplish. I rolled up my sleeves and joined in the work. As we worked I asked 'are we all together in what we want to do, and how we'll get the job done?' And we thought together and we struggled towards our goal. I found myself encouraging the faint hearted. I sought the ideas of those too shy to speak out. I taught those who knew little at all. I praised those who worked hard. When our task was completed, one of the group members turned to me and said 'this would not have been done but for your leadership.' At first I said, 'I did not lead I just worked with the rest.' And then I understood, leadership isn't a goal. I lead best when I help others...to use themselves and focus on my group, their needs and their goals. To lead is to serve, to give, to achieve together."

The shared experience of Common Grounding presupposes that the leader is an active member of the group.

Common Ground

The shared experience of Common Grounding presupposes that the leader is an active member of the group. Visualize and practice it: helpful, full of the joy of learning and doing, attentive, willing to try new things, to listen, to get right in there and play. Then add to it adult planning, observation and control. No line is being crossed over in order to relate to the students...for the Common Ground brings out a new kind of leader, one that can both lead and experience at the same time.

There are some tactics to this. First, acknowledge that you can get bored repeating things. The way to fight this boredom is to look through the eyes of the participants. For them, it is completely new. Because of their newness, you can experience newness, through them! The activity is no longer the issue, then. It's the experience of the participants that's important. Second, let yourself play, and have fun. If you have established that newness, then playing becomes easier and more exciting. Third, your prior experience of doing the activities allows you to identify with them. You've been there yourself! You can speak from experience.

As Bert Harris, a therapist at the Institute of Pennsylvania Hospital, says:

> "If we follow the medical model, we can't know what it means to have cancer, but on the ropes course we can know what it's like to have a similar fear. It does put us on a common ground, and the patients can see us as human beings. When someone is up there and you are holding them on belay and you know exactly what they are going through because the words just come out because you knew what you needed. I can't say what it's been like to not be able to get out of bed for a month, but I can say what it was like to stand on the Zip Wire for 5 minutes and really feel scared. They can see us as human beings who struggle with some of the same things."

Because of the Common Ground, you have more of a chance to operate from inside the group.

Being "Inside" the Group

Because of the Common Ground, you have more of a chance to operate from inside the group. No longer are you the outside "expert." Again, there doesn't have to be any loss of credibility or authority. You can and must step back and operate as the bottom line. The group wouldn't want it any other way. But you are still conveying the message that you are part of them, are human, have feelings, get excited, angry, even make mistakes. You become a different kind of role model on the Common Ground because you are allowing yourself to be known, to be vulnerable.

At the same time you have charge of the situation, and of yourself. Participants are thirsty for such persons to identify with. There is a line that must be maintained in Adventure Counseling, and we are not naive about that. At the same time, that line can be carefully established in the midst of the group, on common ground. You can't cross that line and ask the group for help with profound difficulties you may have. You don't need to "hang out" with them, or get into their personal "raps" to achieve the sense that you belong, either. And there are many activities that you simply cannot participate in with them because of your need to keep control of the safety issues.

Here is a description of a man who works with youth gangs in the San Fernando Valley (Bill Barich, Nov.86):

> "In dealing with teenagers, Manuel follows a single rule, which is that he must never be ahead of them or behind them but always *with* them, refusing to patronize them, granting their world an absolute integrity. He will discuss a pimple, an insult, or a bad lunch. Without comment, he listens to the most baseless complaints, the most absurd bragging, and the grossest expressions of self-pity. He is not always approving, but he shows his disapproval so lightly that it turns into compassion. In his view, every teenager in the valley is a potential victim, easily swayed, easily hooked on drugs, messing around with a number of things whose power he or she cannot fathom."

This Common Grounding is taken to the extreme. Of course he has no power over those street kids. Of course he has to continually "win the right to be heard" (John McKay, former President of Princeton Theological Seminary, in a lecture, summer of 1964). And he has no institutional or parental jurisdiction. He is simply there because he cares about the kids.

That kind of street work can teach us about what it really means to get in there on the same turf with our group members, for in the end, it is the essence of the relationship that we have with them that provides us with the chance to participate in their change process.

...there are many activities that you simply cannot participate in with them because of your need to keep control of the safety issues.

Challenge

When the leader during the Briefing says, "It's important to be able to say at the end of our Activity today that you challenged yourself in at least one way," he is utilizing one of the most effective tools he has. Challenge means going beyond the old, pushing into new territory, new ways of doing things, dealing with fear and accepting help and support. But challenge also is a confrontation with that part of ourselves that isn't sure what it is able to do, or be.

"Naked we stand before the Almighty"

Challenge has the potential of stripping us bare, of getting down to the essentials, the nub of things. When persons in need come to "get help" they are already open and vulnerable. For them, the challenge begins just by committing to a group, and by showing up. They may not act like it. But we must presuppose vulnerability. Think of these scenes:

- A ninth grade boy brought by desperate parents to an alternative school. Just getting out of the car for the interview is a tremendous struggle for him.
- A suicidal patient at a psychiatric hospital working on the goal of being part of a group, this in light of a history of being a butt of peer's jokes, and always on the "outside."
- A student who has worked hard at preparing herself for the Pamper Pole (a ropes course high element), climbs it, then freezes at the top, unable to complete the jump to a trapeze.
- Parents invited to an Adventure day with their child are challenged first by being there, second by being asked to participate in the events their child has been working on. The child is challenged by the presence of her family unit operating in the midst of her Adventure "family."

Challenge is a two-edged sword. While it presents the opportunity for change and success, it also lays bare the issues we are afraid of: losing face, failure and injury.

Challenge is a two-edged sword. While it presents the opportunity for change and success, it also lays bare the issues we are afraid of: losing face, failure and injury. Where there is opportunity for growth, there is also the opportunity for overstepping our bounds, of pushing too far, and thereby retarding the growth we want so badly for our participants.

Challenge is a tool that must be used properly. We must remember that a wholesome environment is our primary concern. Out of that wholesomeness, participants will begin to pick and choose for themselves what they need to do to improve. Because of this, Karl Rohnke, author of *Cowstails and Cobras II* and *Silver Bullets,* coined the phrase "challenge by choice." He explains:

"I've had an extended background in pushing people beyond their perceived capabilities. My role of 'program encourager' began officially in 1967 as an Outward Bound instructor, but had been matured over the years by a certain level of physical self-flagellation achieved in sports and a brief stint in the U.S. Army.

"Pushing people in a program sense was satisfying because the validity of your presence as an instructor depended upon being recognized as more than capable and immersing yourself into the same experiential milieu that the student was experiencing (usually a fearful or physically uncomfortable scenario that involved being hungry, lost, fatigued or bugged).

"Then, because of a change in student population, demographic location and being newly introduced to the public school persona, the approach to 'pushing' practically changed overnight; changed to mellow is probably most descriptive.

"What a change! What a revelation that the simple affording of that choice could achieve more toward growth of self-awareness and image than what used to require large doses of performance pressure. What a relief!

"With the pressure off (instructor and student), the opportunity for growth was palpably different. There was a remarkably sentient feel to teaching that had been masked and blunted by years of ego satisfaction and adherence to a one-minded, often glandular approach."

Challenge by Choice offers a student:
- A chance to try a potentially difficult and/or frightening challenge in an atmosphere of support and caring.
- The opportunity to "back off" when performance pressures or self-doubt become too strong, knowing that an opportunity for a future attempt will always be available.
- A chance to try difficult tasks, recognizing that the attempt is more significant than performance results.
- Respect for individual ideas and choices.

Karl's point is brought home by this example from the Institute of Pennsylvania Hospital: A short-term patient, a lawyer, was very depressed, denying his problems, not involved in anything, complaining of bad back, etc., reluctant to do any-

To force someone to participate would be counter to the kind of group centered spirit we are trying to develop.

thing. He eventually tried some of the activities, and on the last day got up on a high element and completed it. According to the therapist, "He felt he would never have attempted the Inclined Log at all if we had pushed him. The important thing is thet we gave him the decision-making power."

Respect for choice is reflected in accepting comments like: "I've got to come down now," or "My leg hurts too much to play Add-on Tag," or "Man, that's jive, those trust falls." To force someone to participate would be counter to the kind of group-centered spirit we are trying to develop.

But respecting the right to choose doesn't mean you can't challenge. The nature of Adventure activities is one big challenging obstacle course: Climb over this, let go of that, run around and act stupid, laugh and have fun, solve the problem over here, go over and accomplish those things. There's always a surprise, a monkey wrench to dig out of the machinery, a coat that can't touch the electrified Spider's Web.

Your role of leader must be to continually find ways to offer understandable challenges that can be accepted by the group as it maintains its right to make choices. Sometimes it may be necessary to say "This is the way it's going to be. Do it!" You may seem like a drill-sergeant, but groups respond to that mentality, too. A lot of growth can take place when people have no choice as to whether they are or are not going to do something. Just remember that whenever you make choices for the group, you take an essential power away from them.

Granted, there are many different kinds of groups. Passive groups, if given the chance, would often rather not do anything at all. So a line must be drawn there. "You are in an Adventure group, it does activities, has regular meeting times. You made the choice to be part of the group, and because of that there is a certain expectation of you." And we cannot allow participants to wander off or do other things during the Activity. That is not respecting the right to make choices. Challenge by Choice addresses those vulnerable areas where a person honestly feels that he is not able to do something, even if he previously said that he was willing to do it. Or, on the other hand, it deals with a person's right to assess the situation and say, "I want to do the Inclined Log now," or "I want to lead the singing at the rest home this week."

Challenge by Choice addresses those vulnerable areas where a person honestly feels that he is not able to do something, even if he previously said that he was willing to do it.

Here are some principles to keep in mind when you are challenging your group:
- Not everyone needs to do everything. Too often Adventure leaders pridefully boast that each group member did a particularly difficult activity. That may be a good

thing, but it misses the point of Challenge by Choice.

- Utilize the activities sequencing information in Chapter 4, **Sequencing**. Proper activities selection goes a long way toward being able to support the challenge once the Activity is in progress. Intensity decisions are an important accompanying factor.
- Time spent with goal setting is time well spent when it comes to dealing with the challenge of the event. When the participant is clear about what he/she wants to do, it's so much easier for everyone. Remember, goal setting doesn't have to take place only during a Briefing session removed from the Activity. A person may decide to do something during the session. But the same thing holds: Make certain that the person knows what he is doing, and is as clear as possible about what it means. This can involve some strong Counseling on the Run.

- Group pressure is very real, and can be used positively. Members are aided in this when they are aware of each other's goals, and are familiar with each other. That's why it is important, when choosing your activities, to reserve the more intense ones until the group members are more comfortable with each other. Because of the trust that develops in Adventure groups, members will be much more likely to respond to positive group pressure. The agreement in the Full Value Contract to confront and be confronted comes into play here: as long as we are confronting in a positive manner, group pressure should be used. Then it is defined as group support. Certainly there is a fine line here, and it is one of the most delicate areas of Adventure Counseling. Group pressure can go beyond the bounds of caring into aggression and abuse, and it can happen very quickly. Treated as a counseling issue, the crossing of that line can be handled. But if it is ignored, you are allowing figurative "termites" to eat away at the integrity of what you are trying to build.

- Trust (to repeat) is a great support of Challenge. Certain challenges require a strong dose of it. If it isn't there, perhaps more lead-up is necessary. On the other hand, effective challenging can bring about trust. Sometimes you need to take a calculated risk by pushing ahead at a certain time, counting on the trust to emerge.
- Individualize where necessary. Certain participants just will not do what the others are doing. Take the heat off of them. Find something supportive or manual for them to do.

Hard-line Challenge

Project Challenge, a court diversion program in Atlanta, Georgia, takes a hard line with its students: "You can choose to go with us for six weeks of intense Challenge work, or you can go to jail. That's your choice." Those who accept that challenge say that they want to deal with themselves in the manner explained to them when they accept a place in the program. But they also don't know exactly what they are getting into. How do you explain something if you haven't experienced it? It's one of the problems of Intake. They really know only one thing: by taking on the challenge they won't be going to jail, and they will have a chance to get free of probation if they complete the course.

How is challenge used in this context? The word is so important! As a continual reminder? Or a club? Or a tool within the goal-setting process? Their work in Adventure begins with the decision to accept a challenge. It is a choice, albeit a fairly uninformed one. But in the slippery world of adjudication it is a choice nonetheless. It can be ridden all the way through the six weeks. And ridden hard. Those participants know why they are there. And they know there's plenty of work to do. If they aren't willing to do that work, then they are asked to leave. But not just by the leaders alone.

"You can choose to go with us for six weeks of intense Challenge work, or you can go to jail. That's your choice."

The Role of Peer Pressure

Peer pressure comes into play here. Members monitor each other's behavior, and challenge (or confront) each other to deal with their behavior. Project Challenge is incapable of operating without the gut input by all the group members. Those members have the power to judge each other, and even to recommend removing a member of the group to a state lock-up facility. Talk about challenge and confrontation! If the group were developed along the lines of top-down decision making, it never would be able to police itself. The old saw of us vs. them would be continued at the expense of essential group healing power. It's not easy for the group members to deal with each other in this way, and there is plenty of gut wrenching that goes on while it happens. In the words of one member who was sent away for five days, then allowed to come back: " I was furious with them, but being away gave me time to think about what I had been doing. I realized they did it for my own good."

Soft-glove Challenge

On the other hand, take a voluntary counseling group. Essentially passive students have been persuaded to participate. Challenge is best used in short-term goal setting: Negotiating, encouraging, and providing the context for limit expansion. There comes a time when commitment to the group is necessary. Are you here or aren't you? But it comes in different guises, along the way. The principle of group-centeredness and cohesion remain the same. But the issues are different. Because of that difference, challenge is interpreted differently.

Some people need to have their nakedness "bared" in a dramatic way. Hot shot, do everything, "no brain, no pain" types need to be shocked into looking at their vulnerability. Finding the most difficult event "just for them" is something the whole group will understand, though this can backfire: No-brain types often don't recognize danger or difficulty when it is there. They'll just plough right through it. They will need another kind of challenge: listening to others, spotting, support, mundane tasks, to get them out of their "me, me" state. Be careful not to become overly aggressive toward the loud-mouth, either. Watch your own need to control. Try to wait it out. A healthy group will do its own controlling, though it may take more time. It is time well spent.

Instruction

The practical aspects of Adventure activities provide a welcome relief from all the processing/goal-setting/behavior orientation of counseling groups. There are skills to be learned. Step by step cognitive work. Knots. Map and compass. First Aid. Safety. Equipment maintenance. Curriculum for student tutors, activities for the old folks' home. It is good to interrupt intense group work with "listen up" instruction periods, whether there is a specific need or not. It adds variety, gets their minds off problems, grounds them. Because Adventure is so active, the group readily responds to the need to understand how things work. It is in their interest to tie the knot correctly, to know how a canoe works or how to use a compass.

Instruction is especially useful when you need to rein in the group, to remind them that you are still the boss. Your intervening to teach, directly, tells them that now is the time to look at you. There's no Initiative problem solving to it, where everyone has a say. It is leader-centered, and because of that you can change the tempo.

Instruction is especially useful when you need to rein in the group, to remind them that you are still the boss.

So instruction is practical in terms of leader control as well as transmitting necessary "how to" information. The combination of the two elements is important because of safety considerations. There are some Adventure items that are simply not negotiable. Each event has its own safety issues, and must first be mastered by the leader. Then the leader must pass this information down—proper care for the equipment; life jackets at all times in the canoes or boats; knots tied correctly; calls gone through in correct sequence; proper helmeting; no horsing around. Is it too rough, cold, wet, to go out? Will we be endangering our group if we insist on punching through to our goal? Without adequate coverage in this area, the event cannot be practiced. Period.

For several years on our winter camping trip we attempted to get to Thoreau Falls on the Zealand Pond trail in the White Mountains of New Hampshire. We never made it because of time and weather considerations. Although the group was consulted, the leader decided alone to turn back. It's not that the group had no power. Their willingness to try, and to get as far as they did, indicates the strength they had developed. The goal became incidental: They went as far as safety would allow. Who could ask for more? Better to have that kind of "failure" than a group compromised by an untenable situation. In the end, that's a more important lesson than achieving the goal. That kind of "failure" is, in fact, learning in and of itself.

Intervention

When instruction is referred to as taking control, it crosses over into an intervention mode. And intervention takes place whenever the instructor sees the group as needing to stop and take a look at itself and what it is doing. In this way, instruction and intervention take on a similar meaning. Some sample types of intervention include:

- **Substitute a More Relevant Activity**
  The group is horsing around while spotting the Tension Traverse. Stop the Activity. Pretend that someone breaks a leg. They've got to construct a stretcher, and evacuate. Teach them how to treat an injured person. Teach them how to build a stretcher. Have them carry the injured person "out" a distance. Intensity needs dictate whether you want the heaviest member to be the injured one. If there's not enough time, fit this in as an Activity for the next session. Be as directive as you need to be. Combine it with instruction and Initiative. Tie in the First Aid lessons with the seriousness of spotting.

- **Modify the Activity**
  It's getting late, and the group hasn't solved the Spider's Web Initiative (get the whole group through a vertical web of rope). Frustration is running high. Call a time out. Ask them to decide whether or not they want to solve the problem with changed rules, or whether they want to come back and try again. Or you can have them "Freeze Frame" their effort. Group members must "freeze" their bodies where they are. They are then asked to listen to each other,

going over all the ideas that have been suggested. (This technique was developed by Ann Smolowe, Director of Project Adventure's Executive Reach program.) The way you approach it can have a lot to do with the decision they make. If you wait until time runs out before you intervene, there can be no decision. Also, you can use the decision time to slip in some suggestions about what they are doing wrong, or missing.

• **Refocus the Group**

You are doing a community service project, placing Christmas trees on the dunes behind the beach in order to help the dunes regenerate (sand catches in the branches: In a matter of months a new six-foot dune will build up). Group members have made the contacts to do this Activity, and have collected the trees as well. While hauling them out, some of the participants are sneaking off to have a butt and avoid the work. Call the whole group together. Go over what the Activity means, drawing in those who have done the work setting up the Activity. Then let the Activity continue. Instruction and intervention are combined to make a potentially negative leadership experience into a more positive "What are we here for anyway?" and "Let's not devalue the work of your group members." This intervention only becomes necessary when the group is unable to do it for themselves. You need to wait and see if they will correct themselves. Intervention comes when the group has shown an inability to proceed in a certain direction or is going in an unacceptable direction.

When to Intervene

You must have confidence in your ability to manage a group, and you need to have confidence that the group can manage its own behavior and the Activity presented to it. It is the synchronicity of the two that provides the basis for making interventions. Be careful in your judgements, for every time you make an intervention that isn't necessary, you are sending a message to the group that they are weak, that they can't manage their own behavior. On the other hand, if you wait too long to intervene, the group may experience too much chaos, and receive a negative experience from that.

Judging whether to intervene or not is relative to your ability to know and respond to the group's needs at any particular time. Your group at the Spider's Web was having an extremely hard time. This is a pinch point! (See The Conflict Resolution section of this chapter). And the pinch

... every time you make an intervention that isn't necessary, you are sending a message to the group that they are weak, that they can't manage their own behavior.

point might turn into a crunch point. You might decide on a different tactic than intervention. Because of the success you have seen them have at The Wall (a 12-foot obstacle that the whole group must get over), you are confident that they have the ability to manage their conflict enough to handle the situation, even if their conflict has become that crunch point. The judgement to intervene is the by-product of your observation skills, mixed in with experience, competence, and the ability to trust the group.

Empathy

Understanding the participants by actually caring about what they are going through draws the leader closer to them. And developing empathy between the group members is a key element of the "Island of Healing." When a person knows that she is not alone in her struggle, that someone understands, not just in a cognitive cause and effect manner, but in a feeling way, she is much more able to open up, to be vulnerable, and consequently more liable to take the risk of changing.

Risk situations...bring trust and feeling issues to the surface quickly.

Risk situations, whether they are Trust Falls or highly dramatic rappels (coming down a rock face on a rope while rock climbing) and Pamper Poles (a climb to a platform on a ropes course where one is encouraged to jump for a trapeze), bring trust and feeling issues to the surface quickly. A person chooses to participate because it is fun, exciting, and gets the adrenaline flowing. But there is also the unknown quantity of the need to depend on other people in order to complete the Activity. Try doing a Trust Fall by yourself! So the participant may go into the Activity with one goal, and come out with a different accomplishment. (*Thanks for being there. I really needed you. —You got hold of that rope? Thanks for belaying me.*)

Some tools to aid in developing empathy are:

- **Observation Skills**
  People want to be noticed. The trouble is, most observation tends to be of negative behavior when applied to people in need. Of course negative behavior when it requires control must be dealt with. But finding insightful things to say about participants, even if they are in the midst of acting out, helps form a positive bridge. Remember, Adventure activities are about providing positive experiences from which a person can grow.

There's a way of dealing with situations through insight that is non-punitive...that gets across the idea that issues are being dealt with out of a concern for the person, rather than out of a need to simply control the group. So observational insights into what is going on, keeping a mental catalogue or actual notes on what you see, gives the group specifics regarding its work and also lets it know that you are there and on duty. Your observations can be brought up at appropriate times, either in immediate Debriefs, or way down the line.

• **Predictable Style**

Just because a participant is not directly involved with a particular interaction doesn't mean that she is not benefiting from it.

Within the group consciousness there is also the need to establish a method of dealing with situations and issues. Participants watch like a hawk to see how the leader deals with what is going on. Just because a participant is not directly involved with a particular interaction doesn't mean that she is not benefiting from it. You are establishing a gestalt, a group feeling, when you deal with group issues. This doesn't mean you should walk on eggs. And you are allowed to make mistakes. But you need to acknowledge those mistakes, either by mentioning them or through your overall actions. Your overall consistency, and the feeling that you have when you deal with group issues, will establish a modus operandi. In this way, the most unreachable participant may turn around and be the greatest success story, simply from being part of a group that had integrity, and handled its issues with caring, insight and justice.

• **Touching and Hugging**

Many Adventure activities require people to touch each other. Yurt Circle, Add-On Tag, Trust Fall/Spotting Sequence, Belaying (through the very real "umbilical" rope). Because of necessary safety issues, we can take touching out of the intimacy sphere. The messages are more practical. (*You need to do the Trust Fall in order to go to the other activities.*) The two-person and three-person Trust Falls, require spotter(s) to place their hands on the shoulders of the "faller" as an act of assurance, before the fall occurs. Just because the touching has this practical aspect does not mean that other equally important messages are not being given off.

The quality of the experience is greatly affected by how the leader conducts the Activity. For example, the Circle Pass (one person stands in the center of a closely packed circle of 8-10 people, falls back with feet still on the ground, and then is moved around the circle), can be operated gently and slowly, or it can be used as a windmill, where speed is the experience (excesses in this area not recommended). In the two-person Trust Fall, the catcher may, because of her own self-consciousness, straighten up the faller abruptly, essentially pushing that person away. The faller has been caught, but the experience is not a comfortable one. In teaching the Activity, your example is most important.

You must not just talk about the need to be gentle, you must also illustrate it by how you do the catching. It is through your clear knowledge of how attitudes are transmitted through tactile experiences, that you can make a large difference as to whether a participant will be willing to extend herself during an exercise. Trust has to begin during the lead-up activities. Expressions of negative attitudes that are made then, if not dealt with, have the potential of carrying over into later activities. Fortunately, the opposite is also true.

Leaders need to be comfortable with touching, therefore. Their touch accomplishes several things, not the least of which is to help participants relax in an anxiety-provoking situation. A firm, caring touch conveys, "It's all right you fell. We're here. You tried as hard as you could. Try it again." Relaxing is a large part of letting down one's guard. A participant can do the Trust Fall, but still be tense, forcing herself through it. Or she can be relaxed, knowing full well that the group will catch her. The leader's ease with this important aspect of touching will greatly help the group let down their guard and benefit fully from the activity.

Hugging a successful participant, or one that is depressed, or feeling that he has failed, is another dynamic we need to consider. Hugging has many overtones, not the least of which is sexual. But hugging has other messages as well, and does not need to be apologized for. Don't feel afraid of it because of taboos. You need to understand your own relationship to it, and make certain that it doesn't cross lines or get misinterpreted. (One practitioner solves this by keeping her contact somewhat rigid—she makes contact in an encouraging manner, but still keeps her distance.) A hug after an extreme effort, or a hand on the shoulder or arm, can convey a lot of assurance and presence. (*You did it, I'm proud of you!*)

Some people can't stand to be hugged, and resist it by

Don't feel afraid of [hugging] because of taboos...understand your own relationship to it, and make certain that it doesn't cross lines or get misinterpreted.

immediately tensing up. You need to have a healthy respect for this distancing. However, these same people may need that kind of contact, even if it makes them uncomfortable. It can be helpful to wait until a dramatic moment, such as the completion of a Tension Traverse, or a leap to a trapeze off the Hickory Jump or the Pamper Pole. For one thing, attention is focused on an outside event, and away from the interaction with you. Secondly, the person has made a significant physical effort and will be more relaxed because of it. Third, success makes people more able to open up to new experience. Judicious use of hugging can encourage a spirit of empathy in the group.

Cheerleading at a critical point can spell the difference between success and failure.

• **Feeling Presence**

Empathizing has much to do with having a "present" consciousness with the group—that you are clearly with them while they are doing their work. This can be difficult, for a large part of your job is over once the Activity has begun.

You have invested a great deal of work in establishing your program (Bedrock), selecting activities and Briefing the group. Now they are doing the Tire on the Pole Initiative (participants must get an auto tire off a vertical 12' pole, then back on again). You are there to spot, and make sure the ground rules are adhered to. But you have work here, too. You need to be there with them, not only for safety, but to keep track of who is doing what, listening to comments and frustrations, and gathering material for the next stage—the Debrief.

You also need to support their effort. Cheerleading at a critical point can spell the difference between success and failure. Or you may need to get in there and help out, assured that the group did all it could and that an extra hand would be appropriate.

- **Non-Verbal Cues**
  Shaking your head, grimacing, crossing arms, walking around nervously, smiling, blinking, laughing, pacing, kicking the tree, or looking at your watch have a strong impact, even though you may not be communicating with words. Be aware of those cues. Sometimes they can get in the way of the group's experience, of going it alone. Sometimes they are useful. Whatever your decision, they provide powerful messages.

Readings, Fantasy and Journals

Short, compelling readings penetrate to the cognitive-reflective realm, especially when combined with physical activity. The sudden shift of modalities catches a group off guard with defenses down. Members will be able to hear it best when it is carefully selected and germane to their experience at the time. Besides, people like to be read to. The oral tradition is as old as communication itself, back to Homer and before, so it must still be in our genes, in spite of the dominance of other communication modes.

Readings and testimonials contain much of the "folklore" of the outdoor movement.

Readings
Outward Bound programs use readings and testimonials during their Morning Meetings (a time to frame the day, to reflect on one's place in all the intense activity). The same is true for other camps or schools, whatever the affiliation, religion, or purpose. It comes from a universal urge to pull things together, reflect, be clear and unified in what is being done, to call on whatever power and strength is available to help make things sensible. Readings and testimonials contain

much of the the "folklore" of the outdoor movement. That is why many programs compile small books of them in order to facilitate their usage.

Readings are equally effective in Adventure counseling. They can be used anywhere along the Adventure Wave. Either the leaders or the participants can read them. Just as you build your own Activities Base in your particular setting, you can also compile your own base of readings, making it a dynamic process reflective of your group's needs and the interests and experiences of the contributors.

The following examples have been taken from Project Adventure's upcoming publication of readings entitled *Gold Nuggets* (by Mike Stratton and Jim Schoel).

The Story of Howard Blackburn

A reading that can be used before difficult tasks is the story of Howard Blackburn (material taken from the book *Lone Voyager* by Joe Garland, 1978).

> "Blackburn was a dory fisherman. This means that he would leave his mother ship, a large fishing schooner (sail power only), and row out to the fishing grounds with his dory mate in a 20' open boat. This took place at a time when there were no radios for communication between boats or for weather information. There was also no radar, so once out of sight, there was little opportunity for the schooner to contact the dory. There were fog horns, but the sound would not carry very well in a snow storm.
>
> "That is exactly what hit Howard and his mate, Tom Welch. They became lost, fishing in the winter on the Grand Banks (off Nova Scotia, Canada). What were they to do? They had little choice but to bail the boat and row in the direction they thought the ship was.
>
> "This went on for several days. During that time Tom Welch died of exposure. Howard had to make an important decision. 'My hands are cold and wet. Do I try and keep them warm by not rowing, or do I allow them to freeze in the shape of an oar handle so that I can grip and row toward shore? If I do the former, my boat will simply drift and I will be lost.' Howard took the latter course, and after rowing for two more days, was able to get to land. What a feat of courage and endurance. But he wasn't done yet.
>
> "The shack he found on the wild coast of Nova Scotia was not in use for the winter. But Howard, tired and cold as he was, decided to bury his mate before he got into his boat to row down the coast and look for help. It was the only

dignified thing to do. Finally, he was able to find a dirt poor community of fisher folk the next cove over, stayed with them the winter, and returned home the next spring. He lost all his fingers, but his life was saved. He went on to sail a small boat all by himself across the Atlantic ocean.

"So think of Howard Blackburn today, and what kinds of things people are able to endure in this world. If you are feeling some discomfort, or even want to give up, let what he did inspire you."

An Inuit Song

Another example is an old Inuit Song from the book *Never Cry Wolf*, by Farley Mowat, (1963)

I think over again my small adventures
my fears,
those small ones that seemed so big
for all the vital things
I had to get and to reach
and yet there is only one great thing
the only thing
to live to see the great day that dawns
and the light that fills the world.

(Thanks to Beau Bassett, Project Adventure Certified Trainer, and Karen Hegeman, Teacher and Adventure Practioner, for finding this song.)

This reading can be used when the group is all tangled up in some problem and is unable to have any perspective on it. The imagery of "the great day that dawns" indicates a newness, a fresh start, something that can be tied in with the Adventure Wave (there's always another Activity!).

Seeking Out the Challenging Way

Michael A.B. Stratton, a pioneer Outward Bound/Adventure educator (Hurricane Island Outward Bound School, The Carroll School) uses this excerpt from William Barrett's biography of Kierkegaard:

"While he sat at the cafe in the Fredericksberg Garden in Copenhagen one afternoon smoking a cigar, as was his habit, and turning over a great many things in his mind, Kierkegaard reflected that he had not really begun any career for himself, while a good many of his friends were already making names for themselves, getting set up in business or getting published...The cigar burned down, he lit another, the train of reflection held him. It occurred to him then that since everyone was engaged everywhere in making things easy, perhaps someone was needed to make things hard again, and that this too might be a career and a destiny...to go in search of difficulties, like a new Socrates."

Mike comments:

"This reading about the great Danish philosopher Kierkegaard's choice, or need to make a choice, has always enchanted me. Was he going through a midlife crisis? Or was he more than likely alarmed at the acceleration of the industrial revolution (high tech) at the expense of traditional ways and crafts, old values, and a sane lifestyle.

"I have used this reading when opinions about an expedition begin to overshadow the decision-making process. (e.g., 'This sucks!!! We could do this much faster with a snowmobile instead of these damn snowshoes.' Also, motor vs. oars and sail, or MacDonalds vs. a quality outdoor feast, and 'I miss my toilet.')

"This is a great opportunity to discuss why you are out there doing it instead of sitting at home watching Hollywood Adventures. Also, it's a good chance to reconnect with the good old days and ways of life, history, lifestyles and struggles.

"I like to combine this reading with a quote from John Ciardi:

Every game ever invented by man has strict rules to make it challenging and fun. The fun and meaningfulness come from making the hard look easy. Just try to imagine a tennis game without a net and lines.

"So who is right? Mickey Mouse who says, 'Life is a contest to see who can do the least!' Or Helen Keller, who said 'Life is an adventure, or nothing.'"

Peak Achievement
Still another example can be used when you want the group to set goals, or need to help them complete goals:

Hulda Crooks, a 91-year-old mountaineer from Loma Linda, California, reached the top of Mount Fuji in Japan at dawn today after a difficult three-day climb. She is the oldest woman to conquer Mount Fuji. Crooks stepped through a special gate marking the top of the sacred 12,385-foot dormant volcano at 3:45 a.m. as a pink sun rose over the horizon and waved an American flag tied to her walking stick. "It's wonderful," she said, bundled in a down jacket at the summit in near-freezing weather. "You always feel good when you made a goal."

(*Boston Globe,* Friday, July 24, 1987)

A Nugget of Wisdom

Finally, a self-explanatory observation, from Sugar Ray Robinson:

"You can tell what a fighter is made of by how he acts when he's getting licked."

(Thanks to Tim Churchard, PA Certified Trainer and Director of an alternative school, for this quote.)

Readings are also a natural way to blend Adventure activities with an academic curriculum. When linked with the Activity itself, they help participants understand what is going on in two modes: the physical/practical, and the written/cognitive. You can capitalize on this by following up a reading with short answer questions, vocabulary, essays, or even further research. Readings can also be used as part of the Debriefing process. Have the group spend the first ten minutes writing, then have each in turn read his work to the group. This works well for stimulating discussion.

When linked with the Activity itself, [readings] help participants understand what is going on in two modes: the physical/practical, and the written/cognitive.

Journals

Readings can also be tied in with journal writing. The use of quotes from prominent writers' journals (Thoreau and Edward Abbey are good sources) can serve to stimulate the writing imagination of the group. The use of journal quotes (with permission) of either current group members or former participants is also effective and helps the participants identify with the process.

The use of journals can be extended on many levels. They can be used in class, during interviews, or for personal insights; they can be used on City Search or environmental study sessions to take notes and observations. Solo time or time outs are good places to have the group sit down and write (or sketch). You may choose to grade the journals or you may let them stand alone. It is important, however, that participants make an attempt at contributing, since this is a group Activity. Remember, however, that a journal is a private document. Disclosure should never be forced.

Finally, you can transmit the idea that journal writing is a practice worth carrying over into other parts of their lives.

Journals are exciting documents when participants take them seriously. They are permanent records of what is going on at the time.

The following is an entry by an alternative program student about his community service time at the "Folklife Festival" sponsored by the program's support group, Gloucester Museum School, Inc.:

"Last Saturday was really something else. It began with me wondering if I could muster the energy enough to to get through the day. I really wasn't ready for what happened.

"My Gawd there was so much electricity flowing my hair was almost standing on end. I wanted to see everything and try almost everything. But I couldn't.

"All those people and giving of themselves. I really find it hard to put my emotions into words.

"It started with high expectations, and grew quickly into excitement.

"I was overtaken by the people, all going around doing their own thing. Not really caring what others were doing. However unconsciously or consciously they were all working for the same cause.

"There was harmony with each other. But each person was a different instrument and each set up was a different section to the symphony and together there was an incredible sound which fills a really truly interested person's heart.

"I said it while I was there and I'll say it again—the place was just electric. I really enjoyed myself. I put out, but I didn't mind. I got a lot more than I put out. I suppose my most favorite set-up was the scrimshaw. I wanted to work."

A journal entry by another alternative program student reveals some intensely personal things, issues that the student chose to have the staff be aware of (those sections of a journal that students don't want to share can be either stapled closed or marked "confidential"). It reads:

"I have had a few bad experiences with alcohol. Both my mother and father are alcoholics. Though I've grown used to it, it still depresses me often. Their brain cells have been eaten away and there is no talking to them even on the most non-controversial subjects.

"I feel that they are both on their way to becoming insane. I don't want any pity because I know I'm not the first and won't be the last to live with alcoholics. I can

"My Gawd there was so much electricity flowing my hair was almost standing on end. I wanted to see everything and try almost everything. But I couldn't."

never tell when they're lying from when they're not, so I've learned to doubt their word.

"Violence from drunkenness is common. For an example my mom once almost had her tooth knocked out from my dad when she was drunk. I just simply walked out of my house and slept in the truck that night. I've learned to stay out of their fights and not pick sides.

"I think one of the hardest things is that they won't admit it to themselves and seek help. Drinking among kids in town is extremely frequent and it really bums me out to know that many of my friends may be or may someday be alcoholics with kids that will have to grow up (with) the problems I have."

Readings from other journals, by famous people, writers, and the like, or from your own journal or those of former participants, aid in building a sense of value about the endeavor. Handing out copies of readings can help in the participant's search to understand them. And of course having participants share their journals with the rest of the group is one of the best experiences they can have.

Myth and Fantasy

Adventure activities can be enhanced by incorporating myth and fantasy. For example, the Initiative game Spider's Web can have Charlotte "up there" ready to come down at any moment. There's a certain amount of time you have before she makes her appearance. She's a friendly spider, but she's still got to eat. You will make her very happy if you get through the web without hurting it, for she won't have to weave another one. But remember, if you take too long (give an imaginary period of time), well, she's got to eat, and though she'd rather have flies, well, she's still got to eat...

A classic fantasy is the Poison Peanut Butter Pit. It is an imaginary 25-foot area below a rope swing. The swing is the only means by which the group can get across the Pit. The goal is to get a bucket of water to the other side, without any of the group touching the "peanut butter." If anyone touches, or a drop of water is spilled, the whole group is penalized and everyone has to return to the starting point. The water is, incidentally, either nitroglycerin or blood plasma. The nitro will explode on contact, the blood plasma is for a dying elephant. Both fantasy cargoes require that the whole group get across the pit, because "it would be too dangerous to stay behind in enemy territory," or "the elephant needs to be rolled over for the transfusion"—the whole group is needed for the task. Fantasy takes the group away from the mundane and engages their imaginations— the event is implausible, and therefore fun, and therefore more attractive. If they know that there is no attempt to make the event "factually serious" (they know it isn't, anyway), then the aspect of play can be entered unabashedly.

Behavior is still important during play. But play presupposes a step out of time, a release from roles, a healthy regression to a time in one's life when everything was forgiven, forgotten, made new. Play has an open and shut quality —you do it now, then it is over, and we move on. When the "seriousness" of the group "encounter" is removed, the participants can let down their guard, be their natural selves, and laugh. Weaving a fantasy aids in this process. Its best when you make them up yourself, or at least embellish them with items from your own or other group member's experience in the outside world. This makes the experience unique and focused on your group. It can even give group members a chance to deal with some of their real life issues in a symbolic manner.

...play presupposes a step out of time, a release from roles, a healthy regression to a time in one's life when everything was forgiven, forgotten, made new.

Competition

One of the disturbing aspects of competition is that you rarely know or care any more about the opposition than what you need to defeat it. There is a relationship all right, one that has respect, dependency, awareness, but is also mixed in with anger, hostility, submissiveness and dominance. Sounds like a "normal" relationship! Sadly, if we'd be honest with ourselves, a good many of our relationships can be described this way. That's because we carry the competitive model with us in our daily, sometimes most intimate relationships.

Defeating someone can come in the guise of gaining control over that person, getting what you want , manipulating situations to your advantage, or giving something as an "investment" that can be cashed in at a later date. Competition can limit us in our relationships, and cut us off from important shared experiences between people. Many Adventure group members are refugees from the competitive systems that crush, dominate, and isolate them.

It would be easy to lay a bad rap on competition, yet there is something extremely powerful to it that cannot be discounted. Instead of rejecting it as unhealthy, we need to spend time finding appropriate connections to it. Competition is about power in relationships. It is also an avenue for people to become the best they can be at any particular thing. One of our goals is to provide experiences wherein a sense of competency can be derived. The end result may be that a person is no longer satisfied with an entry level job, if her capabilities are greater than that, for example. She must learn to go up against the best, as she goes for the best.

Instead of rejecting [competition] as unhealthy, we need to spend time finding appropriate connections to it.

Alternative Competition

Adventure activities provide an opportunity for *alternative* competition. An experience during a camping trip that because of bad weather required a "bail out" in a school gym illustrates this. That night, we got into a volleyball game. The game took on the normal choose-up-sides, let's-see-who-can-beat-the-other-guy routine. We played that way for awhile, but something wasn't quite right. It didn't feel good. So we tried something different. We started to count how many times we could hit the ball and keep it in the air without its touching the ground. Sounds like Moon Ball, the Adventure-New Games Activity we've referred to, but this took place before any of us knew it as a game.

The whole experience changed. No longer were we playing against each other. We were laughing, and falling down, and encouraging each other. People who had begun to drift away from the volleyball game came back to play this one.

In the Debrief following the trip we talked about why the second game worked so well, and why the first one didn't feel good. It seems that we had developed such closeness during the camping trip that to begin a win/lose game started to tear at that carefully woven fabric. Unwilling to put up with the change, many just left the game. The game they invented (Moon Ball must have come out of a similar experience), included everyone, and had no loser. We were all trying our hardest to keep that ball in the air, competing with the floor, the obstacles, and our own skills and ineptitudes.

Healthy Competition

When we do group work, making another member of the group the "enemy" is counter-productive and potentially harmful. So in order to use the healthy aspects of competition, we need to find other enemies. That's why our games tend toward group goals, or an approach to "us vs. them" that is humorous, and always changing. Add-on Tag has two persons as "it." But those two persons can add on two more with a simple tag, until they become a massive wall of people. No one is really good or bad, competent or incompetent in this scenario. It makes fun of all that stuff! The bad guy is dissipated, because he simply disappears beneath a load of fun. The enemy we are competing with becomes the super self-consciousness that keeps us from being part of the group, to let go and have fun. The enemy becomes that part of ourselves that refuses to let us trust, or to become good at something. We begin to compete with ourselves. When we are part of an accepting group, we are more willing to look at ourselves, to emphasize the good things, and work toward eliminating, or controlling, the bad things.

The enemy we are competing with becomes the super self-consciousness that keeps us from being part of the group, to let go and have fun.

To use competition as a tool we must first acknowledge its power, rather than put it down as a bad thing. Second, we must be able to provide situations where competition will enhance rather than detract from the power of the group, and the individuals in the group. Invoking the Full Value Contract serves us well as we build these situations.

Here are some helpful suggestions:
- Time the events. Let the group work against the clock, rather than against each other.
- See how many you can get on, or over, something.
- See how closely the group can stick to the rules (no touching, don't use the tree).
- Show people "outside" how well you can do: Parents, teachers, the community. Be careful with this, though. Don't develop an us-vs.-them attitude here either. It can injure the overall relationship. At the same time, there's nothing wrong with proving that you are good, and capable. And everyone likes an underdog. Teaching the underdog to like itself is a good trick.
- Talk about those things that keep us from growing as the things that need to be defeated.
- Make certain that participants experience success. There's nothing like success as an antidote to bad feelings and a self-concept of being defeated. Adrian Middleton, former course director at Hurricane Island Outward Bound School, used to say that his goal as an

instructor was to give each of his students at least one successful experience each day.

- Insist on the Full Value Contract. Competition for the attention of the group or of the group leader causes members to work against each other. They do this naturally, as does any family.
- Design games and activities that make a spoof out of competition by changing rules and inventing new ones. Get the participants involved in this. Their ideas can be extremely satisfying to them. This aligns with the Initiative aspects of Adventure.
- Use competitive games when they fit in with an overall group feeling. We've used softball, for example, as a way to simply play, everyone getting a chance to run and catch and hit. Score isn't the issue.

Competition dominates our lives in exams, games, relationships, and jobs. There's more to life than that—shared experience, group feeling, relationships with new and different people, universal encouragement. Presenting this model to our groups provides them with a chance to escape the prison of "us vs. them" and focus on the power of the group to help us become the best we can be.

Centering

Focusing on the present can be difficult for people who are preoccupied with "baggage" or who have a short attention span. It's difficult anyway, for we are taught to plot and scheme about the future, to carry regrets about the past, and to involve ourselves in competition and transference and "measuring up" battles with people and obstacles around us. We miss a lot by doing this. That's why many lessons just don't sink in. If the Activity is so important to Adventure Counseling, we must work on ways to bring people into the present, so that they will open up to the lessons that are presently being taught. Goal setting during the Briefing, instruction/intervention/framing during the Activity, as well as the essence of the Activity itself are methods that achieve a present orientation. The use of centering exercises is another method.

Tim Churchard, of the Bud Carlson Alternative School, relates this story as an introduction to his centering activities:

A philosophy professor from Cambridge University takes a year's sabbatical. His plan is to spend it in a Zen

Focusing on the present can be difficult for people who are preoccupied with "baggage" or who have a short attention span.

Buddhist monastery in Japan. At the airport, he is met by a Zen master. The professor starts talking with the master about Zen, telling him all he knows. He is extremely excited, continuing with his words all the way up into the mountains, the location of the monastery. All this time the Zen master says nothing. After they arrive at the monastery, the master asks the professor if he wants tea. The professor says yes, then continues to talk. He looks down, noting that the master has over-filled his cup, and continues to pour, with tea spilling all over the tray, the table and down to the floor. The professor says, "My cup is full, why are you still pouring?" The master responds, "You are so full. You must first empty your cup, if you are to learn about Zen."

Some centering methods are:

Body Scan: Sit down and focus energy in your gut. Feel your feet. Move slowly up from your feet. Go through your whole body. End up in your stomach. Focusing on the stomach gets you out of your head and into your body. The body is much more likely to be "in the present." The stomach is also a source of power: the base of breathing, the Karate "center."

Breathing: Follow your breathing. Don't hold on to a thought. Breathe slowly and deeply. Observe thoughts, then let them go. Count your breaths. Don't hyperventilate, for that is disorientating. We don't want that kind of dizzying "high." Use breathing exercises during intense effort as a method of taking control of oneself, and thereby following through on what was planned. The Moslems believe that we are all "Abdallah," the children of Allah, and Allah means "breath of life." To breathe out and say "Allah" from the gut is a form of prayer and meditation, and a contact with one's center.

Visualization: See yourself as doing something **right now.** Go through the moves, the obstacles, the feelings. See yourself through the experience. For example, use the Group Trust Fall as a commitment to let go of a problem like substance abuse.

Tai Chi: Deliberate movement as a form of slow exaggerated dance. Go from place to place doing this. It is especially helpful in activities that demand balance and a coordination of eye/hand/foot. It slows a person down, and brings awareness of movements, and what body parts are doing. It is somewhat catlike.

Listening: Ask the participants to repeat what other group members have said or give accounts of what they have done. This can be confrontational, where appropriate. It explores our inability to listen to others, and to see what has been going on. For some participants, this activity must be continually used, drawing them out of their isolation.

Meditation: Use it without a mantra. Ask for quiet, and relaxation. Get comfortable. Close the eyes. Let thoughts come and go. Spend time with this.

Solo: Time alone, without communicating with anyone, even if it is for 15 minutes. It gets them away from the noise and energy of the group. It can be used in many ways, for writing, drawing, the practice of centering techniques, or rest. Pair Solo can be used as an adaptation. There can also be Group Solo, where the group is left on their own to solve tasks, work out problems, or whatever.

Stop the Activity: Ask for complete quiet from the group. Get them to listen to what is going on around them and also to look. This is especially effective in outdoor situations where there might be, for example, a flock of geese, wind in the trees, colors, sunlight on leaves, or rain. It can also be used at the end of an experience. A reading or observation can be interjected.

Some additional resource material:
The Ultimate Athlete, by George Leonard
The Centering Book, by Gay Hendricks

Co-leadership

Working with a co-leader is a demanding, enlightening exercise. Because of the "two-ness" there is a great need for respect for each other and assertion of one's thoughts and ideas. Without this dynamic, a disruptive role model is presented to the group. Following the family analogy, co-leaders can be "mom and dad."

Leadership Competition

Respect comes from seeing your co-leader as a person first, and a skilled leader second. This is because there are all levels of skill and experience. If there is a gap between co-leaders, then the emphasis should be on adapting and compensating for each other. So you start with the person first and move toward the skills. This will not work if there is any faking

Two persons can complement each other when each has skill in different areas, without the necessity of each becoming an expert in the other's area.

going on, however. Playing the role that you know something when you don't is one of the great enemies of co-leadership.

On the other hand, the person who is more skilled can use those skills as weapons to maintain control. In outdoor education, it's known as "mystique." (*I've done all these things, and wear a carabiner key chain, so you better listen to me.*) Not that skills should be devalued. Skills are skills, and need to be utilized. It is how they are utilized that's the issue. Those skills can be taught to those interested in learning them. Then both leaders have the skills, doubling the strength in that area.

The same is true for the leader who has superior counseling skills. We call confrontations in the skill areas "shootouts": gear shootouts (*Look at my Vibram sleeping pad!*); climbing shootouts (*I can do a 5.13+!*); Debriefing shootouts (*Look how I got John to get into his stuff*). Two persons can complement each other when each has skill in different areas, without the necessity of each becoming an expert in the other's area. Teaming an Adventure person with a therapist is a common strategy.

Time for Connecting

Lack of listening, both to the group, and to the co-leader, is another enemy. Group work is intense, and there are no easy answers. The defensive ego must be left home. If you made a mistake, own up to it. If another "way" is being presented, consider it. Mom and dad can have disagreements, but they must be straightened out. Thus the need for meeting time outside the group. It's necessary for planning. But it is also used for the co-leaders to deal with their issues. The meeting time needs to be regular. Don't assume that you can get away without it, for problems have a way of sneaking up.

Co-leaders also need that outside voice, a neutral yet knowledgeable person who is able to listen and process what is going on between the leaders. The practical necessity of supervision and consultation (Chapter 3, **Bedrock**) is used as a tool for maintaining good relations between co-leaders.

It is a reality that there are groups which are not co-led. Make a point if you are in that kind of situation to seek out feedback from knowledgeable peers and supervisors. You may need to go it alone in the field, but don't keep all the issues to yourself.

If respect and assertion is nurtured between co-leaders, a wonderful bond is formed. The group instinctively nestles in with it, safe in the knowledge that communication and caring is being experienced between the leaders. And the bond

The meeting time needs to be regular. Don't assume that you can get away without it, for problems have a way of sneaking up.

provides you with an important on-the-job experience. You look forward to seeing each other. What an antidote for burnout!

Conflict Resolution

"In Karate, the issue is not to meet force head on, but to take the force that is coming toward you and redirect it back toward your opponent."
— Herbie Miller, Karate Instructor, Harlem, New York

We place conflict resolution at the end of this chapter because the issues explored up to this point play as important a role in resolving conflicts as any "tricks of the trade." Having your own voice as a leader, being able to identify and manage your stress, being able to intervene properly, consultation with your co-leader, etc., all are critical points in your management of conflict.

It is natural to be uncomfortable with conflict, and to therefore avoid it. It digs at our weakness, and the weakness of others. It stirs up the placid waters. But the Island of Healing, if built on a solid foundation, will withstand a stormy sea. When drugs and alcohol were found on an Adventure trip, the experience of the group for the rest of the year was enhanced because it was dealt with correctly. Potential disaster was turned into success.

Adventure groups presuppose conflict. We look for it, and even encourage it. Not all the time, of course. It is important to have times that are free of stress, that work without any difficulty, and to reward those times. But the "tunnels, bumps and obstacles" are frustrating "burrs" under the blanket, problems to be solved, issues to be overcome. Most persons in counseling are there because of conflicts in their lives. The Adventure group provides an opportunity to expose people to conflict in a controlled manner, thereby providing them with the possibility of a successful experience. The ability to re-solve conflicts in one arena goes a long way toward resolving them in another. Hence the group goals are worked in first, then the spiral goals. (See Spiral Goal section, p. 107)

We look for conflict so that we can have resolvable experi-ences that form a basis for a transfer of learning. Some familiar conflicts are:
- *"I don't trust you guys"*
- *"We can't do this"*
- *"This sucks. These games are stupid"*

The Adventure group provides an opportunity to expose people to conflict in a controlled manner, thereby providing them with the possibility of a successful experience.

- *"Nobody is listening to me"*
- *"You're a sissy if you don't try that"*
- *"Why are we doing this?"*
- *"I'm scared to do that"*
- Inappropriate behavior, or discounting
- Disagreements

These conflicts will be much more pronounced in the early stages of your group's development. In fact, getting through the first Storming sessions is the most difficult task the Adventure leader faces. Conflict can occur at any time, however. In fact, it can clobber you at what you might think the least likely times, such as right after or during a successful experience. So again, try not to be surprised by it.

Some tactics for dealing with conflict are:
- Proper Intake (exclusion of inappropriate members, and agreements made with group members regarding their understanding and acceptance of the nature of the group's activities. In short, they've agreed to give the group a try, and to participate in the activities.)
- Thoughtful activities selection in your formation of the Adventure Wave Plan (includes having the logistics thoroughly covered)
- The ability to adjust (have a frisbee with you when you attempt Trolley).
- See the group as more important than completing an Activity. Keep your cool in regard to completion. Maintain acceptance. Be able to admit defeat. See everything as a learning experience, and make sure the group sees that as well.
- Stick to your principles. This group is about doing things together! Why are we here? Get back to the basics of goal setting and original commitments. This also includes sticking to the rules (the Full Value Contract). If you don't avoid the conflict, then "pinch points" have a much better chance of not turning into full-fledged "crunch points." (Pinch points and crunch points, referred to in other sections of this book, are descriptions of conflict points that have been developed by J.J. Sherwood and J.C. Glidewell. These writers use them to illustrate the management of psychological contracts. Pinch and crunch points fit nicely into the contracting that is done in Adventure Based Counseling. If the pinch point is addressed, there can be a planned renegotiation. If it is not addressed, then disruption, uncertainty, and resent-

If you don't avoid the conflict, then "pinch points" have a much better chance of not turning into full-fledged "crunch points."

ment will occur, leading to the crunch point. Renegotiation is still possible, but the group has come much closer to a resentful termination than if the pinch point had been dealt with.)

- Keep a sense of humor, and have fun. After all, many Adventure activities are only games. Don't be too heavy about what you are doing. This doesn't mean that chaos should reign. But let yourself laugh, and encourage humor in the group.

- Be able to talk about anything at any time. Use time-outs. Use the talk time to form alliances, to make other plans, to deal with what is going on, to reframe, to remind, to focus, to slow down and rein in. Seek their perception about what is going on, and what to do about it. Plan for the next event with them, if it is possible. Brainstorm.

- Withhold. *(We will go no further until we get a grip on ourselves. So until further notice, this Activity is shut down.)*

- Remove a group member. *(You just can't be here now.)* The importance of co-leadership is seen here, for the co-leader can take the participant away without having the whole group suffer.

- Be a good actor. If the group needs to know you are disappointed, then be disappointed. Choose an effective role for the situation. There's a place for pretending a greater intensity of feeling than you actually have. You mustn't overdo this, for you will be seen quickly as a phony, but some of it is extremely effective.

- Use guilt as a motivator. *(We promised those people that we'd do this! They will be so disappointed that we didn't come through.)* The real-world nature of Adventure activities is an advantage here.

- Don't hesitate to use anger when it is appropriate, but don't let it get out of control. This fits in with the ability to act. If a book needs to be thrown against the wall to get their attention, then do it. But don't do it any more than twice a year.

- Develop and encourage leadership in the group. Talk beforehand with a leader: *(You know how important it is for the group to succeed today. Help out, will you?)*

- Use peer pressure, but only when the group will agree to it. If you are getting across the idea that it is their responsibility to have a successful group, you are much better able to draw on this power. Giving them power in times of no conflict will allow for that power to carry over into times of conflict and crisis.

Conclusion

Leading the Adventure activities requires constant vigilance. No two groups are ever alike. Because of this, Adventure counseling techniques are never "in the can." Leaders with years of experience still scramble during the first sessions, struggling for control of the issues, sometimes just fighting for air as the group deals with the obstacles and tasks presented to them.

We take a risk, too, by stepping away from "normal" techniques, asking people to try activities that are mostly foreign, often awkward, but also fun and exciting. When we challenge and confront people, put pressure on the group to make decisions and play a large role in monitoring behavior, we are presenting an instruction method that many people have never experienced before. We are asking people to go beyond their normal boundaries, and that's hard stuff to do. We must be there with all our attention, ready to praise, pick up, listen, adjust, keep the spirits up, respond to the group's mood, as well as deal with difficult behaviors and significant decisions all the way up to appropriateness for group membership. The Adventure activities provide great opportunities for growth as well as diagnosis.

As we explore the final stage of the Adventure Wave in Chapter 7, **Debriefing**, we will look at how to deal with these opportunities through group discussion.

162   Islands of Healing

Chapter 7

Debriefing:

Processing the Adventure Experience

"Some are chosen to ponder while the world flits by without a glance."

— John Charles Amesse

THE DOWNWARD SLOPE of the Adventure Wave moves the group into a time of reflection. It is the last prong of our three-phase Brief/Activity/Debrief cycle, and for many leaders the most difficult to implement. The action can't sweep the group along in the same way anymore. Often it is much easier to "do" than to think about what we do. Uncomfortable issues make dealing with the Debrief even more difficult. Even though the wide range of groups served by ABC calls for varying degrees of intensity and disclosure, we have found that the following ideas can cross-apply.

In this chapter we will explore some basic issues that can help leaders ease into their group discussions, and facilitate a valuable experience from them. Those issues are:

- **Dealing with Resistance**
- **Listening and Observing Skills**
- **Sequencing the Debrief**
- **Termination of the Group**

Dealing with Resistance

Kids resist talk, and adults, while they tend to talk a lot, resist real talk. Kids will play all sorts of avoidance games in order to keep from "getting down to it." Adults may intellectualize the experience as a way to step far enough away so that they cease to be affected by it. Leaders, too, can resist talk time, often willing to let the experience speak for itself. Why is talk time so difficult? Because the suggestion "let's talk about it" reminds people of negative experiences they have had in the past. The buttons get pushed, and the response is:

"Now I'm gonna get lectured"
"Aah, this is just like a class!"
"I don't want to ruin the experience"
"I don't like sitting around"

Many instructors are gun-shy when it comes to debriefing because they don't feel equipped to lead a discussion, or deal with the group's resistance, or haven't experienced good Debriefs, or feel there isn't enough time, or combinations of the above. And because of the implicit lessons in the Adventure experience, a leader who is reluctant to Debrief can survive without it. A well-orchestrated experience involves plenty of group interaction anyway, with feedback, encouragement and confrontation going on all the time. That's what "Counseling on the Run" is partly about. And there is so much that goes on that we will never see no matter how much we talk about it, things that take years to sink in. We are, after all, dealing with powerful life metaphors. When students come to grip with themselves on a rock face, or have a profound insight into how they work with other people during Blindfold Square, that's their own experience, one that they will continually refer back to. Students are not stupid...they tend to know when things work and when they don't. Just because it is not always fed back to them doesn't mean it didn't happen.

But bear in mind it is common for Adventure leaders to come from an experience feeling that it worked perfectly, and everyone did everything, only to find a whole set of complications. Missing is the perspective of the student who didn't feel supported, or another who felt railroaded. How much better it is for the group to have these issues emerge in a group talk session than in the hallway, or in a one-on-one discussion with the leader. Talking things out in the group gives the group the opportunity to gain strength, and become a more integral part of the change process. And, from family modeling, where conflicts are negotiated and settled in a forgiving atmosphere,

to goal setting, to issues of focusing, understanding, reframing and insight, talk time is a significant part of the Adventure experience.

For example when a student referred to a time when she blanked out and was unable to move (she was climbing a tree that was the beginning of a high "Burma Bridge"), she stated:

"I didn't like Debriefing sessions. But I started to understand how important they were after that time in the tree. It helped me understand what was going on up there, and what I needed to do. Before we talked about it, it was a real mystery."

Rather than no talk, too much talk, or bad talk, we need to be filled in, providing a different sort of talk experience where: "The Debriefing itself is an experiential change process. Once again it is action...albeit verbal action...and not a conscious understanding, which is fundamental to transferability." (Bacon, p. 11) We would add, "And not *just* a conscious understanding," acknowledging the importance of the cognitive realm.

Our addition to Bacon's quote is important, for the Adventure approach to Debriefing relies on the interplay of the action experience and the conscious awareness of implications reflected in decisions and goal setting. This interplay utilizes the strength of both approaches, with the result being a talk session that is action-oriented. Without the sense of action to the Debrief, it is often a lifeless, futile exercise. The Debrief as experience goes back to the Common Ground: Everyone participated in the experience, everyone participates in the Debrief: therefore the experience can come alive in the Debrief. The experience can be relived. The discussion is not a static, safe, merely cognitive exercise. It has feeling, excitement, anger, frustration, accomplishment, and fun.

The event is connected to the Debrief, but the Debrief is also an experience in and of itself, separate from the event being considered. It's delicate balance: We are talking about the past, but we are in the present. To recall the past as present gets it closer, but dealing with the "here and now" gets it closer yet.

The Debrief as Initiative

A way to implement this seemingly contradictory dynamic and to bridge the gap between action and thought is to use the Debrief as an Initiative. Use the principles of Initiative to talk about Initiative-oriented experience. Consider these

The discussion is not a static, safe, merely cognitive exercise. It has feeling, excitement, anger, frustration, accomplishment, and fun.

elements of Initiative that relate to Debriefing:
- Everyone participates.
- The Full Value Contract is in effect.
- Safety/trust issues are paramount.
- The leader provides the structure for the Activity, but relies on the group to provide the solution.
- The group focuses the experience to achieve positive outcomes.
- The group focuses on issues that it is able to handle.
- Group and individual issues are seen as problems to be solved.
- Leader and participants are bonded by their experience together.
- The emphasis is on the present experience.
- Debriefing takes place regularly after every group experience, or whenever necessary.
- Participants are the agents for their own change and gradually need to take more responsibility for their learning.

In order to support the Initiative-oriented Debrief, the following skill areas will be explored: **Listening and Observing**, **Sequencing,** and **Termination.**

Listening and Observing

The tendency to get wrapped up in logistics can cause us to miss important interactions. As an Adventure leader, you've got to think of the sailor's proverb, "One hand for the ship, one hand for myself." Rework it to say, "One hand for logistics, one hand for the group." Keep the ship running, but don't lose sight of the person.

Listening skills are ongoing. No leader just happens to be an accomplished listener. It involves:
- Being clear yourself by getting good rest, keeping priorities in order, staying centered, and not being preoccupied.
- Collecting information, and supporting it with note taking and co-leadership. (Use the GRABBS modality profile.)
- Being an active listener. (Do something with what you hear. Connect it.)

Keeping track of the group begins with keeping track of yourself. If you are preoccupied, haven't had much sleep, feel

Part of the logistics of the activities preparation is preparing yourself, and making sure that you are able to keep a clear head while you are leading.

stressed out, and are generally not centered, your work will be adversely affected. You will forget the students' goals. You will miss subtle interactions. You won't see the struggles they are going through. You won't be there when they succeed. In short, you will have very little material to use in the Debriefing.

Part of the logistics of the activities preparation, then, is preparing yourself, and making sure that you are able to keep a clear head while you are leading. If you are using the counseling format of 2-3 hours, you can without much difficulty maintain the necessary intensity. If you are working for the whole day, or are conducting an overnight expedition, you will need to pace yourself, to take time outs, to go "off duty," letting your co-leader pick up the slack. During these times, take a walk, or meditate, or cat nap. Let yourself escape from the intensity. A former colleague, Perry Gates, said that he would benefit greatly by looking out over the ocean during a lull in the action, keeping an ear to what was going on, but also "checked out." No one even knew he was doing it, but he was getting his rest. If you are in fact exhausted, admit it, and don't try to exercise the mental gymnastics that a good Debrief demands. Be satisfied with a short "check-in Debrief," saving the more thorough discussion for a time when everyone is rested. Of course there are exceptions: Some Debriefing work just cannot wait, and must be labored through no matter what the hour and how tired everyone is.

We must also be collectors of information, both cognitive and practical. What people did, how they felt, and how the group felt. Ease with leading the activities helps us be open to these responses. The more they are second nature, the more thought we can put into our collection. This is an important bedrock issue, freeing us to see, hear and feel. Carry a notebook, or make it a habit to sit down at night and go over the day and think through the work of each of your participants. That's a tough discipline. In Adventure work, it's easy to concentrate on the more dramatic episodes, missing the less obvious, but perhaps more important, interactions. Adhering to the discipline of reviewing each and every person helps you counteract that tendency. Building your collection is better when you can do it in concert with a co-leader. He will see things you don't see, and vice–versa. Occasional use of video tape can aid in the collecting. Participants tend to like it. People like to see themselves on the luminescent screen!

Doing something with what you collect is the next step. The trick is to fit it into the Initiative-oriented Debrief. Again, does Initiative require that the leader be passive? Go back to the above presuppositions. There is nothing there that says the leader can't participate. "Relying on the group to provide the solution" could be construed as that, but in the Debrief, especially in some difficult interpretive situations, the leader must step in. The leader should sit back as long as the group members are providing ample interpretation and feedback. If they aren't, then say something. But don't jump in with both feet! Often we are so excited about the insight we have developed that we can't hold ourselves back from dropping the pearl. Give the group the opportunity to come up with it!

When it is time for us to say something, try to work it out so that the group says it. Often a well-placed question can crack a deadlock and get the juices flowing better than a wizened monologue from us. And remember, the group wants us to be the expert, for experts are safe to be with. They have all the answers. The group doesn't have to think when we are super-willing to step in. Much of their flattery is a method of keeping us on top and them free of the burden of interpretation and responsibility. It is not that you shouldn't share your knowledge. But, in the Initiative-oriented Debrief, you need to get them to do the thinking as much as possible, to dig into their feelings, to build up their own collection of observations, and then act on them. Also, your artful use of silence lets the group "work" on issues, and think about observations and solutions.

Often we are so excited about the insight we have developed that we can't hold ourselves back from dropping the pearl. Give the group the opportunity to come up with it!

Sequencing the Debrief

You receive a payoff for all the careful work you've done with the Full Value Contract during the Debrief. The contract of value, what W. H. Auden called the "law like love," contains a thread all the way back to the Intake. The deal the group has struck has been in effect in every part of the Wave. Reminders along the way have brought it to attention, whether it is casual notes, or "Time out. Let's get down to it" periods. Because of the Briefing, the contract is not something that you are throwing at the group all at once. There are no surprises.

But a group needs to get warmed up before it can get to the nub of the experience. That's why its important to sequence the discussion.

Sequencing of Debriefing issues has been addressed by Quinsland and Van Ginkel (1984, p.8). They relate a familiar Debriefing scenario: After facilitating a two-hour series of ropes course activities, the instructor has assembled the participants in a circle and begins the 'processing' session:

"Well, how do you feel about this experience?"
Silence
"How about you, David?"
"Uh, I don't know."
"Paula?" `(shrugs her shoulders)

We've all been there. We know the students have experienced something. We saw it in their expressions, heard it in their exchanges. So why can't they talk about it?

Examining this interaction, we see that the instructor has jumped right into the most difficult and abstract Debriefing topic, that of evaluation and opinion. The instructor in the above scenario might have had more interaction if he had started at a level congruent with the group. So often we go right to the heart of things! The lack of group response can come from an uneasiness with the questioning rather than an inability to discuss what has transpired.

To answer this problem, Terry Borton, in Knapp's *"The Art and Science of Processing Experience,"* (Knapp, pp. 6, 7) is helpful in structuring an effective Debriefing sequence. She presents three tiers: The "What?", the "So What?", and the "Now What? "

The "What?"

The "What?" helps us ease into the discussion by beginning with the facts. It *"pertains to the substance of the group interaction and what happened to the individuals."* (Clifford Knapp). Because of the "doing" in the Adventure experience, there are plenty of facts, occurrences and interactions to work with. Here are some methods that can help get at these "What?" facts:

The Go Around: Everyone in the group contributes a descriptive sentence. The description can be shortened to one word, as well. (Steven Bacon, 1983, p.18, 19). It could be helpful to narrow down the experience being described by picking an aspect of it. For example, you might pick the completion of the event (getting the blood plasma across the poison peanut butter pit without spilling it), rather than asking them to describe the whole event.

The Memory Game: "One person starts, explaining in detail everything that happened. Everyone must listen carefully. If anyone else in the group thinks that the person talking missed something that happened, say, "Hold it!"…and then explain what is missed. Then, the speaker who said "Hold it" will continue, etc…(Quinsland and Ginkel, 1984, p. 11).

Gestalt: Talk in the present tense, *"I'm now climbing up the pegs on the tree. My knees are acting like sewing machines!"* Because of the present tense, the participants can come close to reliving the actual experience. Gestalt recollection can be especially effective in journal writing. You can give the group 5 minutes at the start of the Debrief to write something in this manner, and then have them read their entries. Or they can take their journals with them and bring them in the next day. Other methods of journal writing can also be used to get the "What?" going, such as standard past tense descriptive writing or drawing. You can also get students to draw themselves or the group doing the experience they remember most.

Photographs: If you take pictures, and rush to get them developed, you are able to generate a high degree of "What?" interest. Participants want to see themselves. Videotape also helps with this kind of interest, and breaks down the nervous resistance.

The "What?" can be the structure for an entire Debrief. Starting with the "What?" leads naturally into interpretation. In experiential learning, specific well placed "What?" questions and ensuing dialogue help participants raise their awareness level about those issues and behaviors that should be maintained and those they might want to change. Once one phase or area or time period has been exhausted, use the "What?" questions to move on into other time periods, and in

You can bounce ahead or go back depending on the needs of the group, but you can always come back to the sequence of events as a way to maintain an orientation.

so doing you can go through everything that happened. This is especially effective with longer experiences, where there are many details that need to be worked over. You can bounce ahead or go back depending on the needs of the group, but you can always come back to the sequence of events as a way to maintain an orientation. The need to keep going in their description or recounting can be a method of getting the group out of a "no win" situation as well.

The "So What?"

Active listening presupposes that we do something with what we hear. The interpretive aspects of the "So What?" provide us with the place to do that. Because we've gotten the group to talk, it's much easier to get into this arena. According to Borton, it *"pertains to the difference the experience made to the individuals, the consequences, and the meaning for them."* (Knapp, p.6). It is here that group members are abstracting and generalizing what they are learning from the experience.

You can use the above "What?" techniques in the "So What?" by simply shifting from the descriptive to the interpretive. For example, you can use the Go Around as a way to describe how they feel about the event. You can also ask each group member to come up with a one word or short sentence definition of a key term, such as "spotting," "discounting," "belaying," "helping," "involvement," "leadership," or "confronting." Perhaps some of those key terms will arise from the Go Around or the Memory Game. You can then build upon what they are already talking about. In addition, try:

The Whip: "Do a short round robin or a positive non-threatening "whip," in which each person completes a short statement like "I'm glad that I..." A quick, clear whip can often loosen people up and focus their attention. Because everyone is on the spot briefly, they may be willing to risk sharing a small piece of themselves." (Quinsland and Ginkel, p. 24) The "I'm glad" scenario also focuses on the positive emotions, a point that should be kept in mind about Adventure Debriefing. We want the session to be as positive as possible, attempting to keep out the "I know you are bad" attitude, that is so easy to slip into when a group is being asked to achieve, or even function.

Going into the Debrief with the thread, or rope, of goal setting gives us another effective entry. We start with the "What?" where we are able to get the group warmed up and relating to what they have done. We next move into the "So What?" where we are able to get the group to interpret just what transpired in the experience. It is here that group members are abstracting and generalizing what they are learning from the experience. We can also ask them to reflect on the goals they have been working on. With this scenario, we have plenty of material, an outline so to speak. There should be enough to work with! And because of the Initiative-oriented Debrief, we can ask questions, and let the group solve the problems as much as they are able.

Evaluating Group Goals

The question "Did we honor our Full Value Contracts?" gets us into those group goals. It is a general, non-threatening question, one that could be asked after every experience. It's a safe place to start because you are not focusing on any individual behavior. It translates as: *"Did we treat each other well, or did we discount each other?", "Was there support, or devaluing?", "Did we stick to the rules we set up?"* The group is seen as an entity that needs to be taken care of, much as we take care of a person. The group members are both the change agents and the persons to be changed. We can say, "Without a healthy and responsible group, we are greatly diminished."

For example, after a community service project, a group was asked whether the Full Value Contract was kept. Some responses were:

- *"We did a good job painting the boats and picking up trash in the boatyard."*
- *"Some of the kids were throwing putty, and didn't do any work."*
- *"Mr. Montgomery (the owner of the yard) thought we did a good job, and he complimented us. But he also said, 'Some of you work awful hard, some not much at all. Some kids went back to the bus without helping pick up the tools.'"*

Though individual behavior was discussed, what the individuals did was in relation to the overall group. Behavior was seen reflected in the mirror of the group. The good and bad things that happened had a bearing on the image and "feel" of everyone else. Interaction with a community person brought the reality of Full Value to the forefront, for they wanted to have pride in their group. The external voice provided a kind of natural monitor (*How did we do in his eyes?*).

We can look at Full Value in light of Nancy's experience on the Criss Crotch (see p. 113). There was no escaping the reality of the fact that the group left her "on the wire," and she was forced to get off. We had discounted her. There were all

Interaction with a community person brought the reality of Full Value to the forefront, for they wanted to have pride in their group.

kinds of excuses, but the fact remained that she was left alone. There were no grey areas. Individuals were the ones who left her, but it was ultimately a group issue because no one confronted the group as they left.

Another example of the power of the group is seen in an incident that took place on a canoe trip with court-referred youth. At the end of the trip, which had been frustrating for some members (a lost paddle, and a lack of cooperation on their part), these particular students were wising off to some people on a bridge above the pull out point. They almost got into a fight. Group was called immediately. The group zeroed

in on and confronted what was going on, and what had been happening throughout the day. The group as "person" just could not tolerate the kind of feelings, behavior, and image it was projecting. Equipment had been lost. There were bad attitudes. Fights had almost broken out and anger had been expressed toward outside people.

In the Debrief, the group strictly monitored its behavior, and produced some appropriate consequences. For one boy, this was a "last straw"...he was sent back to "lock up." For another, some privileges were taken away. They also used the group time to set new goals for their next Activity, looking at what they had learned from the day's experience. It all took place on a riverbank, in the dark, during a slight drizzle. Please note that when we say "The group monitored its behavior" we do not mean that the instructors were passive. The instructors, as per the Common Grounding, were a part of that group while maintaining control over it. Everyone understood that. Because they had been listened to, because affection had been building, because there was an obvious

Because they had been listened to, because affection had been building, because there was an obvious respect for them, the participants were willing to operate in collusion with the leaders. It was an "unequal partnership" that everyone accepted.

respect for them, the participants were willing to operate in collusion with the leaders. It was an "unequal partnership" that everyone accepted.

Instructors are not free of being nailed by the Full Value Contract. Jim Schoel relates this experience:

> "One time while belaying on a rock face, I had a friend show up whom I had not seen for several years. I was very excited to see him, and we immediately started talking. Though my belaying was technically correct and I never lost sight of it, I had emotionally left the climber. In the Debrief, he confronted me, expressing disappointment that he had been devalued. It wasn't important to him that I hadn't seen this person for a long time. He was concerned with a difficult climb, one he had been working himself up to. He wanted me there with him, not jawing with someone else. I had to admit that I had been wrong, that I had discounted him. His confronting me was an important experience for him as well. It was a clear-cut case. He was right and I was wrong. Because we had spent so much prior time making the Full Value Contract, he had a vehicle to use. If he hadn't confronted me, he would have been discounting himself, as that was part of the agreement."

"I had to admit that I had been wrong, that I had discounted him. His confronting me was an important experience for him as well."

The Full Value Contract came into play on an expedition. The group had specified no drugs or alcohol, along with the other group and individual goals. During the trip, one they had worked especially hard to pull off, several joints and some nips were found. The group was confronted with this. Everyone knew what had to be done, because the agreement had been made beforehand: We had to pack up and go home. There was no plea bargaining involved. They were forced to walk by with their equipment in front of their school mates, who asked, *"Why are you back so soon?,"* etc.

The group Debrief used Full Value as its vehicle: "What did we do to our group?", "What individual responsibility was violated here?" A great deal of time was spent on the issue, with many students admitting their complicity. The issue of the trip coming home became a theme for the year. They were determined not to let it happen again, and were eager to prove themselves. A negative experience became a positive one, for a new group goal was hammered out, this one having some meat of determination on it.

The growth orientation of Full Value is evident in this dynamic. Full Value is not a rule of denial, it is a law of growth.

"But we try" is the theme. We are not perfect. We will fail. But we want to do it the right way. Give us another chance. Each Adventure experience after that "bummer" (colloquial for bad experience), was analyzed in light of what they had gone through. At the end of the year, they were able to say "We turned it around."

Evaluation of Individual Goals

Individual goals are also subject to review. We ask questions like:

- *Does anyone want to talk about whether he achieved what he set out to do?*
- *Did anyone see anyone else achieve anything?*
- *Can any "buddies" talk about their partners?* (The buddy system has members team up in order to monitor or keep track of each other during the group experience.)

Journal time can be helpful here, too. Let them have 5 minutes to look over their written goals, and make comments about how they did. Then let them read from the journal to the group, much as the Gestalt exercise. Through this process, behavior issues become a natural benefit of what individuals have agreed to accomplish. We are again escaping the punitive mode. Using the Full Value Personal Action Plan (what you want, how you are going to get it, what support you will need, agreement not to devalue, show evidence regarding achievement) can provide an overall structure to the Debrief, weaving these other activities around it. It can also be groundwork for new goals, moving into the "Now What?" section.

An example of reviewing an individual Activity goal is Bill, who wanted to make a particular rock climb. He really worked on it, but he still "failed." This failure wore on him, for he was a success-oriented person. In the Debrief, his partner who was coaxing him up the rock spoke about how hard he tried, and how important that was. Another observation revolved around the fact that he put so much effort into it, to the point where he was thrashing at the rock, and not being effective.

The group's advice was, "calm down, think more, go more easily and smoothly." He revised his goal with that advice in mind. The next week he tried it again. He failed to complete the climb, but his approach to it was entirely different than the week before. This time, after putting all his effort into it, he came to the realization that it was too difficult for him. Perhaps he needed to work on his arm strength, or stop smoking. His revised Personal Action Plan reflects the new perspective:

Through this process, behavior issues become a natural benefit of what individuals have agreed to accomplish. We are again escaping the punitive mode.

What you want: "To make the climb up the crack at Stage Fort Park."

How you are going to get it: "Listen to the group as they give me advice"

What support you will need: "Support in solving the problem of how to make the climb, support at the rockface regarding actually making the attempt."

Agreement not to devalue: "To not put myself down if I fail, and to try to keep from getting too mad at the rock and at myself."

Show evidence regarding achievement: "How I did on the climb this time."

Evaluating Spiral Goals

Spiral Goals, because of their removal from the group experience, are more difficult to monitor. However, if participants are learning anything from their Adventure experience, they are naturally spiralling or practicing what they have learned. The group, through the shared experience learns to trust whether a participant is for real in his goal setting, also. If a group member is sincere and effective with what he does in the context of the group, what he does in the world will be believable as well. That's why we start with Activity goals, in order to establish a reality base within the common experience. The need for this is corroborated by Cindy Simpson, director of the Atlanta, Georgia Challenge Program that deals with court-referred youth:

> "The smallest thing a kid does here (in group), if he isn't willing to change that behavior, he will do much more of it out on the street. That's why we teach the kids from day one that they cannot let any negativity go by without dealing with it."

Here we are going into the delicate area of what our participants will be doing on the "outside." If they are part of an enclosed program where they are away from home, then much of the spiralling is expressed through the metaphor of the group and in their living situation. If they are in a setting that includes traffic with "the world" then spiralling becomes more than metaphorical. They can actually go out and try to achieve their goals.

The strength of the on-site Adventure group is evident when we deal with spiralling, for that kind of group allows for outside "in the world" reality testing while still relying on the strength of the group to act as a supportive backup, or spotter.

Participants are continuously "spiralling off" new behavior wherever they are, and monitoring spiral goals in the Debrief occurs in much the same manner we monitor activities goals.

So when Wendy wants to leave her house, she sets up her personal action plan, and it is monitored by the group. Because of the delicate nature of some of these action plans we do not look at monitoring as a heavy-handed "did you do this?" Rather, monitoring is supportive in nature: "How's it going?", or "Are you still getting hassled?", or "You sure got guts to do that."

The "Now What?"

The persistence of the Adventure Wave means that there will always be another Activity. The "Now What?" is a structure for planning that next Activity with the group. Activities selection comes to bear here once again. What are the overall objectives? What is the Sequence that we have set up? What are the group needs at this point? Do we need to adjust? Am I using the GRABBS checklist?

If you can negotiate the next Activity with the group members, you are building a sense of power with them. They will also have a period of time to visualize it, think it through, and prepare. The "Now What?" contains the hope, the newness, the chance for better things. As in any dream, it's easy to get carried away with fantasies about something that hasn't happened yet.

New group activities, new behavior, spiralling, all are "Now What?" issues, and they need to be carefully managed. As you manage the planning stage, keep in mind that you are walking a tightrope between what people would like to happen and what can and should happen. New goals are wonderful, but they must be realistic. At the same time, too much realism can kill spontaneity and change.

It's helpful to treat the "Now What?" along the lines of creative problem solving: Allow the creative process to run, put the associations on the board, and don't edit anything. Let them do a lot of the thinking. If a group members throw up obstacles too soon, encourage them to hold off their reservations. A plan can then be developed that is their plan.

The kinds of projects the group wants to jump into are often inspiring but demanding. Say the group wants to put on a Christmas party for the Down's syndrome kids they've been working with all fall. This will take a lot of work. Someone needs to be Santa Claus. There need to be games, food, transportation to and from the site, and presents. Or, during a hike the group gets excited about cleaning up the trails. This

If you can negotiate the next Activity with the group members, you are building a sense of power with them. They will also have a period of time to visualize it, think it through, and prepare.

178   Islands of Healing

is a wonderful opportunity; the group has seen a real need and wants to do something about it. Key questions are :

- *Will anyone get psychologically hurt by attempting these ideas?*
- *How does the Activity fit into our goal setting?*
- *Is there a new angle on our goals that has emerged here?*
- *Will it so disrupt our sequence that we will not be able to accomplish our goals?*

It may require a change in your whole sequence, but in the end, it may help you meet your overall group objectives in a better way than in your original sequence. An important part of the Full Value Contract is the ability to generate new goals along the way. You have to measure whether the group can handle these things.

An important part of the Full Value Contract is the ability to generate new goals along the way.

Transferring Learning

The "Now What?" is also the process of taking lessons from the experience and "reapplying them (those lessons) to other situations." (Rhoades, p.104). We call these "transfer points." It is a standard culminating device to ask a question like, "*What lessons did we learn by doing Blindfold Square that we can use when we do the Tire on the Pole Initiative?*" at the end of the Debrief. Taking the learning in one Activity and moving it over to the next Activity helps the group connect what they have been doing to a larger picture. Often we will see clearly what can be carried over, but the group will not have the foggiest notion. It is important to help them make the connections.

The "Now What?" is a place to talk about spiral goal setting, as well, using the energy of the experience to stimulate the group to think about what they can do in other areas of their lives. For example, the spotting energy that a particular person exhibited during Tire on the Pole could be suggested as a lesson that can be applied to being able to concentrate during an academic class, or the caring that is necessary to hold down a job.

An example would be the way to deal with Megan's problem of excessive school absences. She had an alcoholic mother who kept Megan home from school when she went on benders. Though the background of this hadn't come up in the group, she clearly wanted the group to

help her come to school. It became a group issue out of necessity. *("If we don't do something about this, we are going to lose Megan.")*

Megan had done well in the group, completing some crafts projects and participating in the activities. Through this interaction the group had learned to value her. The group responded to her truancy problem by drawing up a contract for her that said, "I will not miss one day of school for the next two weeks." Everyone in the group signed it, and promised to support it. The group signatures were their idea.

So Megan was able to receive important support from her group members at a time when she needed it. The group, if one were to be objective in their measurement of its developmental stage, was not ready to do this, for they were still Storming. They were resistive to almost everything that went on. But they were able to respond to the reality of Megan's conflict. So they expressed caring, and helped her with a spiral contract. They deserved praise for this action, and they received it. This took place during a Debrief that they fought vigorously: (*All we do around here is talk talk talk.*) The leadership tactic of sticking to your principles paid off. (*We have important things to deal with in this group. Look at what Megan is going through. You have issues, too, and we can help each other.*)

The principles need to be ridden like the wildest bucking horse right through the resistance. Just at the point where it appears that another group Debrief would go by without a breakthrough, something like Megan's contract will emerge.

When working on spiral goals, realism is also important. We want Nancy to have a successful reunion with her father and her new stepmother. Her plan needs to be talked through. She needs support. Some of that support may need to come

from a social worker, or therapist who is outside the group. Indeed, in many cases the Adventure group can do only so much, needing to refer participants for in-depth, one-on-one counseling, or specialized counseling groups.

You can use the energy of the group to begin work on a certain issue, extending that work through more private sessions. If we send a group member off on a spiral goal without the necessary supports, the results can be disappointing. Helping a participant get a job that is too demanding and has no liaison connecting the employer to the group is a common area of failure. The participant makes a mistake, comes late, is ashamed of it, and stops going. Good preparation for spiralling helps prevent these problems. But support during the effort is also necessary. If the support cannot be supplied, it can be better to not make the attempt. Not that there aren't inherent risks involved in the whole process. But as we think of the Initiative-oriented Debrief, the leader must be the bottom line for safety. We must keep the danger margin extremely close. We are there to be the bottom line spotter. Failures can be turned into successes, as in Bill's rock climb. But they can also be devastating, and extremely difficult to patch up.

One spiral goal will lead to another, especially if the participant is experiencing success. The Counseling on the Run strategies come to bear here. Often the participant will get into gear in such a way that new ideas and plans are virtually tumbling out. There is no reason that you and the participant can't goal set on the run, as long as there is check in time with the group, and group sharing and feedback where necessary. Let's reconsider Bill, who "failed" on the rock climb. He found success in a job making futons (a japanese mattress), a job we referred him to. The job provided more evidence that he was a good person, and that he could be depended on as well. (The boss at the futon factory was particularly sensitive, an important resource for people who are just "going out.") He added a job at a fast food restaurant. All through this time he couldn't wait to get out of school. From every angle we could think of we would tell him of his abilities, and that he should push himself further than high school. The rock climbing scene came up: The approach to the climb was the important thing, not whether he made it or not. And it was also how he lived his life, how he challenged himself, took care of himself (he recently stopped smoking, a goal set in the group). He took into the real world his successes, and his new-found strategies for dealing with life situations. The affection the group had developed for him was also a great deal of help in his "spiralling out."

One spiral goal will lead to another, especially if the participant is experiencing success.

Connecting with the Community

If Bill simply had a series of great experiences where he learned to feel good about himself, that may have affected his overall view of himself. But the nature of the ABC group is to make appropriate connections with the community at large. This is accomplished through:
  • The community base of Adventure.
  • Community related activities (service, interviewing, job referrals, study projects, interest counseling).
  • Family, school and agency follow-up.
  • The long term nature of many ABC groups.

Termination of the Group

Any participant's taking leave from the group must be looked at seriously. Too often a group member simply fails to show up for the next meeting. The loss is two-fold, for the departed one  and for the other group members. The experience of loss when something comes to an end is painful enough. To simply disappear makes it much worse. It is therefore important to deal with leaving the group, for the individual as well as for the group as a whole. If the participant can't or won't show up, at least spend time discussing what happened. Whatever the reason for that person's termination, you should attempt to make it as positive as you can, focusing on the good things the person did. Embellish the truth, if you have to. Everyone will understand what your effort is.

The following examples illustrate two distinct termination situations:

One individual (or more) leaves before the group has ended
Matt was, after a diagnostic period, deemed inappropriate for the group. He was overwhelmed by the school setting, and required an outside placement. He didn't agree with the decision, but was forced to go along with it. During the Debrief, the fact that he was leaving was discussed, but no reasons were given. He had a chance to voice his displeasure. Then he listened to the good feedback: *"You are a wonderful artist." "You do very well in science class." "You did good on the bike-a-thon."* He left with a fairly good taste in his mouth, and with a goal of getting himself together enough to come back for another try. Each group member had the chance to say something about him. In this way, everyone knew 1) that he was leaving, and 2) where he was going. They also had a chance to say good-bye in a positive manner.

Termination of the entire group
This must be dealt with in the same serious vein. Richard Weber calls this process "transforming." As discussed in

Chapter 3, **Bedrock**, there are two choices for the group. One is to start again with a new agenda and time period. The other is to disengage. Whatever happens, a decision must be made and the group needs to be a part of that decision. The group can either use the lessons they have learned to form a basis for that new agenda, or they can use those same lessons as a basis for taking leave. Without going through the termination process, the group will have no chance to finalize their time with each other, thereby leaving the participants with a sense of incompleteness.

Here is an Activity that can lend a positive note to the termination process. It is called "Accepting Yourself." (Thanks to Dr. Arthur Underwood.) Using a sheet that the participants fill out either with their partner, or by themselves, they are asked to investigate their strengths in relationship to how they operated in the group. They then are asked to share their findings with the group. This is the form for the handout you can give them:

Accepting Yourself

In this exercise, you will be asked to discuss your strengths openly with the other group members. This is no place for modesty. You are not being asked to brag, only to be realistic and open about the strengths that you possess. Take five to ten minutes to think it over and make notes. Follow this procedure for the exercise:

1. Think of all the things that you have done well while doing the Adventure group, all the things for which you feel a sense of accomplishment.

2. In the group as a whole, each person should share the full list of his or her strengths. Then ask the group, "What additional strengths did you see in me?" Add these to your list.

3. Think about your successes and your strengths. Think about how your strengths may be utilized to improve your relationships, school, work, etc. Then, set some goals around these issues.

This exercise works well because it stresses the positive aspects of the participant's experience. It can be scary, because the individual becomes the focus of attention. But it is a worthwhile risk, if the group is ready for it (the group needs to be securely in the "affection" stage), because the feedback is extremely rich, reality-based, and usable.

A Positive Ending

An end of the year final Debrief took place on a small boat in the harbor. Everyone sat around in a circle. It was a warm June afternoon. The group had participated in a day trip, and felt good about it. Nothing strenuous, or conflict producing. Just fun, and a chance to say good-bye through this last Activity. We took time at the end of this day to review the year. First we listed all the things we had done. It was awesome. The list went on and on. We talked about the highs and lows. We had laughs. We had touching moments.

Then each group member had individual time as the focus of the group's attention. It came time for Billy. Billy was a learning disabled student who three years previously had been barely able to make a sentence without stuttering, and was so disconnected from the world that he was unable to relate to any of the other students. Billy was leaving the alternative program to spiral off to a vocational school, so this was his last time with us. As we did our "go around," a well of feeling began to surface:

- *"We called you 'trucker' because you were always willing to help everybody."*
- *"You did everything. You never missed a trip."*
- *"I could always depend on you."*
- *"I looked forward to seeing you every day."*
- *"You keep on trying, even though you make mistakes."*
- *"You put up with all of our B.S."*
- *"I know you'll make it at the Voke, because you did so well with us."*
- *"I respect you because what you see is what you get. There's not a phony bone in your body. You are a totally honest person."*

Well, we had tears in our eyes. It was one of those moments. Three years of work. Three years of growth. He's still a trucker, too. Graduated first in his class in carpentry. He's working for a construction company. The only complaint is he tends to talk too much on the job. But they love him there, too. And considering how far he came, we'll allow for a little too much talk.

Conclusion

The Debriefing process has the potential of forming a safe Island where the group can consider its Activity. The leader's confidence in how important Debriefing is helps the process become a meaningful experience for the group. It is a skill like any other, which must be practiced and honed by both leader and group. Debriefing has certain principles that need to be remembered, such as:

- Don't be surprised by resistance.
- Make the Debrief Initiative-centered, where the discussion is connected to the group problem-solving experiences so important to Adventure activities.
- Train yourself to listen and observe during parts of the Adventure Wave prior to the Debrief, and utilize that material in an appropriate manner in the Debrief.
- Sequence the Debrief in such a way that it leads up to the more gutsy issues.
- Make sure that when it is time to finish the group, you have provided an adequate place for Termination issues to be dealt with.

Debriefing, or the group discussion process as a whole, provides a model of how the ideal family should operate. We know that disasters within the family unit often come as a result of poor communication between members. A successful negotiating process, capable of dealing with issues ranging from conflict to praise, is a primary Adventure Based Counseling experience that can subsequently be practiced in the outside world.

Section 3

Applications of Adventure Based Counseling

The following program descriptions are specific applications of the Adventure Based Counseling model. They were selected on the basis of their exemplary design, accessibility, and effectiveness. Each specific application bears the stamp of the personalities leading it as well as the geographic area concerned. These leaders have developed their own unique Adventure base. When taken with the more generic information of Section 2 on program design, the specific program information of these applications should help those interested in designing an effective new program or refining an existing one.

188   Islands of Healing

Chapter 8

Schools

"I regard it as the foremost task of education to ensure survival of these qualities: an enterprising curiosity; an undefeatable spirit; tenacity in pursuit; readiness for sensible self-denial; and above all, compassion."

— Kurt Hahn

THE GREATEST NUMBER of adaptations of Adventure have taken place in schools. It was a natural step therefore to adjust Adventure curriculum to areas that need a counseling format. Generally, the adaptation requires smaller groupings, co-leadership, selection and Intake processes, and an Activities Base that reflects the growth needs of the students. In some places the ABC group takes the place of a more traditional counseling group. In others, ABC is used to supplement already existing counseling activities. It is used as a focus or learning tool for a broad range of students who would not be construed as needing counseling. And ABC is also taken as the management metaphor for entire school programs.

The common thread of these adaptations is the ability of Adventure to aid in the socialization process, and to help build a sense of competence. Kids in schools don't know how to talk to each other, or to their teachers, very well. They are therefore unable to properly express their needs, or their real feelings. And because of the competitive nature of the traditional schools, they often are left in the dust academically. This leads to a variety of problems: alienation, poor attendance, failure, acting up behavior, and many forms of abuse. Issues surrounding sexism, racism, cliques, career and life choices, relationships (both sexual and friendship), drugs, marriage and families dominate school life today. It takes trust to be able to form the courage to speak up, and to examine areas that others might laugh at, or scorn. There is a direct correlation between the success adults have and the social skills they developed during their school years. We hope the following school adaptations will show how versatile ABC is in its ability to respond to a variety of needs. Those programs are:

- **Youth Challenge**
  Manchester Public Schools
  Manchester, Massachusetts
- **The Bud Carlson Alternative School**
  Rochester, New Hampshire
- **Adventure Based Counseling**
  The Gloucester Public Schools
  Gloucester, Massachusetts

Youth Challenge

A full-year Adventure Based Counseling program
for all eighth grade students.
Manchester Jr./Sr. High School, Manchester, Massachusetts

"Do quality work and it will grow from that seed"

Youth Challenge began as an entry program aimed at introducing Adventure curriculum to the Manchester Schools. The initial idea was to involve a small number of students in Adventure in order to give them some satisfying, non-competitive experiences. A target group of a mixture of learning disabled, shy and passive students, those who were generally not making it in the school social structure, was selected.

Because of the success of this initial venture, counselors began to refer students to the program. Some parents also began to request it for their children. This pressure brought about an expansion to three groups in the next two years. Success breeds success. Within five years, the entire eighth grade was participating in one of the Adventure groups.

The staff feels that kids taking Adventure at this juncture, with the counseling framework of co-leadership, small heterogeneous groups, and once-weekly meetings, are better prepared to handle such pressures as achievement, cliques, substance abuse and other troublesome issues. It is because of the grade-wide heterogeneous groupings that we consider Youth Challenge to be an excellent Prevention Model.

It is because of the grade-wide heterogeneous groupings that we consider Youth Challenge to be an excellent Prevention Model.

There are many benefits to this format. One is the school spirit that it is able to encourage. Because mixtures of kids have been involved with each other dealing with the range of Adventure activities, there is a natural carryover into the later years of High School. They have had a chance to get to know each other, and to appreciate each other's strengths and weaknesses. No, they are not all friends. But there is an awareness of each other, and an appreciation, that goes a long way toward overall closeness in a school. Secondly, students are able to benefit from the learning that takes place in the Adventure group regarding how to talk about things, from solving problems to dealing with personal issues. A common language develops, and it is carried over into other areas of the students' lives. Third, in this school, all eighth grade teachers meet together in team meetings.

Because of the assessment capabilities of the group, the group leaders are able to share perceptions about students from a non-competitive angle with those teachers. Often a hint regarding learning style will emerge, something that the team has missed. Or, an effort made on the ropes course can be gently carried over into a class.

The structure, then, sees all eighth grade students heterogeneously grouped in small sections of from twelve to seventeen participants. "Youth Challenge provides a setting to enhance self-confidence and positive inter-personal relations. The activities are a means to provide the environment in which different behaviors can be evidenced. It is through this experience that adolescents become aware of positive, healthy behaviors and develop the ability to generate behavioral alternatives." (Youth Challenge Curriculum book) The objectives are:

- To develop communication skills (listening/speaking)
- To develop self-confidence and self-esteem
- To improve problem-solving techniques
- To learn to trust oneself and others
- To strengthen decision-making skills
- To gain better appreciation and respect for others
- To learn how to better cooperate in a group
- To gain better control over impulsive behavior
- To develop an appreciation and respect for nature
- To participate in a variety of physical activities
- To become aware of social responsibility

Students are evaluated twice each quarter. They receive Physical Education and Health credits.

Two instructors are assigned to each group as co-leaders. Each is trained in the Adventure Based Counseling model of Project Adventure and one is a certified school guidance counselor. The instructors are assigned common planning time and work together to plan for group and individual needs. Each Manchester program has been observed and accredited by the Project Adventure Staff. The Youth Challenge Program has been highly commended by the PA Accreditation team.

Each class has four segments: Warm-ups and aerobics, Briefing in terms of goals for the day's principal Activity, the Activity itself, and finally, Debriefing the Activity.

Because of the length of the Activities and the time required for Debriefing, the classes meet once a week for two consecutive blocks or one hundred total minutes. Each class has four segments: Warm-ups and aerobics, Briefing in terms of goals for the day's principal Activity, the Activity itself, and finally, Debriefing the Activity. There are frequent time outs taken to focus on group or individual performance. While Activities and Initiatives have been divided into units of emphasis, it is important to note that the Activities are interrelated and weave together the various goals outlined. Activities listed under a particular heading are not exclusively concerned with that topic. A trust/ communication/problem-solving sequence is followed through the course of the year (These activities can be found in the Activities Selection Chart in Appendix B.) There are times when a group may need review of previously emphasized goals, however. A solid foundation of trust, good communication and cooperation are much more important than a tall but wobbly scaffolding of experiences.

A solid foundation of trust, good communication and cooperation are much more important than a tall but wobbly scaffolding of experiences.

The key to Youth Challenge is its inclusive approach: Every student in the eighth grade participates. Because the groups are smaller than standard classes, and because there is co-leadership, supervision, and the involvement of a counselor, it is called Adventure Counseling. This broad approach makes it possible to develop a thematic curriculum. If a school system wants to concentrate on Substance Abuse, Sex and the Family, School Climate, or Community Service, the structure that encourages group process is in line. All that has to be done is to adjust the flow of activities. The building of trust that an ABC group demands can be carried over into these areas. The sensitive issues that come out when these issues are considered can then be dealt with in effective and responsible ways.

Adventure activities are continued on an elective basis in the ninth to twelfth grades, during Physical Education classes. Also, older students come back to help with leadership, and chaperone the day and overnight hiking, boating and canoe trips.

Mixing within the groups helps build strength. For example, toleration of others is often a problem with high achieving students. One girl, Lorraine, was vocal, academic, and athletic. She believed she was an honest person, very fair and equitable. But she would take the mother role, tell other students what to do, especially Frank, who was a high energy, nervous, low achieving misfit, new to the school that year. Lorraine would run roughshod over Frank.

It took about half a year for the kids to be able to focus on this problem, and do something about it. When they confronted her with it, it was a shocker to her. She disagreed. But gradually she began to see, and to deal differently with Frank. They didn't become "friends," but this insight affected the way that they treated each other. Frank, in turn, began to say "This is bothering me" when he felt himself being ordered around. Frank had been getting frustrated in the group, anyway. He would walk away from a problem, and sit in a corner. The kids tell him: "You got upset we didn't listen to you. But you want to be listened to only on your terms. So when you go sit in a corner someone else will come up with the solution to the problem instead of you." Frank made a goal for himself: "I will try not to withdraw." Now, he's not getting in a huff. He is attacking the problem more thoughtfully. He's also being accepted. In fact he made a point of coming into the counselor's office (Mr. Ananian) and announcing, "I have a friend!"

Another girl who was extremely timid both physically and in her interactions with the group, had to be coaxed to go on cross country skis, and found it difficult to navigate even the slightest hill. But the group encouraged her to keep at it, and she showed a lot of improvement. This change was carried over to the Beam Initiative (the whole group must go over a horizontal log tied up eight feet high between two trees). She was very emotional getting over this obstacle, feeling good about it. She was in tears going down, as if something had let go inside her. She continued to grow in confidence throughout the year, and became a happier, easier person.

She was very emotional getting over this obstacle, feeling good about it. She was in tears going down, as if something had let go inside her.

Adventure groups provide a framework for discussion of incidents that occur in school over the course of the year. The typical homeroom may have the time for such discussions, if

194   Islands of Healing

there is an extension, but most often there is not the framework to deal effectively with issues. For example, Manchester had a drug incident. The decision was made to deal with the issue in the counseling groups exclusive of whether the students in the groups had been involved. The school had a structure to deal with a specific problem. "We are not threatening to the students. Because of this model (the ABC model), they open up to us." The ABC group established a level of relationship that can be carried over into the High School year.

In conclusion, please note that this adaptation of Adventure started as one small group. "Do quality work, and it will grow from that seed," says Dick Ananian, guidance counselor at the school.

Bud Carlson Alternative School

Rochester Public Schools
Rochester, New Hampshire.

"It took awhile to turn it around."

"Less is more" is the spirit of this 12-year-old program. When the students give away $3-4,000 dollars that they have raised, they get a lot in return. This willingness to serve is seen in the following evidence:
- Each student participates in community service at least one day per week.
- Students have raised $25,000 dollars over a period of 8 years, and have in turn given it all away.
- The school is named after a community person who represents this spirit of giving (Bud Carlson was a school committee member who volunteered his retirement years to helping others).

A letter from the Rochester Visiting Nurse Association, Inc. to the School goes further:

> To All of You at the Alt:
> For your years of generosity in working for, and sharing with, those in need in your your community, a sincere thank you.
> We are most grateful for your $300.00 contribution which will help us to care for the sick and the needy in the

Rochester area.

It's hard to say which is more appreciated...the gift or the givers. I am always personally inspired by your efforts.

Sincerely,
Leslie Dupee
Executive Director

The Bud Carlson Alternative School serves 25 students, ranging from grade 8 to grade 12, and age 13 to 18. Its primary function is to reintegrate students into the school system. Participation in the school is voluntary. Students may be truant and abusive, but they must also be "workable" in the sense that the Intake procedure and the early diagnostic period (30 days probation), leaves the staff with sufficient proof that they want to be part of the school, and will participate in the activities. In this sense, extremely abusive students cannot be managed by the rather slim teacher corps: two full-time teachers and one teacher three days of part time.

The re-integration program develops in the students an overall enhancement of self-image. This is broken down into the elements of:

- Commitment
- Trust
- Responsibility
- Caring for others
- Skills
- An appreciation for learning

They have their own triangle: Love for Kids, School, and Teachers. "If one side falters, the other brings it up."

The staff members are trained as counselors, special needs teachers, and outdoor leaders. There is a director. All are available to participate in all the activities. One of the staff, Lauriann Couture, is a former student at the Alt She is especially attuned to what the students are experiencing, and is able to work with them effectively. When questioned about what it is like "being back," she responded: "When I think of when I was first a student at the school, everything was unclear and dark. As the years went by they became lighter. By the time I graduated things were bright and shiny. That's the way I look at it now."

The school has its own separate space, operating in a storefront one mile from the Junior/Senior High School. This separateness is important to the staff, and to the students, for it gives them a sense of control. The responsibility to maintain the space is theirs, and they make it a part of their overall educational experience.

The staff is able to meet every morning for one hour before any students arrive. All students take some classes at the Junior/Senior High School, where they get U.S. and World History, and Science classes. The Alt provides instruction in the following subject areas:

English: Reading in the great books, writing of letters, the student's own progress reports, and journals

Math: This is a key subject. Students are tested, and through an individualized program, they move through a structured sequence

Social Studies: Through community service, and such topical issues as interviews with local people, sex education, personal hygiene, drug issues, CPR, and hands-on construction projects

Physical Education: A regular scenario of Adventure experiences including a weekly four hour "action day"

They conduct group meetings every day, ranging from 10 minutes to 3 hours, depending on need. The counseling model is highly focused on Activities, with the staff making the choice of responding to behavior and problems as they arise

rather than providing specific sessions devoted to dealing with issues. If students are discipline problems, they are placed on a contract, and a discussion with the parents takes place. If the problem persists, then the student will be asked to return to the Junior/Senior High School.

A week's schedule looks like this:

Monday	Regular classes (at the Alt and at the Junior/Senior High School).
Tuesday	Community Service Day; everyone participates, serving in settings ranging from day care to the library to the police department. Each 90 hours of community service produces 1 credit.
Wednesday	Regular day (same as Monday)
Thursday	½ Regular day, ½ Action Day
	Adventure Activities: Ropes course, rock climbing, cross-country skiing, canoeing, games and Initiatives. (They keep the group close together during all the Adventure Activities, feeling that it is better to wait and be together than participate alone.)
Friday	Regular day (same as Monday and Wednesday)

In addition, there is a sequence of expeditions:

October	In the first week, a two-night camping trip with the whole school. The purpose is to get everyone together.
November	Beginning "winter" camping in the mountains
March	The "Ski-A-Thon" which is the main fundraiser for the community service give-a-way project. Ten students must qualify for this event by: • Passing all classes. • Raising $70.00 in pledges. • Illustrating strong commitment to the program. • Having good attendance. • Staying out of trouble. • Standing up in front of the School and telling why they think they should be chosen to go.

Qualifying students then participate in a 25-mile trek in the mountains by snowshoe and ski, sleeping out in cold weather and preparing all meals "in the wilderness."

Two more camping trips occur before school is out, involving hiking, canoeing, dory rowing and rock climbing.

The year ends with a banquet. The money raised by the students is given to the community groups that have applied for it, and have been chosen by the students as deserving. Ski-A-Thon participants are awarded a group picture commemorating their involvement.

Other activities are added to this basic structure when necessary.

A cadre of student leaders is developed to support the program. These are called "sherpas." Students must qualify for this position. In order to qualify, a student must:
- Participate in the Ski-A-Thon.
- Show 90% attendance.
- Show a mastery of outdoor skills.
- Earn the title of "designated belayer."

The sherpas provide important leadership role models for the younger students, and for other groups that utilize the resources of the program.

A parents' group meets once a month, in the evening. It is used as a group that supports the school, but student issues are also discussed. This group puts on a fundraiser "spaghetti dinner" every spring.

The Alt has overcome the odds in its ability to weather twelve years of existence. Community service means community support. A school in a store front requires that support, for people trained in traditional settings just don't tend to understand what happens in these places. But they do understand when they see decent kids who have been in one or another kind of trouble giving of themselves to their community. It is simply something that can't be argued with. Add to the political support for such endeavors the fact that community service is a sound educational activity, and you have one potent mixture. It is a main "transfer point" for the Islands of Healing, this associating students with other "islands" in their community. Everyone at the Alt subscribes to the notion that the service component is the reason for their survival.

The kids had some things to say:

> *"The banquet. You just can't describe how good a feeling it is [where they give the money away]. I can't talk about it. There's not words [to describe it]."*
> *"I like the rock climbing the most. The ultimate. Scary. Challenging. Do it."*
> *"My sister went here. The counselors at the Jr. High told me about it. My friends told me what the school does for people. If somebody calls, they give help. Students give help."*

> *"Students trust each other, listen to each other."*
> *"It's like a family here...a prison up there [at the High School]."*
> *"I know everybody better down here. Small groups. We're around each other all the time."*
> *"In the meetings, everyone says what they feel."*
> *"People say what's on their mind. You don't feel embarrassed. No one laughs."*
> *"It's not a hangout. We don't just sit around. [We] work at our own pace."*
> *"We set goals like being less quiet. My strategy is to be called on in class more, and give my opinions in the school meetings."*

"My goal was good attendance, and get all my academic credits. My strategy was to do homework, and let the other kids pressure me when I was absent."

"Here, everything is our responsibility. If we break a commitment, it's like breaking a big promise."

"The promise reflects on the school. Whenever we do something wrong it comes back in our faces. The school has done a lot of things for the community."

"Before I knew about this school I was in trouble every day, detention every day."

"I've made new friends. Could never express myself that good. Or talk about how I felt. Feel better about myself. I plan to go on the Ski-A-Thon.. I'm qualifying. Last year I didn't have great attendance. Rocks scared me, so I skipped. This year I began to trust people more, because I saw other people trusting each other. Tim [Tim Churchard, the Director] helped me out a lot in that area. Never even climbed a rock until end of last year. Now, I climbed this year. I'm also a belayer. Will be a certified belayer this spring. Also, I teach guitar. My community service is with the Homemakers of Stratford County. I shovel snow, mail letters, do inventory, stuff like that. Found out about the school through friends. I wouldn't be in school...be off skipping somewhere...if it weren't for this place."

"Tim found out I was having trouble in 8th grade. Wouldn't go [to school]. Hated it. Bad up there. Teachers think they know everything. Don't get to be yourself. Don't care about you [at the High School]. I quit. I go to night school now [for her academics, in addition to her work at the Alt]. The Alt is a support, helped me out. Everyone figured I'd quit night school, too. But I didn't. This place has supported me. My first year, I was nervous, skipped a lot. Middle of year...realized this place could help me. From my teachers...caring, friend. Talk about personal things. Doing really pretty good. It took awhile to turn it around."

The important thing for this girl is that she found a home. Certainly her generalizations about the High School are not all correct. They are, however, a reason why some Alternative Programs get a bad name. Just because it is a student's perception does not mean that the program as a whole should take this stance (note the need for institutional congruence as discussed in Chapter 3, **Bedrock**). The Alt in this case is operating as a mediator between two forces, student and institution, recognizing plus and minus value in both, but making sure to emphasize the positive side of both.

Life at the Alt is a continuous series of events: service days, action days, expeditions, academic course work, interviews, etc.

Life at the Alt is a continuous series of events: service days, action days, expeditions, academic course work, interviews, etc. The teachers, because of the staff time they have each morning, their understanding of the students, and the community service "heart" of the program, feel productive and hopeful, and very much in charge of these events, weaving them in such a way that they are both connected thematically and related to the students. And because the students have 2-4 years to experience this scenario, the change has the potential of being far reaching. It can take awhile to turn it around. But in a program with as much "heart" as this one, there is a willingness to wait.

Adventure Based Counseling

The Gloucester Public Schools
Gloucester, Massachusetts

Adventure activities have been practiced in the Gloucester Public Schools since 1974 when High School Social Studies teacher David Wise participated in the Project Adventure Workshop "Cape Ann Investigations." His use of the activities in his classes and a subsequent on-site training workshop attended by 20 teachers and counselors, provided the impetus for a broad range of Adventure adaptation. The significant area where the practice of Adventure has been maintained is in counseling. In fact, the concept of Adventure Based Counseling had its beginnings in the Gloucester School

System, in conjunction with the Cape Ann Mental Health Center. From elementary to high school, Adventure experiences are available as part of the counseling format. This is how it works:

- **Elementary:** Adventure Counseling groups;
- **Adaptive Physical Education:** Work with disabled students in combination with a counseling component;
- **Middle School:** Adventure Counseling groups and "House Plan" Adventure experiences for regular education students;
- **High School:** Two Alternative Programs,
  The Alliance Program (within the school building)
  The Gloucester Alternative Program — "GAP" —
  (located off grounds).

In addition, Adventure activities are used in "Personal Growth" classes as part of the Social Studies department. For our purposes, we will explore the operation of:

- The Middle School Counseling groups
- The Alliance Program
- Adaptive Physical Education

Middle School Counseling groups

"The student was not liked by many."

Adventure Based Counseling as a generic approach to counseling had its beginning when Paul Radcliffe, at that time a Gloucester counselor and School Psychologist, saw the opportunity to combine PA growth experiences with strategies representative of more traditional group counseling models. From the start it has been essentially a "hospital" model, that is, bringing clinical procedures into the school setting. This was aided by regular consultation with the psychiatric services available at the local Cape Ann Mental Health Center. This was a sound approach and surprisingly easy. The procedures made sense because (a) they are thorough, relying on the checks and balances provided by several decision-making "tiers," and (b) they are in line with the professional screening, referral and staff supervision procedures that function in a clinical setting.

The program goals for the ABC group are:

- To increase self-confidence and self-esteem in a challenging and supportive atmosphere where growth is encouraged and in which the positive is emphasized.

- To realistically define personal goals and strategies for implementation.
- To develop and implement new behaviors and approaches to coping with peer and adult relationships.
- To foster appreciation and respect for individual differences existing in a group.
- To learn increased responsibility and social maturity by practicing interdependent behaviors within a cooperative success-oriented framework.

Staffing consists of a co-led team of a school counselor and teacher, both trained in the use of the Adventure Based Counseling format.

The referral process operates in the following manner:
- Teacher refers to principal
- Principal refers to school psychologist
- School psychologist pulls together a team. The team prescribes a treatment plan.

Once the student is selected for a group, the Intake operates like this:

First Meeting: One-to-one, with the purposes of (a) discussing the program (the "what"), (b) ask "soft" questions (the "so what"), such as, "How does the student see his world? Why was he with a counselor? Was he getting into trouble?" The session is closed by saying "Take a week to think it over. We'll get together in another week to talk further in order to decide."

Second Meeting: One counselor with 2–3 students, all of them having done the first round. This is a chance for the kids to ask questions, do some thinking, and deal with the safety issues. ("Will there be any bullying?" "Will I be scared?" "Will I be safe?") The counselor asks, "do you think you know enough to be involved in the group?" Here's where the choice and commitment come in. If the answer is "yes," then the third meeting is scheduled. This meeting also involves beginning goal setting: "What do I want to change? Why do I want to be here?"

Third Meeting: With the parents. If their O.K. is given, then it is time to set a date and start the group.

This Intake procedure serves to establish a seriousness to the counseling, "Hey, this isn't just choosing sides in a ball game." There is clarity regarding purposes for all involved, as well.

The groups meet once per week, for a two and a half hour session, during the regular school day (this varies depending on scheduling issues). These groups continue to function for the whole school year. (It takes the first month of school to do Intake, and formulate the groups to such a point that they can begin to operate.)

The first few group meetings help paint a picture of just what the group is like. The activities selection process is an aid during this diagnostic time. A sample Activity sequence covering a ten-week period is given in Chapter 4, pp. 74-76. Sticking with warmups, acquaintance and de-inhibitizing, the counselors store up information about the students. They do things that relate to the student's interest level, not pushing too hard, going slowly as the group begins to take shape, making certain that the group can be successful with them.

The Full Value Contract is introduced early on. It impresses on the students that the group is not just about getting out of class and playing on ropes. The group is about *changing*. "What am I here for, and what goals am I going to set for this 'changing'?" By the third week, each student should have come up with one goal. At the end of each Debriefing session thereafter, the students are asked to think about a goal for the next week. The goals are constantly being worked on and reformulated, in this manner.

After each session, it is important for the co-leaders to get together and Debrief the activity. They do it while it is fresh in their minds. This provides a basis for planning the next activity. The group's success depends on this.

Examples of the kinds of interventions that can take place with these age groups is seen in the experiences of Terry, Jack, Jim, and Bill.

The group is not just about getting out of class and playing on ropes. The group is about changing.

Terry

Terry was a 13-year-old middle school student. He had low self-esteem, illustrated inappropriate behavior, and was a low achiever, though not retarded or learning disabled. He was not liked by many. The assistant principal had referred this student. He had been having a great deal of trouble with his behavior and appearance (long hair and army coat). The assistant principal had ordered Terry to "clean up your act," but had been refused. Things were at loggerheads. The principal didn't know what to do with him. So they decided to refer him to the ABC group, going through the above mentioned process.

Terry ended up being sullen, and quiet. He would skip

classes, but he always came to group. The co-leaders represented two trusting people to him, people who cared for him. He opened up and talked about his problems with the principal. Going through the group process, he could be seen as making gains. Things relative to those gains came to a head when he participated in a full day "peak experience" rock climbing trip to Crow Hill in Leominster, Massachusetts. It was a simple climb with a slight overhang. Terry was the last one to go.

He was huddled up. Everyone else had done a climb. His resistance and fear were obvious. "I don't want to do it. I really don't feel well." The co-leader said, "Give it a shot."

So he got on the climb. He went all the way to the overhang. There, he lost it: "I can't go any further."

The co-leader questioned himself: (*When do I push, when do I back off? If not sure, always back off.*)

Terry said, "I want to go back down, you bastard."

"Do you really want to go down, or stay a couple of minutes?", the leader said, practicing "planned ignorance," not hearing the word "bastard." "I've known you for three quarters of a year. Why don't you try it some more?" He got him to a point.

"I want to try it."

Terry almost made it, coming very close. Once he was back down on the ledge, he said "That's it!"

The leader said, "You did so well. Why don't you take one more shot at it. Be more committed. Throw yourself at it."

In the meantime, there were some Army Special Forces guys in the area, and they were looking at him. This was both good and bad, but very real. It intimidated him, but he also realized they were pulling for him. They cheered him! (This is real "community education!") You could see the care and concern of everyone, kind of like an orb had settled around him on that rock face. The conflict the leader felt was, "Will all this help, or is it too much?"

"Terry," the leader said, "you came inches from making it."

"I want to try it one more time." This time, he came within an inch of making it. He lost it and slid down. He cried, "Let me down." He was exhausted. He pounded his fists against the rock, cursing. After going through that, he rallied. "I'm gonna give it one more try." Rather than going at it straight away, he went a little to the right this time. It was a little different move, and this time he made it.

In the Debrief that night, he ended up talking about how that rock face was the principal with whom he had been having the difficulties. For two years he was the rock face. He

In the Debrief that night, he ended up talking about how that rock face was the principal with whom he had been having the difficulties.

could see it as if looking at the rock face in a hallway. What he felt he needed to do was move to the right, instead of running directly into him. "I need to change how I come at this guy."

Jack

Jack approached everything as a tough guy. He's a big kid, 6' 1", 225 pounds, but he's also very fragile. He was climbing up the rock face. Although it was steep, it wasn't very high. But he was scared to death. He tried to make it, trying to be cool and not let on that he was really scared. So he started talking about his sneakers not being the best kind of sneakers for this kind of thing. We encouraged him and he made it to the top and we said, "You know what you just did? Look around you."

He looked over the ocean and we said, "When you're an old man, you have grandchildren, and you're around them some day, you'll start thinking, and say, 'See that place over there, you know I climbed from the bottom to the top. Nobody could ever take that away from me.' It is a solid accomplishment. You can't take it and hold it in your hand, but nobody can ever take it away from you...you climbed that."

The leader (Frank Bonarrigo, Middle School Psychologist) said, "I emphasize the accomplishment. Some kids who have been incarcerated, had things taken away, they have all these defenses built up about how they feel about the world—that crazy world. They develop mechanisms that work for the environment. So they need to accomplish things, to feel good about things. A couple of kids have made a real good try and maybe gone up 10-12 feet, so I talk to them about that, how trustful that is. Maybe some of the others made it all the way, but I could see that these guys were really trying and I like that. That too is accomplishment."

Jim

Jim was heading for trouble because he was unsuccessful in school. Although he could hardly read, he somehow managed to get by in his earlier grades without any problems, but it was catching up with him. He used to go and sit with the custodian to get help with his reading. The custodian was talking to the counselor one day and he said, "There's something wrong here," so we did an evaluation and found the learning disability.

It turns out that the whole family has pretty much the same disability. As part of his education plan, he became a member of the ABC group, and he made it a home. Though he had never been sure of himself, he kept good attendance and

He used to go and sit with the custodian to get help with his reading. The custodian...said "There's something wrong here," so we did an evaluation and found the learning disability.

an excellent attitude. He was someone who made you feel good just to be around him, with a ready smile and a joke and a laugh. Never in any real trouble, he needed a place where he could accomplish things, to feel part of a group. His ABC group carried over into the alternative program at the High School. He graduated as a student leader and earned an award as the best Adventure student. Because of the coordination of his counseling program, from the point of assessment in eighth grade right up to graduation, he was able to maintain his spirits, learn, and give of himself to other people.

Bill

Bill was referred to the ABC group because of his bullying and dominating behavior while he was in seventh grade. He acted it out through actual physical encounters with his peers. In the preliminary activities, an autocratic leadership style took over, where he was actively directing people. During the

Nitro Crossing, for example, he would say "Tim, you do this, Mark you do this, Bobby you do this." His physical presence had a lot to do with it. Other kids were willing to defer to him out of fear.

Blindfold Square, Spider's Web and Nitro Crossing were used to assess the group early on. They were successful at none of these activities because of Bill. The leaders let this lack of success continue, choosing not to intervene. In the goal setting with Bill, his goal was to be a leader. What he meant by that was to "get things done on time," with no sense of how you become a leader on a team. That dynamic was an ongoing one, and it wasn't really confronted until three months later on the Mohawk Traverse.

The group was failing, falling off, not working together. Bill finally ran out of ideas and energy. On his own, out of desperation and frustration, he became quiet. He had no more to offer. The co-leaders decided to intervene. Debrief in the middle of the activity. They asked questions: "What is working?" "What is not working?" "Why?"

At that time Bill remained quiet. He had become willing to listen. One of the kids, Mark, sized up what they needed to do to be successful. The other group members listened to it. And Bill was not able to listen to it. It was a strategy of how group members could support each other, be interlocked, on that long traverse. They got back to the activity and completed it.

Bill was first confronted during the Debrief. Three kids (this tells you a lot about the inner work of the group, for it had become safe to make the confrontation) told him, "Bill, your goal is to be a leader. Good leaders need to listen to others on the team." So Bill amended his goal. He wrote in his journal, "My goal is to be a leader, but in order to be a leader I need to be a listener." (The second part was penned in under "What I need from others.") That was further modified in weeks to come. He realized: "(a) how hard it is to be a listener, and the reasons why it's hard to listen; (b) that other ideas are not always consistent with my own, (c) I will be losing center stage; (d) I have an image that leaders always have power and control."

Three months later, the group took a three-day hiking peak experience to Zealand Falls (spring, snow on ground, hills, cross streams, a tough trip for this group, though do-able). The goal for the day was to get to the hut. Bill got frustrated. He was dealing with his timetable, and the group wasn't meeting it. Kids were putting out, but they didn't have his stamina (you only go as fast as the slowest).

Then a student fell in the snow. He took off his pack, and refused to go further. Bill was on him: "Get the pack on, Tim. We gotta make the hut. It's only one hour away." The other kids were watching. They were afraid. They wondered if the staff was going to make it safely.

The leaders let it play out, ready to intervene. Tim mustered the strength to confront Bill, right back to the Mohawk Traverse, saying, "You're right back to shoving people around [Tim was screaming at him]. Haven't you learned anything from the Debrief of the Mohawk? You need

Tim mustered the strength to confront Bill, right back to the Mohawk Traverse, saying, "You're right back to shoving people around."

to listen to what we need, too! And what I need right now is to be able to rest!"

Bill somehow was able to hear it. And he was able to negotiate with Tim as a result of that hearing, coming up with what Tim needed and what Bill needed. They worked out a 10-minute rest for Tim. The other kids didn't mind taking it, either. After the 10 minutes, Bill also carried Tim's pack for 20 minutes. For the next two days on the trip, the lesson stayed intact. This became a central experience for Bill, and for the group as a whole. Bill went on to finish High School, is married with two kids, and is a car salesman at an agency in town.

The ABC group in the elementary and middle schools can serve to pick up on either real or potential difficulties in terms of student adjustment. Those difficulties can then be traced and dealt with during the students' schooling. Use of the Adventure metaphor and approach can provide a consistent "language for this work, both for the students and for the staff."

The Alliance Program

"The first time I went to the Adult center (a recreation center that deals with a significant group of people suffering from Alzheimer's disease), I felt I belonged. I felt at home right away. By helping them out."
    —Karen, an Alliance Program student

The High School Alliance Program is a full-day alternative voluntary program geared to
    "...those students who have not been productive in the mainstream, seldom complete assignments, are often absent from school, and generally have difficulty following the rules and policies of the school." Students may or may not be identified as special needs students. It is an alternative focused on small group interaction and a close relationship between staff and students, with a range of therapeutic opportunities during the school day and week.
    "The purpose is to reintroduce students to school through a supportive model which would eventually result in their returning to the mainstream. The program provides flexible structures for students in that it mixes their alternative program experience with regular high school classes. The mix is determined by the students'

ability to participate in regular classes successfully. If a student is judged "not a good risk for participating in regular classes," then more classes are scheduled in Alliance and fewer or none in the mainstream.

"As some students progress with their coping skills and develop improved self-image, they re-integrate completely into the regular program. The Alliance Program consists of a set of Core Experiences. All students who are enrolled in the program participate in them. They take place during three consecutive periods daily. Some students are assigned to classes in the Alliance Program during the morning periods, depending on an individual student's need for additional structure and support."

(From the Alliance Program proposal, Dr. Charles Symonds, Principal)

The Core Experiences have four purposes:

- To foster an involvement with the program: this purpose will be accomplished through group activity, Adventure experiences, and meetings of the community at large.
- To foster prevocational and vocational/career abilities and interests: students participate in a series of projects and activities relative to career exploration, vocational choices and task completion. These projects and activities involve community service, participation in work placement, vocational counseling, career exploration and personal development.
- To foster the use of expressive language: project experiences and community experiences are used as vehicles for students to improve speaking skills and writing skills.
- To attend to the personal development of each student in the program: students participate in two decision-making counseling sessions per week.

Staffing consists of three teachers responsible for a maximum of 33 students. One is the "head teacher," and also has special needs certification, with the capability of testing and assessment. The others are regular education teachers. All the teachers have counseling skills, coupled with varying degrees of Adventure skills and experience, from ropes course, rock climbing, camping and canoeing, to small boat handling and cross country skiing.

The Alliance Program practices Adventure in the areas of thematic academic classes (environmental studies), integrative experiences for the "project classes" (each student participates in a project class, which includes an activity-oriented counseling group), and some of the physical education classes.

The activities available are:
- Ropes course (the complete curriculum)
- Rock climbing
- Rowing and small boat handling
- Canoeing
- Community service
- Environmental service (maintenance of a five acre island used for camping and environmental study)
- Tutoring and activities with Down's syndrome students
- Recreational activities with the elderly at the Adult Community Center
- Hiking
- Camping
- Cross-country skiing
- Hands-on woodworking and other crafts (boat construction and maintenance, equipment repair, ropes course construction, landscaping, cemetery maintenance)
- Folk-Life Festival (a day-long celebration of the town's history sponsored by the Alliance's support group Gloucester Museum School, Inc.). Students run a concessions booth, have a display of Alliance Program activities and provide logistical help.

Each Alliance teacher uses the above activities according to his skill level, personal interest, and student interest and ability. Like Bud Carlson Alternative School, the Alliance Program places a great deal of emphasis on community service. It has proven to be a central "curative factor" for them.

Students do fundraising to defray costs of field trips and other activities. They do this through a 20-mile bike-a-thon, a fish fry, and help put on a yearly auction that benefits the Alliance Program activities. These activities not only raise money, they become a conduit for student energy, resulting in greater investment in their program.

Here's a group interview with students presently in the program5:

What do you like about the Alliance?
　　All: "It's the togetherness, the trust, love, real friendship, community, all getting together, a lot of caring people always looking out for each other. There's not too many groups like that that are so positive. Other groups don't have that communication and caring."

Why?
　　All: "Because you just get together, you'll hang around with a tiny group, it's not everyone together. The little group is just there doing their own thing. This group is like a family. You walk in there, feel open. Don't need to hide things from each other."
　　"Well, sometimes you try, you can be open, but not all the time."
　　"The teachers and the kids all are working on the same level. They work together as one."
　　"In other classes there's lots of pressure. If you don't keep up, you fall behind. It's do this do that. In Alliance, everyone is working at their own pace. It's more realistic than the regular classes. The teachers talk with you and understand you. Not as many kids in the classes, either. Teachers are able to get to know you."

You do a lot of volunteer work. What do you like about that?
　　Marty: "It's a good feeling. Helps you communicate more. The first time I went there, I didn't talk [in reference to working with Down's Syndrome kids]. I was nervous, I felt uncomfortable. Later on, you start talking."
　　Karen: "The first time I went to the Adult Center [a recreation center that deals with a significant number of people suffering from Alzheimer's disease], I felt I belonged. I felt at home right away. By helping them out. It makes you feel more important if you are doing something for them. I wasn't feeling too important before that. Things were going lousy."

Did the staff value you there?
　　Karen: Yes, because all the other people were older and I was a kid. Knowing that someone my age cares, and can handle it [what the people were going through, their condition]. A lot of people our age can't handle

that. I can't work with the retarded kids. I can work up there."

Bob: "If I was an Alzheimer's person, I wouldn't want a kid asking me if I wanted to draw a picture. I don't want to be patronizing. I'm more comfortable with the STEP kids [a Down's syndrome program]. Makes me feel better about myself. Important. Doing something for someone else besides myself. A good feeling."

Susan: "It gives you compassion. Makes you feel better about yourself. Not always looking out for number one. When I first got into the program I felt bad because I was messing up. I felt bad for myself. I got to see people, look at them and see how good that you have it, healthy. They don't even have the chance to mess up the way I did. How fortunate I was. I changed. Stopped screwing up. Because I have the chance and they don't."

Rory: "Sharing part of yourself, not asking anything in return."

What about the other Adventure experiences?

Steve: "We're in the Alliance, we need socialization. Everyone wants to participate. If you don't, you're the minority. We do group activities. Field trips. Ropes course. Like getting everyone on the square [Prouty's Landing], working together, give support, receive support. Organizing for camping trips, for the Christmas party we put on for the STEP kids; we worked together giving and receiving."

Susan: "Get in touch with nature by the outdoors thing. Learn about respect for nature. By looking at the world and how messed up it is. All the trash on the streets. Get mad. Look at nature as pure. I never really looked at anything. Walked right by it, threw a candy wrapper on it. Now I appreciate it more. Rock climbing, I never appreciated the ground more than in climbing. I'm wicked scared of heights. I hated it."

Steve: "I liked the adrenaline."

Rory: "Learned I'll never do it again" [rock climbing].

Fred: "Red Rock is mad. I liked rappelling off it."

Denise: "When you reach the top it is the best."

Marty: "I can't believe I got up there. The rock is a challenge. You feel you can conquer a rock or mountain or cliff."

Susan: "If you don't make it, you feel terrible. You see everybody shinny up the rock. Couldn't make it up the rock."

Rory: "I love going on nature hikes. But I don't like the seats [Swiss seats]. I don't feel safe. Like I could get hurt. I never want to do it again. But it wasn't a negative experience. It was fun. Positive experience seeing other people. I liked trying. I'm scared of heights."

Martha: "I like rowing. Fun, teamwork, physical strength, got wet 'cause people splashed."

All: "The ropes course. Did Heebie Jeebie, Swing to Platform, Tires, Pamper Pole, Spider's Web.... Makes you grow up, face reality, changes your attitudes toward things, makes you feel important, needed, teaches you responsibilities."

Interviews with students who have been away from the program for a period of time can be especially valuable when it comes to measuring long-term effectiveness. Both of the students we will discuss here appear in other parts of the book. In this format, we will hear directly how they feel about their experience four years after their involvement.

Katy:

"I found out about the program through my sister, who had taken it the year before. The school psychologist, Joan, also urged me to take the class. When I first came into the program I was extremely quiet, in fact 'shut down.' The program got me motivated. My first impressions were not good, because I didn't like anything. I wasn't close to people. I didn't want to be touched or hugged or anything. The way the class was structured it forced me to get involved. I thought it was good. That's what I wanted. I wanted to get more involved but didn't know how. Wanted attention, and got it. Wanted people to ask me questions and see if I was O.K. It made a new life for me. Wouldn't be where I am now without participating in the class.

"I was shut down because of the way I was brought up. I was so used to being shut down and closed in. It gave me spirit and openness. Before the class I was messing up. Because I like it so much, it encouraged me to go to my other courses. So I'd be able to keep going. I made the honor roll. Did excellent the last two years of high school. I was thinking about withdrawing from school my sophomore year.

"I liked the class because the activities made me see a lot of plus points in myself. During rock climbing, I would pound on the rocks and hurt myself. Now I don't make such a big deal

The way the class was structured it forced me to get involved. I thought it was good. That's what I wanted."

out of it. It wasn't just the frustration of not making the climb, but the frustration of dealing with my family that was coming out on the rock face. Me not being able to finish some of the climbs, I would feel bad about myself, but in the Debrief I was able to see a lot of good qualities in me I was never able to see before. That's why I liked being in the class.

"I made a lot of friends. Eileen and Jim. Some of the kids in the class, I wasn't able to get along with outside. When they tried to be nice to me, I thought they were teasing me and putting me down. I wasn't hearing them.

"Being at school, it was like a home away from home for me. My college is like that for me, now. The things I wasn't getting from home I was getting from the class: support for the things I was doing. I'd go home all excited about something I did. I'd tell my mom about it, she wouldn't show any sign of appreciation or support. I was getting it through the school. My mom has changed. She's gotten a lot more supportive now. Before, she wasn't good at expressing things. Now I see it, because I'm looking in from the outside. And she's feeling better about herself.

"Isabel [an Alliance teacher] came up to me and asked me once whether I was O.K. I was glad you teachers didn't feel sorry for me. I didn't want that. You pushed me, knew what I wanted and needed. I wrote a paper about myself [in college] called 'The Wall.' I fought my way out of it, with help.

"The activities gave me hands-on experience. Most of the stuff I learned we didn't only learn the skills and techniques but also learned how to teach it. Provided me with the resources I could use in the future and pass it on. I remember the ropes course. I was up in a tree. I got a bloody nose. You helped me down. The Debrief made me feel better. Because it [all these things] made me feel so good I'd like to teach it to others, so that they can feel the greatness I feel. It's so exciting it's too hard to explain. That's why I like working with the summer camp: working with little kids, doing the same thing. Having fun, and not putting themselves down. People get a lot more doing things hands-on [rather] than just a straight lecture.

"Now, I'm coordinating a group of 150 Girl Scouts for a one-day experience. I have them broken into eight groups. The activities are: Map and Compass, Low Ropes, Outdoor Cooking, Animal Tracks, Nature Hike, New Games, Indian Lore, Woodsman's Team. I'm the director. Not doing the activities, just organizing.

"Now that I'm working with other kids, I see some of me come out in them. I think of how I was dealt with. I remember one camping trip and remember throwing skis around and doing dangerous things. They do similar things. I remember me being real violent. I see other kids being violent. Dealing with it can be real hard."

Gary:
"I got into the class because I needed a History credit. Also, I had done some of the activities in Personal Growth class and I liked it. I liked the camping trips, rock climbing and ropes course. I was doing O.K. in school if I wanted to. Flunked math. I found it so boring. Didn't like school. Enjoyed learning things. But the high school format wasn't down my alley. How do you learn best? When you teach yourself. How did I relate to other kids in school? O.K. I was quiet. I was not really outgoing. Would have gotten along better if there had been an outing club.

"Only had casual relationships. The kids in the class? More common bonding. We shared more in common. More identifying with each other. But the use of drugs with the kids was so prevalent. So ingrained in their life. Again, I drew the line at casual friendship, though we had more in common. That's why Katy and I got along so well. We didn't do drugs. This was not a problem that the class created. It came along as dirty laundry. The program was short of being a rehab program. Dealt with underachievement, mainly.

"The program made a direct corollary between input and output: you work for a period, then get to see what you've done.

"The program made a direct corollary between input and output: you work for a period, then get to see what you've done. I experienced this in the boatbuilding class."

I experienced this in the boatbuilding class. This versus math, where you struggle, get a grade. I liked the reading, and the group Initiatives. There was good problem solving going on, good group interaction. Leaders, followers, procrastinators getting to know each other. Unless we all succeed, nobody succeeds. Individual Initiatives such as rocks and the heights. You are up there yourself. Individual's support comes from those below. Bond with the belayer. So many levels of it. Up there, either complete it, or don't. Can't spend your life up there. It's really complicated.

"The expeditions. There is no half-way: once you leave the high school it's like a roller coaster ride. And you leave the gate, you gotta finish the ride. Have to do it all. Tough to quit on a trip. An important part, they were fun, but at that point it was an escape. *At the time*. The thing about it, as you are escaping, if you want to think about it later, you can. Get away from it all. Escape. I needed to escape. The class changed the direction of my life.

"Looked at each individual in the program. They can't identify with the saying, like 'never try, never win.' They've had no success. They get burnt out with life. Get people who turn to different levels to find out what life is about. There has to be more to life than 9–5.

"The class gives a sense of accomplishment. Feel something new and different. Once in a long time I feel great it wasn't because I was drunk or high or broke into a house and got away with it. Not artificial stimuli. I did something legitimate. But many of the students don't know it because they are not articulate enough to say it. They don't have the handles. It's a beginning, a new beginning. You have to endure it, putting up with our tents, canoeing at night, the idiot next to you, sleeping in the rain, putting up with yourself because there's no escape from yourself. Dangling on a rock. Only one thing: start addressing yourself. That's a scary thing for a high school kid. If there hadn't been a lot of support....

"After I graduated, I started the criminal justice thing. [He's a student at a local college]. And it was for the same reasons I could identify with the same things in the class. The reason I could see the same things is that I knew what to look for. It's an approach to things. It's like fine food. When you've eaten some, you keep on looking for more of it.

"What's next for me? One and a half years of school? I'm torn. Part wants to join the service and be a pilot. Other part: take what I've learned and apply it. Pilot or duty. Both could be comfortable. Help with relationships with people? After I found out that there are similarities between people, but they

"You have to endure it, putting up with our tents, canoeing at night, the idiot next to you, sleeping in the rain, putting up with yourself because there's no escape from yourself."

are just below the surface. I started to realize that I had more in common with people than I thought. As a result of that I can be more outgoing, can be more helpful, can see that you have something more to offer than just your presence. You wake up and the world is round. There's more to people than the flatness...which it appears to be."

The direct recall of students who have participated in this program is astounding. Living in the same town, we continually run into them. They are able to go right to the good things we did together. The filter of time makes those good things even better, again underlining the importance of positive experiences, and the search for meaningful activity.

Adaptive Physical Education

"Humps, tunnels and obstacles"

"If I had my choice, I'd do Project Adventure all the time, because I can do everything in the context of it." So says John Doberman, an adaptive Physical Education teacher. He has woven Adventure activities into his Physical Education instruction in pre-school, elementary and junior high/high School classes. These students all have combinations of developmentally delayed, mentally retarded, physically disabled and speech- and learning-impaired special needs. What John means by context is that he can adapt and modify similar activities for a broad range of groups.

Planks, ropes, mats, special belay systems, increased spotting, can all be used to help the students achieve understandable and valued objectives.

   He contrasts Adventure programming with traditional physical education competition. "I can only go so far in adapting street hockey for someone in a wheel chair." Getting a group of disabled students to participate in a problem-solving exercise is an adaptation. Planks, ropes, mats, special belay systems, increased spotting, can all be used to help the students achieve understandable and valued objectives. Humps, tunnels and obstacles which are scattered around every educational area can be used—bleachers in the gym, piles of mats on the floor, a big rock outside the back door. Parallel bars or padded horses can be climbed, straddled, tunneled, or slid along. And the traditional ropes course can be modified where a wheel chair paraplegic can be hoisted up to do traverses, and even the Zip Wire. Or they can participate in specially designed Accessible Challenge ropes course activities. [Note the work of Judith Hoyt and Dr. Chris Roland referred to in Chapter 4, "Group Formation Considerations."] Everyone participates. There is a group harmony that develops. Special populations have a deep longing to relate to their group in things that bring them close, that make them proud, that help them deal with the extraordinary, and with fear.

Not that competition isn't valued. Certainly the Special Olympics concept underscores the value of it. But as an overall program framework, Adventure activities, according to Doberman, give him greater flexibility to deal with the needs of the students. For example, an Individual Education Plan (IEP) may stress "needs to develop communication skills." Because of the Brief/Debrief method, the student in question receives the framework for a crucial part of his plan. Traditional competitive games do not provide this opportunity, forcing the teacher to create a separate communication session. Often that kind of session must be fabricated. Here is the recurring theme of "real life action" and the necessary talk time that surrounds it.

Doberman feels that these students need a context in which they can learn a "healthy dependency."

Doberman feels that these students need a context in which they can learn a "healthy dependency." They have been saddled with the "handle with care" label since birth, or accidents have rendered them disabled. It is easier to "do for" these students, rather than have them "do for self." Robert Perske (p. 24), clarifies this issue as he makes the reader aware that parents, advocates, and those persons "who work with the handicapped, impaired, disadvantaged, and aged tend to be overzealous in their attempts to protect, comfort, keep safe, take care, and watch. Acting on these impulses at the right time can be benevolent, helpful and developmental. But if they are acted upon exclusively or excessively, without allowing for each client's individuality and growth potential, they will overprotect and emotionally smother the intended beneficiary. In fact, such overprotection endangers the client's human dignity and tends to keep him from experiencing the risk taking of ordinary life which is necessary for normal human growth and development."

The goals of group- and self-initiative go a long way toward breaking the dependency mold.

The goals of group- and self-initiative go a long way toward breaking the dependency mold. This kind of change comes slowly, taking years for small increments, but because the activities are growth-oriented, the instructor can have the patience to wait for it. And because these students tend to stay with the same teachers for a number of years, there is time for the change. In fact, this long-term staying power is a great advantage that public school special needs teachers have.

The goals for the program are:

• To increase body awareness through sensory

integration.

- To increase muscle strength, tone, coordination and control through a range of physical activities.
- To improve balance and play skills by hiking, climbing, and use of a range balance exercises and games.
- To increase awareness of the natural world through environmental explorations.
- To increase self concept and a sense of inner direction through cooperative games and Initiatives and Challenge Activities.

John has a degree in Physical Education and Special Needs for the moderate and severely disabled. He has taken the Adventure Based Counseling and Advanced Skills and Standards workshops, and has studied special topics in Environmental Education. He has utilized Adventure activities in his classes for 10 years. He also teaches in a Project Adventure Summer Camp.

Co-leadership for his groups is provided by those Special Needs teachers and aides who have overall responsibility for the students. Supervision comes from the Assistant Superintendent for Special Needs.

Some of the activities available for these Adaptive Physical Education Adventure programs are: hikes, structured play sessions utilizing cooperative games such as Blob, Octopus, Weave, People to People, Body Snatchers, modified Initiatives such as Prouty's Landing using a climbing rope in a gym, hula hoop activities where a small group goes for their hike inside the hoop, "group pick-ups," a Swedish box for a modified wall Initiative, mats that can be made into tunnels. Low ropes course elements, bouldering and rock climbing activities are also used.

In our interview, John referred to a range of concerns and insights he has about the different aspects of his work:

"Fortunately my pre-school program is located near a large open space with plenty of trails, hills and boulders. Just taking a walk along the paths that lead away from the school offers numerous challenges to this population.

"I recall one little fellow who had cerebral palsy. The rocks and tufts of grass made walking very difficult for him but he wanted to get out there so much that he struggled to maintain his balance. For the others there was an additional challenge, 'Mr. Doberman, how do we get back to school?' What surprise and accomplishment they felt when they retraced their steps along that same trail and finally saw the flagpole over the tree tops! This led to other hikes on other trails, remembering specific 'markers,' trees, rocks, boulders, that would lead them back safe and sound. It was a real challenge for them and surprisingly some leaders arose out of the group. It was great confidence building for four or five year olds. Speaking of challenges, do you know how big a boulder looks to a pre-schooler? Here's a great challenge for them: get the group onto the top of a big flat-topped boulder. Careful spotting and having everyone sit makes it possible. Make sure there are plenty of staff to keep control.

"The *Cooperative Sports and Games* book has been an unending source of activities for all of my groups. Hula hoops are so versatile for group Initiatives. Again, you have to be careful with these little ones, they tend not to be aware of danger or the possibility of it. I tend to keep things at an even pace, like a group walk inside a hoop. Slow and steady wins this race. Therapy balls and physio balls are other must pieces of equipment, for little bodies need as much sensory feedback as possible. Group pick-ups are a real challenge.

"Nothing beats New Games! I use them extensively to achieve both behavioral and physiologically related goals for all my classes. If I want to address cardiovascular endurance then it's 'tag' games. They love them all. For strength and body awareness modified bouldering is great. Usually I incorporate some game along with a hike and also the bouldering. What I usually do is pick a particular glacial erratic that has several easy climbs on it. Here on Cape Ann there isn't any shortage of them, anywhere. What I've found also is that for my students it doesn't matter if they are only a few feet off the ground, it might as well be fifty! They are still scared and are faced with a real challenge. Spotting is crucial and I continually monitor the group and individuals to keep them in control, for they tend to get carried away very easily.

"Indoors I've adapted several pieces of equipment that any gym has. Balance walks using several low beams, 2x4's and benches with plenty of mats. In addition I take an old Swedish Box, place mats all around it and produce a modified Wall Initiative. It works just like a full sized climbing wall. The advantage here is that stacking two of them can double the height. Again, spotting is crucial, so have additional staff on hand.

"These kids love to swing, so using the old climbing ropes found in many gyms is ideal. These can be used in a modified Nitro Crossing/Prouty's Landing. Instead of a platform use one or two hula hoops. If you need an additional aspect to this simply place a low balance beam on one end. I've found that using these ropes gives most of my students a greater surface area on which to hold, as well as a larger knot to possibly sit on or wrap their legs around.

"One thing I've come to realize in attempting Adventure programming with moderate to severely disabled individuals is their multitude of limitations. Just taking a hike in the woods surrounding their school can present apparently insurmountable obstacles. A steep grade has struck sheer terror in some of my students and actually turned into an Initiative all its own. The group had to wait, encourage and finally help this person down the slope. It was a real obstacle for him. Now when we go on hikes he still hesitates, but he has previous accomplishments to draw from. At times you have to operate at that level before going any further with your programs.

"When you present group problems you might want to be part of the group. Otherwise the failure and dissent can be devastating to morale. A lot of these students have had everything done for them, and I mean everything! To present them with a decision that has to be made within time limits and with no additional help is a real challenge."

"When you present group problems you might want to be part of the group. Otherwise the failure and dissent can be devastating to morale."

In conclusion, here are some of Doberman's principles of adaptation for dealing with disabled young people in a traditional public school:

- Stress the team concept, and the non-competitive aspects.
- Use the environment: old gym equipment, plenty of mats, outside areas—walks, rocks, trees. Get them out of the school environment.
- Maintain a completion/success orientation.
- Have action days—activity time to be looked forward to, the peak of the Wave.
- The Adventure goals of personal and group Initiative can be hammered away at and built upon year by year.
- Incorporate excitement and newness.
- Have shared Adventures—integrated groups of able-bodied and disabled students participating together in activities.
- The type of games that involve close contact are real barrier breakers.
- Watch out for upper body strength, for it's lacking in most of these students.

Chapter 9
Hospitals and Treatment Facilities

May the long time sun shine on you,
All love surround you,
And the pure light within you
Guide your way home.

— Song of the Voyageurs

THE ADAPTATION OF ADVENTURE
to the hospital setting is a productive and at the same time
complicated process. Definitions of treatment modalities,
competition for treatment time, intensity decisions, staffing
and training issues, and the appropriate Adventure Activities
Base are some of the things that hospitals face. The benefits,
on the other hand, are great: modeling of adaptive behaviors,
group issues expressed in practical and usable ways, the
combination of the physical and emotional spheres through
the Brief/Activity/Debrief process, opportunities for controlled behavior manifestation and treatment of such, and
more.

The past five years have seen strong growth in hospital adoptions. We have done interviews and explored the program designs of four hospital and clinical settings as support material for this section. They are:

- **The Institute of Pennsylvania Hospital**
  Philadelphia, Pennsylvania
- **Elmcrest Psychiatric Institute**
  Portland, Connecticut
- **The Solstice Residential Adolescent Treatment Program**
  Rowley, Massachusetts
- **Charterbrook Psychiatric Hospital**
  Atlanta, Georgia.

We will use the Institute of Pennsylvania Hospital program to demonstrate the application of Adventure in the hospital setting. The Adventure work at the Institute is instructive because of the long period of time they've been in operation (12 years), the large number of staff fluent in Adventure techniques (over 20), and the complex web of treatment responses they have devised.

The TREC Adventure Program

The Institute of Pennsylvania Hospital
Philadelphia, Pennsylvania

"That stuff's powerful medicine down there."

Rick Thomas, a supervisor of the Activities Therapy Department, director of the TREC program (Training on Ropes Experiencing Challenge), and a Project Adventure certified trainer, cites this interaction:

"I remember this person as having no affect. I saw him walking out to the activity... He was stiff and unresponsive. I saw him again after the activity. They got rained on, so they came in one half-hour shy. They were in the workshop making hot chocolate. The man walked up to me. His whole body was different. He didn't walk like a schizophrenic anymore. He walked like a normal person. He had full range of motion. Normal gait. He talked to people in the group and said, 'Do you have any marshmallows?' This was a significant change. People in the group said: 'This happens to him after TREC group.' His whole persona had changed. He didn't seem like a schizophrenic anymore. A woman therapist who also recognized this commented, 'That stuff's powerful medicine down there.' Not that this group cured him. Being related to others helped him to relate with himself. Combine this physical experience with a group experience. The experience was integrative: all his senses."

Rick goes on to expound on the need for a competency model:

"We want to help patients be more independent, decrease their feelings of helplessness, and get away from the idea that someone else has the secrets about their well-being and who they are. We try to educate patients about their strengths, not looking for pathology. The people we see need experience in doing differently, to experience themselves as different. They're not ready for insight. They need to be brought up to another level before they acquire that. They need to learn by *doing* first. They simply do not have the ability for abstract thinking. Generally, if they do abstract, it is merely a form of intellectualization, with few feelings attached. As Glasser says, 'Act differently, even if you don't feel differently.'"

The following example of a higher functioning patient under-

"The people we see need experience in doing differently, to experience themselves as different. They need to be brought up to another level before they can gain insight, they're not ready for insight."

scores this principle of the competency model. Judy Lieberman, an Activities Therapist, had this to say about a lawyer hospitalized because of a suicide attempt:

"Donald was very depressed when he came in. He denied much of his illness. He would not involve himself in any hospital activities. It was hoped that TREC would give him a chance to break out, make him accept his being in the hospital and being with other patients. He started off the TREC program with a range of somatic problems, claiming a broken ankle and hand, a bad back. The staff's approach was to say, "It's up to you. You make your own contract. You can watch, help, or participate."

"He did some of the activities at the beginning, but in difficult ways. He needed a lot of our support. At the end of the fourth day he said: 'I feel better about participating. More risks than I thought I'd ever take. I'm doing things I didn't think I'd ever accomplish.' He has written letters thanking us for the help he got.

"I like the leadership stance of not putting any expectations on the patients. Empowering them to make the decision is very important."

This treatment group worked for Donald because of the emphasis on his strengths in terms of his decision-making ability. It was also effective because of the collaborative aspects of goal setting: he not only set goals for himself, but he set them in relationship to the group. In addition, he was able to provide the same kind of support to others as they worked on their goals. This was accomplished without in-depth reflection [during group time] regarding the cause and effect as to why he was hospitalized and on suicide watch. This is not to say that he wasn't working on those issues in his individual psychotherapy. Or that those issues would not come up during the TREC group. TREC provided a complement to, and in effect a laboratory for, that individual psychotherapy. Material generated in the individual psychotherapy hour would fuel the interaction in the TREC group., and vice versa.

In the overall structure of the hospital, all patients receive individual and group psychotherapy. As a tool, then, TREC supports the work done in the psychotherapeutic areas by providing an Activities Base from which groups of patients can work on important growth issues in a supportive, challenging, physically and socially connected environment.

According to Dr. Sandy Melnick, the Institute's Assistant Medical director, "TREC works best where the course lends itself to the person's needs. If I have a patient who has particular needs, I would talk to the TREC therapists [during TREC activities they are called TREC 'leaders,' illustrating the attempt to downplay the distance between clinician and patient]. A therapist doing TREC would translate that."

At present there are five populations served by TREC at the hospital:

Mixed diagnosis general adult groups
The population that is served by TREC within the mixed diagnosis units is more dependent on referrals by therapists than by the alignment of specific disorder categories with the operation of specific groups. For example, eating disorder patients are mixed in with a young adult group that may have persons on suicide watch. Criteria for admission is the ability to participate in a group in such a way that is satisfying to themselves and others. This is determined by a group interaction assessment (small observable group tasks that require interaction). They also participate on a voluntary basis.

Adolescent treatment groups
The adolescent treatment program consists of approximately 25 beds on a mixed gender unit plus 15 beds scattered throughout the adult units. There are two groups within this population. First is adolescents abusing drugs and alcohol. This is a thematic group, with the focus on dependency issues. The second group is composed of the remainder of the population who are encouraged strongly by their therapist and or treatment teams to participate. Their focus is on general issues of adolescence.

Drug and alcohol groups
The third population is patients hospitalized in the 28-day drug and alcohol program known as the "Strecker Hall Program." Starting the Tuesday of the second week every patient is required to spend a full morning and afternoon on the TREC course. The goals are:
- Community building.
- To gather further assessment on their individual strengths and weaknesses.

...TREC supports the work done in the psychotherapeutic areas ...patients can work on important growth issues in a supportive, challenging, physically and socially connected environment.

- To further enhance a positive connection to the treatment culture. Within that group further discussion of the Alcoholics Anonymous and Narcotics Anonymous steps is provided.
- To demonstrate the role of the activities therapist in their treatment, because TREC is the model of how the hospital conducts all its activities groups.

Attendance at that initial group is a prerequisite for referral to the voluntary Intensive Group or Intensive TREC Group. It is here that participants get into more intense goal setting, problem solving and high elements.

Staff development groups
The staff development groups fall into two categories. First, staff groups approach TREC leaders with their desire to have an educational experience about what TREC can offer, and to have a stimulating group experience away from the clinical unit. The second type of staff group is one that is in a crisis generated by the conflicts endemic to the clinical setting. This kind of group will use TREC to help them identify the problem areas and facilitate change.

Wilderness Program of Pennsylvania Hospital
Outpatient wilderness group participants must be referred by a physician within the Pennsylvania Hospital treatment family. Some of the outpatients come to the hospital for various kinds of treatment including individual psychotherapy, involvement in the activities therapy outpatient program (including the work therapy program), and the Wilderness Program. Centered around a camp in the Pocono Mountains, a variety of courses are available for individuals actively involved in outpatient psychiatric treatment. Some of the experiences include hiking, Initiative games, ropes course, group living and food preparation, and solo time spent evaluating personal values and reassessing one's potential. Outdoor skills and athletic ability are not required. It is generally conducted on weekends, Friday to Sunday. The cost is $50.00 per day.
The objectives of the Wilderness Program are:
- Increased self-confidence
- Compassion and tolerance of others
- Willingness to take risks
- Ability to trust and be trusted
- Health and physical fitness
- Appreciation of the natural environment

Dr. Melnick sees the the general objectives of the TREC Adventure program in this way:

- Provide success experiences with things that are perceived as challenging and difficult.
- Create improvement in self-esteem.
- Help participants complete organized tasks.
- Take into another setting and another context the same issues and struggles the patients have anywhere. It defines them symbolically as they occur in the setting of the course.
- Give those fearful of new experience an opportunity to attempt to experience new things. They can use the safety of the gradual group experience to do that with the support of the other people.
- Provide opportunities for people to look at how they function. Here, the group and individuals overlap... How they function with other people, what roles they take, did they contribute or not, hold back or invest themselves.
- Help people function better with other people and try out new behaviors in that setting. (e.g., "I'm going to attempt to volunteer to go first because I'm usually so afraid to reach for new things. I'm going to try the Inclined Log and the Wire.")

First-hand interviews with the staff bore out the objectives of these programs. They stressed the importance of the socialization and group experiences, or the ability to acquire group interaction skills. These skills are listening, talking, caring, confronting, timing, being sensitive, trusting and being trusted, and giving and receiving support. The TREC group provides a tangible place for the patients to have these experiences.

The TREC staff consists of activities therapists from a range of disciplines: dance, recreation, music, art, drama, and occupational therapy. The important criterion for TREC leadership is that they master the Adventure Counseling methodology, and are able to lead groups safely in the activities. To this end, they conduct extensive on-site staff training and updating, and also send their therapists to workshops. Staff persons start actual TREC work by co-leading with experienced personnel. The training comes mainly from those experienced TREC leaders.

They also use the TREC/Adventure activities for their own staff development, finding it useful in breaking down communication barriers and other organizational issues. According

"In terms of staff development, in terms of getting people to work together more effectively...[TREC/ Adventure activities have] accomplished more than all the hours of supervision and sitting in the room talking."

to Suzanne Corry, the Director of Activities Therapy, "That has been one of the most helpful...in terms of staff development, in terms of getting people to work together more effectively. That has accomplished more than all the hours of supervision and sitting in the room talking. That's an area where we haven't really begun to realize the potential of this..."

The Structure of the TREC program relates to the specific needs of the groups. There are some general guidelines, however.

- It is important to compress most TREC experiences into one week because of the shortening length of stay (the average length of stay is 37 treatment days as opposed to 170 treatment days four years ago). In the one-week model the group will meet for two hours each day of that week. Patients can repeat the group if it is appropriate, either as second or third timers, or as leaders.
- The compression of the experience is needed because of the coming and going of patients. There is much less chance of group disruption over a one-week period.
- The TREC group, when taken at the end of some patient's stay provides important reality testing for them, a lead-in to the world at large. In fact, some participants actually come back to their group after discharge. Another guideline revolves around activity selection.
- It's good to start the activities with some assessment Initiatives such as the Trolley (moving the whole group on two 4x4's that have hand ropes next to each foot of the participants. The purpose is to get to group to coordinate and move together). After that, the selection process comes about through scanning the group needs. A 20-element ropes course, plus a range of trust activities, games and Initiatives, is available to them. Referrals from the Inpatient TREC program are made to the outpatient "Wilderness Program."

The TREC group, when taken at the end of some patient's stay provides important reality testing for them, a lead-in to the world at large.

Helping Patients Get "Unstuck"

Interviews with staff and patients present an intimate look at life at the Institute, and bring alive many of the the issues mentioned above. A therapist, Bert Harris, says:

"It is helpful when patients are feeling stuck ('stuck' is defined as any form of impasse or blockage in the treatment), and we can bring in an experience on the ropes course, then they can imagine it the same way they were on the elements: visualize yourself succeeding at that...

Be able to recall the experience and bring it back that way. We do need to remind them of that sometimes, to dig it out."

John Berns, the co-therapist with Bert, adds:

"They don't remember it the same way. They don't remember the success or the struggle so one way they can demean the success is to say, 'Oh yeah, I got over the log and it wasn't anything.' Then when they see the video [they will use videotape as part of the sessions], and watch themselves really struggle up there and then do it, or not do it and just be pleased with the struggle, that's a really powerful thing. This provides a high level of interaction. It's one thing when we have groups and we talk about trusting and supporting people and it's a whole other thing when we go backwards into a crowd of our peers. Someone is taking someone's life in his hand. I've seen people here get very close in their groups, often closer than in their therapy groups where they may be good for six months to a year or two. "

John and Bert go on to relate TREC work with the Gestalt technique of experimentation:

"Ask them what is happening when they try things. Use it to get at their awareness. It is experimental and supportive at the same time. Do cognitive things: 'What are you telling yourself when you are up there? What kind of statements do you make?' Metaphors. Modeling. What does it mean to you to have trouble balancing yourself? Use mental pre-visualization. People have trouble with an element. Go through with their mind successfully experiencing that. Rehearsing. We've found a lot of success... People getting through elements they haven't gotten through before by visualizing themselves successfully accomplishing, putting down the anxiety enough to get through it. Gestalt is here and now... Visualize it as here and now. If it's too scary for someone to do something then ask them how they can imagine it. They also become more relaxed about it when they experience the fun side. And, once they hear that you can relate it to their life, and it will help them, they become more at ease. We don't emphasize

Gestalt is here and now....Visualize it as here and now.

getting over the net or getting down the zip, but being 'here and now,' trying and seeing what comes up in you.

A young patient named Al had been in the hospital for a year after a suicide attempt:

"My sister is at Harvard. I always competed with her. My family is very competitive, expected all A's and B's. She is better than me at athletics, etc. I always felt put down. My freshman year at college, I was living in a dorm. I didn't know anybody. Would go to the cafeteria and eat alone. I found myself compulsively going to class, even if I didn't need to. Started to skip meals because there was no one to dine with. Didn't know how to interact, get along with people.

"I find it hard to ask people for things. I've always got to do it for myself. If I get into a position where I ask people for help, I push them away from me. I am trying to work on being able to interact, and get along with people. It takes a long time. Old habits die hard. For example, I'm trying to listen more during the Initiatives, to let the other patients have ideas. I used to butt in and insist that my way was right! When someone else was doing a good job, I was able to accept their leadership. But if they were totally making a mess out of the activity, I would step in and correct it. That gets me in trouble sometimes, because people don't like it. They don't have a chance to do it their way.

"The group would give me feedback. That's one of my goals. And I want to see myself as able to do things. I tend to have such high expectations of myself. That's what I expected. No big deal. If I can't do it, that's where I get mad at myself. Nothing is good enough. It is common knowledge! TREC is a good place for teamwork...where everybody is working together to tackle the same things. Rather than competing. I find myself getting into the competition role...Who can do the Two-Line Bridge more eloquently than anyone else? Rather than saying I did it better than I did it last time. What I want competition to be is to compete for the common objective. The Spider's Web. I'm going to get through that thing myself, not for the team, but for me.

"I don't know what happened, but eventually I gotta help everyone through. A personal challenge for me is to get the whole group through. I got out of myself for a little bit, with a lot of support from the other members. One thing that's taught me has been the Wall. You could use a

"One thing that's taught me has been the Wall. You could use a ladder, and everyone would go over individually. I tried thinking about ideas, like running and jumping over the Wall. You can't get over that Wall by yourself."

ladder, and everyone would go over individually. I tried thinking about ideas, like running and jumping over the Wall. You can't get over that Wall by yourself.

In a similar vein, a dentist who ran a clinic was hospitalized for manic depression. He was overworked and suicidal. He was in the hospital for four months. He used TREC the last month he was there. At that point he was able to hear feedback. TREC was given to him as an option. His problem was that he had to "do it myself." His dilemma: no girl—no fun. He needed to learn to just be with people, rather than get hung up on the sexual stuff. He used TREC to look at himself. His goals were not to go first, and to listen. We helped him with those goals. He took those lessons and applied them when he became a representative of the floor at the Patient Council. He learned to go with the floor's agenda, rather than with just his own.

Eating Disorders
Eating disorders can be impacted by addressing body image and self-esteem. According to Sue Mitchell, another TREC therapist, these patients' experience with TREC is "similar to someone turning on a light. Something about the physical nature of this group and how you use yourself with other people, use your body… They are just stunned by what they learn. I don't know what it is all about yet, I have a lot to learn about what they are going through. They perceive themselves as so huge and clumsy and they are not. There is a big impact on me just watching it. My style is that they almost don't know I'm there. I really pull back. I watch and listen and let them do the processing. They are mixed in with E.D. [emotionally disturbed] patients. I would love to do it just with women eating-disordered patients, with two women staff members. That would intensify for me all the information I'm getting. That's a goal for me. An 'eating disorders' TREC group."

Substance Abuse
Substance Abuse is another form of "stuckness" addressed by TREC. The concept of support is explored here in terms of using the TREC experiences to establish the ongoing need for Narcotics Anonymous and Alcoholics Anonymous groups once the patients are discharged. The ability to rely on others, and to ask for support is a critical element of those groups.
According to Dean Wille, an addiction therapist, many patients have come up to him and said that it is easier for them

to act on their feelings, to get involved in a task, than sitting in a group and talking about it. That they have gotten more out of their groups than they did get of other groups simply because they felt safer, and it's more concrete. They felt safe because they could concentrate on the task. They weren't conscious of their behavior during it.

They felt safe because they could concentrate on the task. They weren't conscious of their behavior during it.

The substance abuse program had been conducted in the unit on a weekly basis for two years every single week (as of April 1986). It is a 28-day program, with people coming in and going out.

Week One	Orientation. Specialized groups. Basic issues of addiction. Use of Trust exercises, and Initiatives, in order to assess what their issues are.
Week Two	Come into a group: Group issues. Group building, cohesiveness, communication, problem solving, decision making.
Week Three	Discharge issues. No new patients. More trust activities.
Week Four	The individual needs of the patients are addressed. Some patients will choose to start a new TREC group. Some will opt to participate in the Wilderness Program.

They tend to stress the nurturing model, rather than concentrating on negative behaviors. However, they also tend to downplay the optional aspects of some experiences. This strategy underlines the fact that substance abusers are great con artists, and will do anything to avoid facing the important issues that have them hung up. So when they are on a high element, for example, the leader may be somewhat more coercive about their completing it than with another kind of group. This points up the ongoing choices that the Adventure leader must make in relation to group type and specific individuals and how to relate them to the activities.

...substance abusers are great con artists, and will do anything but allow themselves to face the important issues that have them hung up.

If the problem is more severe than the program can handle, the 28 days can be treated as diagnostic. For people who are resistive to the treatment, the staff will have them for 28 days, then refer them to long-term treatment for drug and alcohol. That long-term treatment may be more behavior-oriented, where all their possessions are taken away and must be "earned" back. Rick Thomas reminds us of a further complication: "Many abusers, once they have dried out, will manifest deeper psychological problems." These patients will be assessed and referred for appropriate long-term treatment.

Steve Golodner, another activities therapist, reinforces the need to establish a positive group culture through the "Anonymous" system (Alcoholics and Narcotics Anonymous). The TREC group provides a concrete model to tie into all the time. He uses the example of a favorite Initiative, Acid River (The group must go from stump to stump by moving boards to connect them):

"In the Briefing, I said, 'If you are going down don't grab at someone, 'cause you'll pull them down with you.' A woman in the group took it as 'don't reach out for someone and ask for support.' The response of the group was, 'Someone wouldn't reach out and ask for help until they were on a board and falling and so out of control that there was no way to get control back, whereas if they had felt they were a little shaky and at that point reached out for support before they lost control they would have stayed on the board.'"

That's a common problem for alcoholics — they feel that no one is available to help them, especially when they are out of control and already down. They can sometimes reach out for support when they are only just a little shaky. In one sense abusers are always getting people to rescue them — that's how their family systems run. Understanding this kind of manipulating behavior will help you realize that failure is a possibility, and that the patient often contributes to the "failure"?

Acid River, to Steve, offers a realistic analogy to the life of the abuser:

"Only 3 of 10 made it across. I told the group that the percentage that made it across is the same as the percent of this group that will recover. Recovery is on the other side of the river. We had an experience where I called time after 40 minutes. Everyone had fallen in. Two people on the rock. They took it as failure. I said, 'You were in a safe place, as safe as could be. You are never sure you are going to make it.' They were as successful as they could be at that moment. There is no assurance of a successful recovery. All you can do is make sure you were at the safest place for you at any given time."

Steve goes on to talk about the high elements as illustrative of the fact that you have to do things on your own, with supports:

"We had somebody right at the top of the Inclined Log unable to make the step over to the wire and we wouldn't rescue him. We interpreted that as his not being ready to make the step to recovery. He kept saying it was the group. He was angry at us for pushing him. That's the dynamic in his life—laying it back on others. But we said, 'You didn't make it.' We allow them to fail more than others, because they tend to be higher functioning patients. When they've had a failure we'll talk about the failure and replay the same thing. You have choices to do something different."

"We allow them to fail more than others, because they tend to be higher functioning patients. When they've had a failure we'll talk about the failure and replay the same thing. You have choices to do something different."

Harriet, a former patient who had been out of the hospital for two years when the interview took place, will conclude our time at the Institute: "I don't remember the different elements....Even my journal. More about the quality of the experience. The whole thing about support systems. I came away with the feeling that it is urgent for me to establish much better support systems than I had. I have done that." She then gave us a copy of her journal. It reads:

Ropes Course – Spring 1984

These are my goals as of 4/4/84:
1. To allow myself to totally trust my support system.
2. To learn to trust myself enough to take risks.

Really enjoyed the session this morning. Had fun. Able to let go. Not as self-conscious as usual. A lot of feeling for group…liked the fact that group was small!

4/11/84 — It was tough today, to put it mildly. Came face to face with a lot of stuff: fear of incompetence, my own judgement of my performance, over-coming negative programming and shit in order to move on, etc. When I fell off that cable, being vulnerable in front of people, accepting support, I thought it meant I'd failed at something I'd just watched someone else succeed at. A few hours later, I can't even remember why I reacted so dramatically. Why didn't I just get back up on the thing and try again, instead of making a drama out of it? I'm glad my healthy side won out in the end, but getting from here to there was hell. If I can let go of some of the judgement about not being perfect and just try, it'll go alot better.

Another thing I need to let go of is a feeling of competition with and jealousy toward Gina [Another participant]. She's doing it for herself, I'm doing it for myself. Gotta remember that. We're two separate people, with a separate set of problems sharing an experience. [Harriet's comment in the interview: "This is a huge pitfall for me, comparing self with others. I learned a lot about doing it. I still catch myself. I'm much more able to abort it."]

4/18/84 — Much better experience today. I let myself be supported a lot on the log, and I was pretty good about accepting the support without judging myself or needing it. Also, it was fun to work on the log problem with Gina and Dave, great feeling of accomplishment at the end (a real rush), and felt closer to both people afterward. Really "got" that group determination can carry me through when I'd be inclined to give up. The theme was definitely support.

5/2/84 — Good moments, bad moments, felt like a failure when I couldn't make it across Monkey Bars; then felt a little more confidence when crossed Fidget Bridge. Last stuff was best...power of visualizing helped me reach bar and then falling back from High Log was terrifying but I knew they'd catch me, and they did, and I felt better. But will there always be people to catch me when I fall? Physical movement in and of itself felt good. *(I Have to Move.)*

5/9/84 — Another good day on the course. Even though I didn't do as much as I could have, I pushed myself as far as I needed to. I'm still somewhat stuck in the competitive mode, but I think I'm making progress with that, too. Walking across the log involved a lot of trust (on my behalf), that my spotters would catch me if I fell. It felt good to actually feel that trust, not just pretend it was there. The more of the course we do, the more I think an Outward Bound [course] would help me. I'm sending off that application today!

5/16/84 — Good experience. Didn't judge self for lack of perfection and took all risks asked of me. Performed well, which was a plus, but not essential. Noticed resentment toward Gina for doing as well and for her little girl's giddy enjoyment of the whole thing. That's O.K. I refuse to judge myself for any hostile feelings I might have. I'd like to understand why I feel that way. On the whole, I feel like I'm making real good progress toward my twin goals of accepting support and taking risks.

Outward Bound, here I come. Doing well, taking risks. Climbing, jumping, walking high, falling free, feeling free, letting go, trusting them, trusting me. Progress in human endeavors, getting hold of something that's mine, inside me.

5/30/84 — An hour inside today because of the horrible weather. It was a lot of fun as well as pretty instructive. I noticed that I'm far more willing to accept 'whatever' in this small, trusting group atmosphere than anywhere else. It's a nice feeling and I hope I can generalize it more. One other point of interest is that the game I felt least willing to play was the role of the clay in the sculpture thing. I didn't like the helpless, vulnerable feeling I got. I'd like to be more willing to risk spontaneity in situations where the risk is calculated (like in the program)."

That was the end of the journal. Due to time/work constraints Harriet was never able to go to Outward Bound. She concluded the interview by relating an experience she had with her boyfriend:

"It was an interesting experience on issues of support. Walking through a park in West Philly with my boyfriend. Huge tires there. You can play on them. He is a big physical risk taker, agile, excellent with balance. I have a fear when it comes to physical things. He leapt up on to the tires. Said 'c'mon.' I froze. And I thought (I was frustrated) if I were on the ropes course and had the support...that I had there and knew I was safe I'd be all right...but there I felt completely inhibited by fear. He didn't give me a hard time. It was a negative experience. Annoyed with self that I didn't feel I could do it alone and his support wasn't enough. It reinforced the concept of needing a support network and needing to feel safe. Occurred a few months ago. If I had forced myself to take that risk it wouldn't have been an honest thing. The inhibition was honest. That's just where I was."

Conclusion

The Institute of Pennsylvania Hospital is a pioneer in the use of Adventure Based Counseling within the hospital setting. Key to their success is the wide range of staff that is trained and feels comfortable in implementing the model. This has many benefits: The practice of ADC is not limited to a few knowledgeable practitioners; the relations at the hospital are positive because of extensive use of Adventure activities in staff development; and therapists use the program as part of the patient's treatment plan, making certain that it is not isolated in a recreation department as just another in a series of experiences.

242   Islands of Healing

Chapter 10

Programs for Court-Referred Youth

"In nature there are neither rewards nor punishments. There are consequences."

— R.G. Ingersoll

EFFECTIVELY SERVING YOUTH who are in trouble with the law is one of the larger issues of our time. The prison population of the country continues to grow, and lack of effective prevention and treatment models for youth is one factor in this growth. Outward Bound, the Eckerd Foundation and many other private and state agencies have provided through their wilderness programs viable options to the dilemma faced by those who conduct the penal systems. Young offenders are referred to these programs because of the personal and interpersonal growth they are able to experience.

The two programs explored in this section are based on the

ABC premise of integrating programmatic Adventure techniques (which include wilderness experiences) into an institutional setting that has a community base. This approach builds on the successes of wilderness programs while adding the important elements of community-based education and follow-up. We will look at two programs:

- **Project Quest** of Sussex County, New Jersey, is a primary prevention model and is targeted for those adolescents who are on probation for a first offense. Based at a school site, it offers an example of school and court cooperation for early prevention intervention.
- **Project Challenge** of Atlanta, Georgia, is a treatment model. It was developed by Project Adventure, Inc., in cooperation with the Georgia Division of Youth Services as a community-based program for seriously court-involved youth. Challenge participants are typically referred to the program after a second or third offense. The alternative to success in Challenge is usually a secure lock-up state facility.

Project Quest

Sussex County Vocational Technical School
Sparta, New Jersey

> *"At the beginning of the program when we started this
> I thought this isn't going to go right. After the second one,
> you get along better. You start trusting everybody... It was
> exciting, something to keep me out of trouble a little bit...
> This changed my attitude, I'd say. I had a bad one."*

This quotation is from a "termination summary" each participant in Project Quest filled out during their final Debrief. The
student's cycle involved ten three-hour sessions and a three-
day culminating activity (camping, hiking, and rafting). His
short-term Adventure Counseling Group was geared to meet
the needs of a mixture of court-referred youth who live in the
Sussex County area.

Recognizing that traditional approaches to ameliorating
delinquency haven't worked very well, the State of New
Jersey has enacted sweeping changes in its juvenile justice
code. This involved decriminalization of Status Offenses
(incorrigibility, truancy, running away) and the creation of
Family Crisis Intervention Units and Juvenile Conference
Committees. These new agencies are diversionary in nature;
their purpose is to keep juveniles out of the court system.
While the creation of these agencies indicates a welcome
change in philosophy, they employ the same traditional counseling and probation tools that the previous system relied
upon. The chosen new intervention was an Adventure Based
Counseling approach. The program title for the Sussex
County New Jersey intervention is Project Quest. Since its
initial introduction Project Quest has been designated part of
the Sussex County Mental Health Master Plan. A dissemination model has been set into motion, as well as a method for
training more facilitators to consult with and staff new start
up programs in local school districts.

Project Quest is a 10-week program for youth who have
been referred by either the County Probation Office, the
Family Crisis intervention units or the Juvenile Conference
Committees. The referrals, male and female, are interviewed
by the two group co-leaders who select a group of 10–12
participants they feel can benefit from the program.

The program's objectives are as follows:
- To provide short-term group experiential counseling to
  groups of court-involved adolescents.

- To significantly improve academic performance as measured by a standardized testing instrument and grade point average.
- To significantly reduce school-related difficulty (truancy, and disciplinary referrals).
- To significantly improve the self-concept as measured by standardized testing instruments.
- To provide a counseling model that will improve the problem-solving and socialization skills.
- To provide ongoing support for the adolescents upon program completion through utilization of home school district personnel.
- To improve parenting skills by offering Active Parenting workshops.
- To assess the overall effectiveness of the intervention approach, looking toward a state-wide adoption based on the same model.
- To lower the rate of court-related offenses.

There is an additional objective for groups involved with substance abuse:

- To coordinate ongoing involvement with substance abuse treatment groups, such as Alcoholics Anonymous, after termination of the ABC group intervention.

Project Quest meets for one 3-hour session per week over a ten-week period. In addition to this group counseling, a two- or three-day culminating activity (or expedition) is scheduled.

Follow-up is a key element of the program and is made easier by the fact that the students are drawn from the same school district.

The program staff have a wide breadth of counseling knowledge including extensive training in group process and Adventure Based Counseling techniques. Additionally, there is expertise in working with alcohol and substance abusers, and adolescents. All co-leaders must minimally hold a Master's degree in counseling or a related field and have at least five years' experience working with juveniles in an educational or counseling setting.

Follow-up, a key element of the program, is made easier because all students are drawn from the same school district. A faculty member of the participating school is provided training in the ABC techniques at a Project Adventure four-day training and is assigned to the group as it leaves the Project Quest program. The staff member holds periodic meetings (at least monthly) to provide a security net for participants, and to continue the growth process of goal setting and contracting begun in the primary intervention period. The original Project Quest facilitators are available to the faculty members for consultation and further training during the year.

A six-session parenting program is offered in conjunction with the Quest cycle. This group meets with a group leader for six weeks, two hours per week. Xerox's Active Parenting program provides video-taped scenarios of parent/child conflicts around common family issues. These are used as a springboard for dialoguing, and role-playing solutions to problems. The program employs Rudolph Dreikurs's "logical consequences" with children, and culminates by modeling the Family Meetings as representative of democratic vs. autocratic parenting. Aside from the more structured material, the meeting time affords parents an opportunity to feel they are sharing a common experience. Groups are encouraged to continue meeting upon completion of the six-week cycle.

An evaluation component is built into every Quest cycle. In addition to student self-report, termination summaries, and group and individual progress notes, various standardized measures are employed. Clients are pre- and post-tested on two self-concept measures. Pre/post school-related data is also collected on each client including attendance, disciplinary referral rate, grade point average, and standardized achievement tests. All data is analyzed using various statistical procedures. Although data analysis on the first two Quest cycles have not been completed, preliminary examination of results indicates significant positive change on self-concept measures for all participants. An extensive evaluation report will be completed in the near future.

The sequence of activities may vary, but the leaders attempt to keep to the following Wave plan. After each activity, the co-leaders would write down their observations. Segments of these observations are included in the following Activity sequence.

Week One
Introduction and Icebreaker Activities, followed by an explanation of the program structure and components.
Conclusion: Rappelling practice for Week Two activities.

Co-leader Maizell comments: "The initial session met with tremendous resistance. The group, however, rapidly became committed to the process as a result of the activity progression. We chose to take them cliff rappelling the second session in order to meet the power of their resistance with a high impact activity. This decision put us in a position to be in an early Common Ground and bonding experience, while creating an appropriate disequilibrium in their usual experience."

We chose to take them cliff rappelling the second session in order to meet the power of their resistance with a high impact activity.

Week Two
Cliff Rappelling
Rock Climbing

Maizell: "The activity made tremendous strides in establishing a sense of group and of a shared experience. Initially, there was again much resistance to participation. However as the distance from school increased, the stereotypical acting-out behaviors began to decrease. All but one boy participated. [He claimed the instructors weren't paying close enough attention.] The weather deteriorated into a cold rain during the activity but the group persevered and really drew from the activity."

Co-leader Gary Trunnell: "That trip was a real pivotal point early on, especially with 'V.' I don't know too many gals who would stand out there as cold and as rainy as it was and support the boys in the group. The closeness and warmth, especially with 'J.' and 'C.,' was really interesting. Off and on, throughout those eight sessions, those three had a special relationship. The stress of the rappel combined with the unfamiliarity of the experience, allowed for healthy nurturing to occur, the innocent asking for warmth from another human being. The rock climbing put things into perspective and allowed the boys to fail gracefully, as the contract protected them from the usual ridicule. The nature of that kind of fear draws the line for you. Then there is the technical quality of the activity that forces absolute dependency within the climber. The climber can, at times, not be in control of his own safety. The message is that I can be out of control and still survive. This is contrasted with the rappel which the climber does control. The contrast offers additional power to the latter experience. Trust became a visceral experience. The activity provided the underpinning for the rest of the 10-week experience."

The rock climbing put things into perspective and allowed the boys to fail gracefully, as the contract protected them from the usual ridicule.

Week Three
Debrief Rappelling
Trust Sequences (builds on the trust established in Week Two rappelling)
Tour of the Local Challenge Course
Trust Fall and Hickory Jump completed

Maizell: "The next meeting saw the re-entry into the group of a number of previously non-attending members, with one new participant, as well. Although a number of students had to leave early due to either negotiated or unavoidable commitments, the day went exceedingly well with the remaining participants. It is hoped by the next meeting that the full group will be intact. The nature of the population has resigned us to the inconsistency of attendance. If it improves over the remainder of the sessions that will be a positive sign. The day was spent on running through the Trust Sequence. The clients took this quite seriously, and all managed to complete the Trust Fall and Hickory Jump activities. Again, in the 'artificial and accepting' environment of the group, the discounting and hostile attitudes tend to fall away, replaced by real concern for each other's safety. The group, to a person, was able to relate that as a result of the day's experience, they were much more comfortable with entrusting their physical safety to the members of the group. This will, to some degree, be reflected in outcomes during the high elements."

Trunnell: "The Debrief was interesting, in that a number of clients attempted to discount the process by throwing sticks and calling attention to themselves in other ways. This could be attributed to nervousness, dealing with interpersonal stuff, a problem with self-disclosure."

Week Four
Further Initiative and Trust Activities

Maizell: "Attendance of all members is a continuing issue. By Week Four, three members of the original 12 had dropped out and had been referred back to the Probation Department. Overall the attendance had been better each week. We recycled through some of the Trust Activities to integrate the two members who had missed the previous session. The Trust Activities were Debriefed by a student who drew out from each of the returned students comments on how it felt to physically trust others. A thunderstorm interrupted the Meuse [an Adventure Activity] and caused a 'disappearance' of the group for over 35 minutes as they went inside. This provided a good opportunity to get into the original contract and purpose of the group. The final activity had better participation as the group had bought back into the original contract once more."

Week Five
Low Ropes Initiatives
First Individual Goal-Setting Session

At the end of the session each client fills out an Individual Goal Assessment Sheet. This sheet serves two purposes: to allow for clients to cognitively integrate feelings and activities and to act as an assessment tool for monitoring change specifically related to the Project Quest model.

The major counseling exercise of the day was Duo Goal Setting. The group was asked to pair off and have a serious conversation about the following issues:
- Concretely define and operationalize a number of important goals that each individual wished to work on.
- Concretely define what group resources would be needed to obtain the goal.

Individual Goal Assessment Sheet

The purpose of this sheet is for you and the group leaders to keep track of your goal-setting during the ten-week experience. This should be completed during the time between each activity meeting, and handed in at the following meeting. We will make a copy and return the original to you. Please write the goal you set on the space provided:

_____

_____

1	2	3	4	5
completely false	mostly false	partly true and partly false	mostly true	completely true

Please circle the response to the questions below using the above answer key as your guide.

1. I achieved the goal I set for myself this week	1	2	3	4	5
2. I used the support of the group to achieve my goal	1	2	3	4	5
3. I achieved the goal on my own	1	2	3	4	5
4. The goal I set was important to me	1	2	3	4	5
5. This session made me feel good	1	2	3	4	5
6. I tried my best to achieve my goal	1	2	3	4	5
7. I trusted the members of the group	1	2	3	4	5
8. Trying my best to achieve my goal is what counted	1	2	3	4	5
9. I felt good when I achieved my goal	1	2	3	4	5
10. This group is important to me	1	2	3	4	5

- Concretely define personal strengths that would assist in achieving the stated goals.
- Concretely define personal weaknesses that might get in the way of achieving goals.

The following goals were identified as being representative:
- Learn better to deal with and express strong feelings.
- Get along better with parents.
- Feel better about oneself (self-concept).
- Be supportive of everyone's efforts in the group, and be trusted by others.
- Do better in school.

Strengths were identified as:
- has leadership skills
- speaks one's mind
- is supportive of others
- has specific knowledge
- is not a follower
- is independent
- is willing to try

Weaknesses were identified as:
- poor control (temper)
- gives in to peer pressure
- poor self-esteem
- poor attitude about school

A group goal was also identified for the next week: *to get organized more cooperatively and avoid the usual 35 minutes of settling in.* Additionally, the group requested that a group support phone list be generated so that group members might stay in touch and help each other out during times of stress or loneliness.

Week Six
Further Goal-Setting Contracting Activities.
Introduction to High Elements.

Maizell: "This day was spent on finishing off the Duo Goal-Setting process, then attacking the first two high elements. Once again, the compactness of the process became evident. The high elements are, for the most part individual Challenge activities where the client must face his own self-doubt and inadequacies in dealing with the perceived risk involved in each event. There is group support and spotting of activities, as well as the relationship between the student belayer and the climber. However, each element takes time to complete and therefore the group tends to fragment a bit.

For the following sessions a low element will be used to knit the group together as part of the experience. The day went well, with a minimum of gathering hassles. During the goal-setting Debrief, however, a fair amount of distracting behavior continued to occur. This took the form of throwing sticks, a worm, and some discounting remarks. It is still somewhat difficult for the clients to remain tuned in for long periods of time when discussing issues."

Week Seven
High Elements

Maizell: "This session was held on a Thursday due to rain cancellation. The change in date seemed to correlate with attendance, which was way down. It is suspected that any alteration of schedule is difficult for this population to handle. The group worked well together, although the same transitional period seems to be needed between school/ABC. The residue of the school experience is powerful."

Week Eight
More High Elements

Maizell: "We set up the Burma Bridge, and the Pamper Pole. The discounting was at a minimum during Pamper Pole experience. Everyone watching was supportive and helpful, in terms of spotting the initial climb. The most striking difference in terms of the experience was the lack of success in completing the element. The self-control and determination that was certainly not reflected during the earliest sessions was clearly in evidence. The clients attempted the element again and again, with no displacement of blame onto the object or the rest of the group. There was no sense of failure when a client missed the trapeze, or abuse from the onlookers. Also absent were the usual mumbled obscenities and the giving up that is often present with these children. There was the demand at the end of the day that the trapeze be set up again for another attempt the following session."

"Also absent were the usual mumbled obscenities and the giving up that is often present with these children. There was the demand at the end of the day that the trapeze be set up again for another attempt the following session."

Week Nine
The entire meeting is spent on expedition preparation. Clients negotiate rules, regulations, and responsibilities such as cooking.

252   Islands of Healing

Maizell: "The balance of this session was spent on packing and distributing gear to the members of the expedition. There was good cooperation in evidence as demonstrated by the willingness of members to carry community gear, and a noticeable lack of horseplay. A number of expedition-related matters were decided upon by the group, such as smoking and safety, especially when on the Delaware River."

The Expedition:
Day One: Canoe Trip
Day Two: Trail Hike

Day One:
Ten hours of canoeing, map reading, selection of campsite, Debriefing.

Maizell: "Real feeling of togetherness; the group really under control. At the first sight of the river, the group was petrified. Sorting of canoe partners, ordering of canoes. Group stays together emotionally and physically en route. Two best canoers get hung up by an old bridge base. The group beached their canoes. 'We can't swim now we have to help 'R.' and 'J." The whole group heads upstream to problem-solve how to reach the canoe by launching themselves from further and further upstream to beat the current and reach the stranded canoe. Lots of verbal encouragement. No discounting around the canoe getting stuck. Finding the campsite required careful scrutiny of insufficient maps. A half-hour was spent on this, with little loss of patience. This occurred after 10 hours of canoeing. Leaders get directive about organizing food at the campsite. 'V.' volunteers to cook and the issue is raised as to why she should. This area of competency was a sore spot, as 'V.' wanted to shine in that regard. A Debrief of the day was also held, around the campfire. Each client was asked to list what strengths he had brought to the day. Other group members were asked to add to their list. The sense of community around the fire was powerful. The shared experience of the day had knit this group together, with intense emotions of satisfaction and group loyalty echoed by all. Went to sleep between 12 and 2:00 A.M. Statement about discounting other people's sleeping time was ignored. This was debriefed on the spot."

"The shared experience of the day had knit this group together, with intense emotions of satisfaction and group loyalty echoed by all."

Day Two
Canoeing to pick-up point. Full pack day hike over 12 miles on the Appalachian Trail.
Dinner out, and the quiet ride home.

Maizell: "The morning trip down the river was peaceful. The kids paddled quietly and joked about the coming hike. This light-hearted mood was maintained as we reached Stokes State forest and traversed a short stretch of Route 206 en route to the Trail. A number of boys decided to put on a display and hold hands while walking along the highway. This was the ultimate demonstration of deinhibitization! Finally the trail was reached. The first half mile of the Trail went almost straight up, with a switchback halfway. This unexpected development quickly sobered the group. 'V.,'an overweight chain-smoking girl, threw her pack into the woods and sat down, announcing in rather colorful language that she was not going any further. The group gathered around and De-briefed the situation. It was decided that 'V.'s' load would be lightened and spread out amongst members of the group. Finally the top of the switchback was reached and the group collapsed for lunch. The hike continued. At our next stop at a fire tower, 'V.'once again stated she'd had it. Another Debrief occurred and the issue was settled. It was truly marvelous to watch the group organize around the established ABC ground rules and work out their differences!! The balance of the hike provided all kinds of grist for the mill, including having to ration water due to the developing 90-plus degree day, a threatening thunderstorm, and growing fatigue. Every member of the group shone at one time or another, and many strengths contributed to overall success. There was 'D.,' who was named 'Packhorse' as he uncomplainingly carried much more than his share. There was 'C.', 'The Timekeeper,' who forced the group into an effective walk/rest cycle and wielded his watch like a dictator. There were 'S.', and 'P.', who got the group singing silly songs, lifting everyone's sagging spirits. Leaders became followers and followers, leaders. And finally the end of the trail, a cool artesian well, a quiet celebration! Then out to dinner and the subdued but satisfied bus ride home."

It was truly marvelous to watch the group organize around the established ABC ground rules and work out their differences!!

Week Ten
Final Debrief and termination.

(This session is attended by the faculty member from the school district who will be working with the group on an ongoing basis. During the final Debrief a schedule is set up for

254   Islands of Healing

further group meetings with the new group facilitator.)

The final Debrief was taped. The children spoke with sincerity and often simple eloquence of what Quest meant to them:

"When I came into the group I was really against it, but now that I started coming to the program more I've found out that people do care. You can trust them. I had a bad attitude when I came in here but now I think I'm better because I am in the group. Because you've all helped me through the times I've been afraid to do something. I haven't wanted to do something, but I did it anyway."

"I learned that you can trust a lot more, and you guys I know I can talk to about just about everything; anything I wanted to. This experience, you know, going down mountains. At first I wasn't going to let anybody put me down this hill, except maybe Rich or Gary, but I realized that you guys are just as much capable of doing that as anybody else. I just want you to know that you are all like sisters and brothers."

"Gave me something to do after school instead of going home and getting into trouble. Met a couple of nice people. Got to do stuff that I'd never done before. Had fun. Not as lazy as I used to be. I'll get up and do stuff around the house."

"This group changed the way I feel a hell of a lot. I met a lot of nice kids. They helped me out when I needed support. You and Gary are super; I'm not saying these guys aren't, but when you needed to talk to someone you guys were there. The kids were there. Like Frank said, 'I tried a lot of this stuff and I never could do it before, tried to anyway.' The group helped me out a hell of a lot. I'm really thankful to the group and I'm really glad I came, because I don't know where I'm going to be ten years from now, but I know where I would have been, would have been in the same place, you know like I was before I joined the group. So I'm really glad I joined it, and stuck with it, 'cause there are a lot of people here that give me a lot of advice and I try to help out a lot of people too. So I want to thank everybody."

"Lot of good times with everybody. Getting to know everybody a little better. I already knew some people who were wise-asses in the beginning, and cooled down. They weren't so hot anymore after everyone jumped on their case. Did a lot of things that I used to do when I was little. Felt good; brought back a lot of memories, except I never did them safely. Like I said, I met a lot of people in the group; grew closer to a lot of them. We laughed a lot; and shared a lot of our past experiences; what our lives were like."

"I had a great time with you guys. It really helped me out in my home life. Like before this, me and my mom were like at each other's necks. Since we've both been coming to this group we're getting along a lot better. Talking to each other when we need to, and she finally came out and told me how she really felt about the guy who's living with us. I'm not going to repeat her words... I learned to trust you guys a lot."

"At the beginning of the time when we started this I thought this isn't going to go right. That first meeting that we had, you know. That one in the bleachers, hell bent for leather. That's something to remember. After the second one, you get along better. You start trusting everybody. A little. This changed my attitude, I'd say. I had a bad one. Changed my attitude the way I was, like nothing's worth anything."

"Mine is basically the same as everyone else. There were two new people that I met, which were 'C.' and 'S.' And I didn't trust anybody, and I can trust everybody. Except the discounting, I just get off-hand with discounting, especially the one that happened today but, these are my friends and they helped me through everything, and I can trust everybody. I never did anything like this before. It was great. I still hope we can have some more meetings, be with each other more. I just had a good time."

"Well, at first I had a bad attitude and didn't want to be here. I guess you could tell when I first came that I didn't want to be here. Anyway, it's different now, because we got to know each other. I had a lot of fun, just like I'm back in the Boy Scout troop. Changed me, I calmed down, can stay cool. I don't go right at brother's throats when they say something, you know. My father and I are getting along better. Rich here has helped me along, in trying to keep me out of trouble. The group really helped a lot, cause they were there. I'd just like to say thank you."

Conclusions

Project Quest is relatively new (two years old). Some preliminary "hard" data are available. A small sample group of nine students was pre-tested in March 1986 and post-tested in June 1986. The instrument used was the "Culture Free Self-Esteem Inventory," by James Battle, Ph.D. (Children's Hospital of San Francisco, Publication Department, P.O. Box 3805, San Francisco, California, 94119 (1981). The definition of Self-Esteem for this test is: "...the perception the individual possesses of his own self-worth. An individual's perception of self develops gradually and becomes more differentiated as he matures and interacts with significant others. Perception of self worth, once established, tends to be fairly stable and resistant to change." Self-esteem was measured in the "general," "social," "academic," "parental," and "total" categories. Significant positive change was recorded in all areas except "parental," where no significant change took place. The combination of the self-esteem inventory and the final student Debrief provides us with what we view as excellent preliminary results. More information regarding the test results, and the facilitation of this test, will be available through the Project Adventure office.

Project Challenge

"Not a stone unturned"

Project Challenge is a six-week alternative program providing "court diversion" for juvenile offenders in Atlanta, Georgia.

This community-based alternative program addresses the educational, social and personal needs of juvenile offenders. Developed by Cindy Simpson (Director of Project Adventure, Incorporated, Atlanta Office), Project Challenge contracts with the Georgia Department of Youth Services to do five to six Challenge sessions per year. As a model, Project Challenge seeks to maintain the intensity of a wilderness course while keeping vital connections to home communities, and the work, educational, and social issues that they offer.

The cornerstone of Challenge is group talk time, or simply, "group." All activities—wilderness, Adventure, academic, role playing—are subject to group discussion, with the use of the strategies of point system incentives, threat of lockup, and peer pressure. The activities play a vital role in drawing out the behavior of the students. Through a system of rules, values, goal setting and group caring, students teach each other to take responsibility for their lives, speak up, confront each other, assess themselves, take risks, and lay realistic plans for the future.

Twelve or fourteen moderate to severe juvenile offenders meet daily Monday through Friday from 8:00 a.m. to 3:00 p.m.. Some of the essential motivation for completion of the program is acquired through the student's placement by a DYS screening committee and the knowledge that successful participation can shorten his/her incarceration obligation to the Division.

The goals of the program are:
- Provide an alternative resource to placement in a Youth Development Center for youth committed to the Division of Youth Services.
- Provide youth committed to the Division of Youth Services with the socialization skills, self-confidence, and motivation necessary to succeed in the public school system.

Evaluation of the program from October 1983 – June 1986, with 175 youth served, produced the following results:
- 94% of the youth starting the program completed it.
- The academic performance of the participants was enhanced:
  Reading skills went up an average of one grade level
  Math improved 0.3,%
  Spelling improved 0.2.%
- The recidivism rate for a three-year period following completion of the program has held at 15%.

For every 12-14 students there are two leaders, with the leaders balancing themselves in skill areas: special needs, academics, criminal justice, counseling expertise, Project Adventure skills. The leaders must be flexible enough to work some evenings (parent support group), and participate in expeditions. They must also have the capability to relate to families, agencies, schools, the courts, and the business community. Probation officers and other social service people often participate in the activities, gaining important Common Ground in the process. This is of great help in transferring the learning back to the community.

The Challenge Curriculum is constructed so that a contin-

Probation officers and other social service people often participate in the activities, gaining important Common Ground in the process.

ual mixture of academics, discussion, and Adventure activities is offered. Each day of the 30-day cycle is carefully outlined. In brief, the curriculum has the following segments:

Days One to Three
Games and warmups; presentation of daily point system along with a thorough discussion of the rules:

Goal Setting	3 points
Games	3
Class	3
Break	4
Class	3
Games/class	3
Class	3
Goals/class	3

Goal setting presented and acted on; testing; personal code of arms (students list their strengths and produce evidence of them through pictures and descriptions); definition of family, and the Challenge group as family; Georgia state laws (a discussion); discussion of the juvenile system, and where they are placed in the system (and where they will go if they keep on screwing up); court-related words and definitions.

Day Four
Visit to the Milledgeville Prison (this is a 10 point day trip).

Days Five and Six
Debrief of prison; written commitment to Challenge; games; quiz; journal-keeping introduction and practice; goal contract.

Days Seven to Ten
Prepare for 4-day ropes course trip: issue camping gear; shop for food; cook; set up camp; play games; low elements (Trust Fall/Spotting Sequence, Tension Traverse, Wild Woosey, Nitro Crossing, Prouty's Landing, Mohawk, Wall, etc., stressing group activities). Debrief every activity after it has been completed. Prepare for high elements, then do them: Cat Walk, Inclined Log to Two-Line Bridge, Dangle Duo, Zip Wire, Pamper Pole. Last day pack up to go home, after framing the next sequence and Debriefing the whole experience.

Days Eleven to Twenty-one
Debrief trip, hand in homework; phone interviews, including

role-playing; personal skills and abilities exercise leading up to personal references and implications of having a record; discuss interview techniques, and role play interviews: one secretary, one boss, one person to be interviewed as a job of their choice. This is all lead-up to an actual job interview (it is practice, but done in a real setting with a real employer). Discussion of a living budget (all the issues regarding cost of living). Discussion of food chains, along with definitions and quizzes. Day Sixteen is a family day (½ day): families are welcome to join in games and Initiatives beginning with the Trust Fall/Spotting Sequence. After the Trust Falls, staff will be meeting with parents and their child for family conference. Biology collection nets, continued discussion of the food chain, continued use of the journal. Voter registration forms. Loan application issues (complete loan application in pairs). Pond study and marsh walk (students fill out a work sheet and keep an observation journal). Study the Georgia state map. Family planning situations: several days of discussion. Compass walk, map and compass instruction. Preparation for backpacking trip (clothing, food), divide into groups of 3–4, then spell out tasks.

Days Twenty-two to Twenty-six
Take backpacking trip. Living together, camping, cooking,

traveling, group discussion time, free time, and assignments and journals. Continual review and setting of goals and the daily compilation of points is practiced. Given time, the last mile of the hike is done as a solo. Students begin hiking in 10-minute intervals with staff members going in the beginning, middle, and end. Students are given assignment of answering questions about themselves and the group (the essay is due on Day Twenty-seven of the course).

Days Twenty-seven to Thirty
Debrief trip, hand in essays, journals, and lists. Plan and put on the graduation banquet. Conduct a City Search. Conduct a community service project. Review all goals, and set spiral goals. Go over academics: math, spelling. Fill out "values"

worksheets. Discuss peer pressure and being able to say no; that trust is something that will have to be earned back; priorities of grades, sports and jobs (time management). Do the Fallout Shelter exercise. Final testing. Wrap up the goals. Final group discussion: What students liked and disliked about the program and what each student is worried about concerning being at home and or back at school. The banquet takes place on the last night (graduation).

Follow-up for these students is conducted through interaction with parole officers and school counselors. As stated, many of these players get involved in some way with the Challenge cycle, and are thereby able to carry their relationships over into the daily lives of the students.

Individuals

Our interviews with students, a social worker, and the staff impressed us with the fact that the manner in which the staff conducts "group" is the key element of Challenge. Our observation of the program took place during the fourth week. The first day there, a two-day canoe expedition was planned (you could see the canoes waiting patiently on a trailer outside the window), this while the group was absorbed in five hours of discussion. One and a half hours more were spent around the campfire, after dinner, in the dark, for a total of six and a half hours in one day! The attention of the students was rapt: they stayed "on task," confronting each other, listening, waiting, responding.

The attention of the students was rapt: they stayed "on task," confronting each other, listening, waiting, responding.

Donnie

This example underscores the way the Debriefing process helps keep the group on the "talking" task. Donnie was being threatened with lockup because of his irresponsible attitude. He had failed to bring in his homework.

> *"You don't seem to care about anyone but yourself."*
> *"You want to isolate yourself, be a turtle."*
> *"You wait for people to take care of you."*
> *"You gotta help yourself before we can help you."*

These were all comments from the kids.

The leader: *"What can you do to help the group?"*
Silence from Donnie, and thought. "Finally: *I want to be part of the group...and get help from you. I don't want to go to Augusta [lockup]."*

The leader: *"What is the best thing we can do for Donnie? We have to decide."*

Cindy: *"Have a detail to do every day."*

Laverne: *"Let him go on the canoe trip…how is he going to act? Watch him. If he blows his chance, we must lock him up."*

Buddy: *"If this canoe trip, and the two days after…this could help him…he could change."*

A basis for their decision is seen in this statement: *"The group can still help Donnie, and Donnie can still use the group."*

Trish: *"The group can do a little more, but I'm afraid that you will forget and mess up, out of habit. You should go to a group home after Challenge, because you don't get the rules from your own home."*

Everyone agrees: *"This is the last chance. Straighten up your act."*

One hour was spent on Donnie. Students not contributing their observations were penalized…by not getting points for the day, and through confrontation by other group members. The students responded to this rigid structure, and you can see by the comment regarding Donnie's need for a group home "because you don't get the rules from your own home" shows how much they want it.

The students called group, so everything was dropped, everyone stood foot against foot in a circle.

Jack

Another incident that gives us a glimpse at the effect of talk time on group was the manner in which the group dealt with Jack's behavior. The incident that brought the issues to the surface was his loss of a canoe paddle, and his excuse that "it sank." He waited awhile before he announced it, diminishing the chance that it would be recovered. During the canoe pullout at the end of the trip he wised off to some men (who had been drinking) nearby. Jim (Jack's canoe partner) got back into his street stuff, and together they put on a show.

The students called group, so everything was dropped, everyone stood foot against foot in a circle. This went on, in the cold and the dark, for one hour:

"It's your attitude, Jack. You just can't do that stuff."

"That's what you'll be doing out on the street."

"You don't seem to care. We were scared of those guys."

"We coulda all been shot."

They got into it with Jim, also:

"That's the old Jim, doin' that jive street stuff."

"You're supposed to be a leader. What ya doin', following Jack like that?"

The next day, in the classroom, during the Debrief of the trip, Jack continued to be resistive. You could see it by the "cut of his eyes" according to one of the leaders, and by his sarcasm. That night the leaders decided to put him into lockup, but wanted the students to take the action. They got their wish: By a vote of 9-12, they removed Jack from the program (no chance of return, it was too late in the program). They told him he would be considered for the new cycle starting in January. He had to stick out the day, pack his stuff, and head off to Atlanta with a counselor where he was admitted to a secure facility.

This example illustrates the value of actual consequences to group decisions, and the value of students having real options. The threat is backed up by action, giving a potency to the kids and the program. Jack is also given a real option which he will lose if he continues to "slide": He knows, from four weeks of hard group work, what he needs to change, and his peers have told him time and again about it. There is clarity.

Because "Youth at Risk" kids don't know how to act, they must be put in situations where they can learn how to act. Because Jack trusted the group he had a chance of accepting what they were saying. Cause and effect. "If I correct these specific behaviors, I will be able to succeed. If I don't, I will be back on the street, and back in lockup." Jack was a shaken, serious boy who entered the secure facility in Atlanta. He took time to work this over, and came back and completed the next cycle. He is back in school, and will be working for Challenge during the summer on a federally funded construction project.

Trish

Trish was a similar case. She experienced 72 hours of lockup at the beginning of the course because the group decided she was out of control (cursing, belligerence on the ropes course). She said, "I hated it at first, and I hated them. When I got to lockup, they gave me a Bible, and I did a lot of thinking about my past. I settled down. Now, I see that these kids were trying to help me." Trish seemed sincere in this statement, and the counselors backed it up by saying that Trish had greatly improved and was in much better control since that experience.

Denise

Lockup is not the only prod that motivates talk time. So is a sense of safety, and trust. On a backpacking trip, Denise was giving all kinds of hints that she was having relations with her father. Finally, because the group was a safe place for her, she responded to their urging that she talk about it. She had been

"I hated it at first, and I hated them. When I got to lockup, they gave me a Bible, and I did a lot of thinking about my past. I settled down. Now, I see that these kids were trying to help me."

having a good experience on the trip, trying new things, feeling freed up, and, as it turns out for so many kids, the freedom that comes from living away from home. The kids were supportive, and able to make her feel comfortable. This is because of similar abusive experiences that they'd had. "This has happened to me." She had been allowing this thing to go on because she was getting what she wanted: a car. But it had been a heavy burden on her, and she was relieved to be able to let go of it. The staff subsequently arranged a family meeting (in company with a Social Worker). The father denied it at first, but his protestations faded. A referral was made for the family to receive counseling.

Tom

Tom, with an extremely low I.Q., had been kicked out of school at 15 because he was incorrigible. He sucked his thumb, drooled, and could not print his name. He would cuss out the other students, and spit at them. His case was made a group issue, and the other members began to be patient and supportive of him. The kids would take care of him, treating him like a little brother during the activities. They made an agreement not to laugh at him anymore. When it came to dealing with his cussing, they decided to put him out of the group for awhile and do cleanup type duties. Tom hated this, "cause he wasn't with his friends." An exciting breakthrough came when he learned how to write his name—*in the sand*—on the beaches of Cumberland Island. He responded to that soft and forgiving medium just as he had responded to doing the other activities.

Fletcher

The group's response to behavior in a problem-solving manner is seen in this example by Kathy Dubois, one of the Challenge group leaders (taken from an article published in the Project Adventure newsletter, *ZipLines*):

"Fletcher glanced at life occasionally and only through the curves of his eyes. When you looked at him, he quickly turned away and hid to the best of his ability. He never spoke up, or even asked questions. 'Yeah' or 'Neah' was the best response we got.

"At times we waited in group for an hour or more for Fletcher to answer a question. Sitting in the center of attention while nine other kids angrily confronted him, Fletcher would hold his tongue rather than risk the embarrassment of saying something stupid. And so Fletcher's behavior continued through the first week and a half.

"If I could pinpoint a time when Fletcher began to change, it would have been during the three days we spent at the ropes course. Watching him over time was an interesting chronology to follow. Day one of the ropes course ended with our trust sequence. During the Trust Fall, the group had to stop between every person to confront Fletcher. He was laughing and walking away during the activity. I didn't know if we'd be able to continue.

"That night we played some Initiative games after dinner and I believe the turning point for Fletcher came at this time. The kids were playing Blindfold Line-up by Number. We gave everyone a number and told them to begin. Fletcher started laughing; we watched closely. Every time someone tapped their number into Fletcher's hand, he tapped the same number back (rather than his own). After this continued for a while, we stopped the game. The group angrily confronted Fletcher and frankly, so did we. To watch Fletcher was to watch a hermit crab pulling back in its shell, curling in each leg.

"While the group decided on Fletcher's consequence, we [the staff] withdrew. We knew that Fletcher was in special education classes in school. Did he understand the game? We thought not. Being staff, we decided to confront Fletcher with this, and the group caught on quickly. Because Fletcher frequently did not understand what was going on, he acted silly to cover up feeling stupid. By the end of the evening, the group [with a little help and direction], decided on two plans for Fletcher. The first was he needed to ask when he didn't understand something. And second, after directions for an assignment or a game were given, the group needed to ask Fletcher if he understood and would he repeat the directions. This was how the group decided they could help Fletcher help himself.

"Sounds simple, yet it was a turning point for Fletcher and his involvement with the group. The second day on the ropes course, Fletcher's goofing off decreased. He usually stood to one side alone until someone in the group gave him a specific task or confronted him. However, now he occasionally chimed in, never becoming the 'spotlight speaker.' Fletcher was involved.

"We were back in the classroom for the next week and a half. Fletcher was beginning to take his school work more seriously and speak up more. His voice was both clearer and louder.

"We returned to the ropes course the following week...the day before we left to go on our backpacking trip. The group started on the Mohawk Traverse and at this point in the group's development, they were able to complete it in an hour and a half. Fletcher, because of his excellent balance, was a key person in helping others across the wire. He was one of the first across and a high point for me was watching Fletcher hustle back to spot others. His encouraging comments were loud and clear.

"I'll always remember his first words when he came down...'Wait for me, you guys. I want to help.' He could hardly get himself unclipped fast enough."

"Later on, Fletcher and his partner finished the Dangle Duo with apparent ease. I'll always remember his first words when he came down...'Wait for me, you guys. I want to help.' He could hardly get himself unclipped fast enough.

"The following day, we left for Cumberland Island. Fletcher earned the highest points for three out of the four days we backpacked. The changes he had made were amazing and I knew when Fletcher would approach someone to ask help; with directions or adjusting his pack, that these were things he would not have done four weeks earlier.

"We awarded Fletcher the Most Improved Person trophy at our final banquet. This was after I gave him the WRAT spelling test which everyone took on Day One and on the Last Day. He spelled two words correctly the first day, and two correctly the second time. However, on Day One Fletcher attempted only two words. On the Last Day Fletcher tried all 46...even *pusillanimous*.

"I realize that not everyone changes as dramatically as Fletcher did. Others improve in more subtle ways and some don't change at all."

Conclusions

Project Challenge is about the mixture of Adventure experience with a large amount of incredibly detailed talk time. No stone is left unturned (that is to say, even the most minimal behaviors are dealt with). Without this approach to Debriefing, the issues around the lockup decisions would not have been as clear, and students would not have had such an investment in the course and in each other. In fact, their approach to Debriefing epitomizes "Debriefing as Initiative." They know why they are in the group, and that the issues being worked on are extremely important for how they are going to lead their lives. That's why the canoes sat on the trailer outside the window during the pre-trip Briefing and no one mentioned their use, or asked "When are we gonna go?"

APPENDICES

Appendix A

Evaluations

Evaluation

Adventure programs in Hamilton, Gloucester, Manchester, Massachusetts were evaluated from 1980–1983 by a summative evaluation management system. The test results demonstrate positive movement on the control goal of the ABC program, the "improvement of self-concept." The Hamilton, Gloucester and Manchester evaluations were focused on year-long Adventure Based Counseling groups ranging from elementary to high school. These programs were evaluated in accordance with funding guidelines of the U.S. Department of Education's Title IV-C grants aimed at developing demonstration projects to improve local educational practices. Formative evaluations were conducted by Project directors William Cuff and Paul Radcliffe during Year One. Summative evaluations were completed during Years Two and Three by Dr. Marcus Lieberman and Edward Devos, Department of Moral Education, Harvard University. Concurrent with these evaluations, the programs were reviewed by the Massachusetts State Department of Education and subsequently awarded validation status as model educational programs with proven effectiveness.

Evaluation Design

A quasi-experimental design was employed which included pre- and post-testing of both the Adventure Based Counseling students and a control group. Separate analyses were performed for upper grade students and lower grade students. The respective sample sizes for the two levels were: 54 experimental and 58 control group students in Grades Six through Ten, and 51 experimental and 27 control group students in Grades Three through Five. The sample size for the follow-up evaluation during year three consisted of 50 experimental students and 26 control group students from the same grade levels. Program participants and the comparison group consisted of special education students who had been formally evaluated and recommended for participation in counseling. Group assignment was based upon voluntary participation decisions by parents following presentations describing the program.

While a volunteer effort may be in operation, it was the parents, not the students, who ultimately volunteered. The suitability of the comparison groups is further suggested by their similarity to the experimental groups on pre-tests (see Tables 1–3). It should be noted that while similar, the comparison groups were somewhat better off before the intervention than the Adventure Based Counseling groups. Such a situation, often encountered when seeking a comparison group for evaluating ameliorative programs, stands as an obstacle to evidencing program effectiveness. The positive results to be reported are all the more striking in this light.

Instrumentation

Enhancing self-concept is the most basic of all the purposes of the Adventure Based Counseling program. Commensurate with this view, the primary evaluation instruments employed were the Tennessee Self-Concept Scale (developed by Dr. William H. Fitts), and the Piers-Harris Children's Self-Concept Scale. A secondary instrument administered in the evaluation study was a Student Attitude Inventory developed by the Center for Urban Education.

The Tennessee Self-Concept Scale is a widely used instrument with desirable psychometric properties. This self-administered test is composed of 100 self-descriptive statements to which the subject responds as being like or unlike her/himself. It is intended for individual or group administration of subjects at least 12 years old with a sixth grade reading level. The manual provides extensive information concerning construct validity, discriminant validity and content validity. The test/retest reliability for the scales used in the evaluation range from 0.80 to 0.92 with a median reliability of 0.89.

The Clinical and Research Form (form c and r) was used in this evaluation study. This form provides a number of measures including response defensiveness, a total score, and self-concept measures that reflect "What I am," "How I feel," and "What I do," with scales such as identity, self satisfaction, behavior, physical self, moral-ethical self, personal self, family self and social self. This form also yields additional scores with six empirical scales in number of deviant signs, general maladjustment, psychosis, personality disorder, neurosis, and personality integration.

The Piers-Harris Children's Self-Concept scale developed by Dr. Ellen V. Piers and Dr. Dale B. Harris is another widely used instrument. By contrast, the Piers-Harris requires a Third Grade reading level and was used with lower grade students in the study. The test provides a percentile and stanine score of the subject's self-concept compared with the normative group. In addition, six subscale scores in behavior, intellectual and school status, physical appearance and attributes, anxiety, popularity, and happiness and satisfaction can be obtained. Reliability estimates, based upon internal consistency, are above 0.85 for the group with which it was used. Test/re-test reliability is above 0.75. The manual provides

ample information regarding the instruments validity and reliability as well as the administration and interpretation of the scale. The psychometric properties reported above, however, only apply to the total score whereas the psychometric properties of the subscales or cluster scores have yet to be established.

Information relevant to tests, manuals, scoring and costs for the Tennessee Self-Concept Scales and the Piers-Harris Children's Self-Concept Scale can be received by writing to:

Western Psychological Services
12031 Wilshire Blvd.
Los Angeles, California, 90025

In an effort to assess student's attitudes toward school, teachers, and classmates a Student Attitude Inventory was administered to all students in both levels. Although the psychometric properties of this instrument are not yet established, the information yielded was valuable principally for its descriptive potential. The inventory consists of 21 easily read questions which require a forced choice response from the respondent. Additional information regarding this inventory and specific descriptive statistics and results for each of the items as used in the study can be obtained by writing to Project Adventure, Inc.

Results and Discussion

The Adventure Based Counseling program's claims of effectiveness were that:

- Students completing the program will significantly increase their self-concept by participating in a series of challenging activities that motivate them to venture beyond previously set limits.
- Students will learn to respect and support each other by working in racially, culturally, sexually, economically, so-

cially, and physically diverse groups to solve problems so that group members must utilize their combined skills in arriving at a solution.

Results: Significant Increase in Self-Confidence

TABLE 1 shows the mean scores for all subjects in each group during the 1981–82 study for the "positive Scores" of the Tennessee Self-Concept Scales. These scores are described in the manual as follows: Total Positive: This is the most important single score on the counseling form. It reflects the overall level of self esteem. Persons with high scores tend to like themselves, feel that they are persons of value and worth, have confidence in themselves, and act accordingly. People with low scores are doubtful about their own worth; see themselves as undesirable; often feel anxious, depressed, and unhappy; and have little faith or confidence in themselves.

Adventure Based Counseling students significantly increase their Total Positive score compared to the control group.

Positive Identity: These are the "what I am" Items. Here the individual is describing his basic identity; what he is as he sees himself.

Adventure Based Counseling students significantly increase their Positive Identity score compared to the control group.

Positive Self Satisfaction: This score comes from those items where the individual describes how he feels about the self he perceives. In general this score reflects the level of self satisfaction or self acceptance.

Adventure Based Counseling students significantly increase their Positive Self Satisfaction score compared to the control group.

Positive Behavior: This score comes from those items that say "this is what I *do*, or

this is the way I *act*." Thus this score measures the individual's perception of his own behavior or the way he functions.

Adventure Based Counseling students significantly increase their Positive Behavior score compared to the control group.

Positive Physical Self: Here the individual is presenting his view of his body, his state of health, his physical appearance, skills, and sexuality.

Adventure Based Counseling students significantly increase their Physical Self score compared to the control group.

Positive Moral Ethical Self: This score describes the self from a moral-ethical frame of reference; moral worth, relationship to God, feelings of being a "good" or "bad" person, and satisfaction with one's religion or lack of it.

Adventure Based Counseling students significantly increase their Moral Ethical Self score compared to the control group.

Positive Personal Self: This score reflects the individual's sense of personal worth, his feeling of adequacy as a person and his evaluation of his personality apart from his body or his relationships with others.

Adventure Based Counseling students significantly increase their Positive Personal Self score compared to the control group.

Positive Family Self: This score reflects one's feelings of adequacy, worth, and value as a family member. It refers to the individual's perception of self in reference to his closest and most immediate circle of associates.

Adventure Based Counseling students significantly increase their Positive Family Self score compared to the control group.

TABLE 1
Tennessee Self Concept Scales:
the "Positive Scores"
1981–1982

Variable	Group[a]	Pretest[b]	Posttest[c]	Adjusted Posttest[c]	Adjusted Gain	Adj. F-Value
Total Positive	Exp	306.8 (28.1)	347.4 (26.1)	325.5	+45.7	80.81*
	Cont	321.5 (37.7)	322.8 (34.9)	317.4	-4.1	
Positive Identity	Exp	112.7 (12.2)	123.3 (10.7)	124.3	+11.6	34.62*
	Cont	115.9 (12.2)	116.4 (11.5)	115.3	-.6	
Positive SelfSatis	Exp	95.7 (12.7)	111.0 (11.9)	114.2	+18.5	62.43[a]
	Cont	104.0 (16.5)	104.3 (16.0)	101.0	-3.0	
Positive Behavior	Exp	98.5 (9.5)	113.1 (8.5)	114.2	+15.7	93.44*
	Cont	101.5 (13.1)	102.1 (12.1)	101.0	-.5	
Positive Physical Self	Exp	65.3 (6.7)	73.4 (6.4)	74.0	+ 8.7	67.30*
	Cont	66.9 (9.0)	66.8 (8.2)	66.3	- .6	
Positive Moral/Ethical Self	Exp	59.2 (6.4)	65.8 (5.6)	67.1	+ 7.9	48.95*
	Cont	62.8 (8.5)	63.0 (8.2)	61.6	-1.2	
Positive Personal Self	Exp	60.7 (8.6)	72.1 (6.2)	72.8	+12.1	79.08*
	Cont	63.4 (9.1)	64.2 (7.9)	63.5	+.1	
Positive Family Self	Exp	61.3 (8.4)	66.6 (8.2)	68.0	+ 6.7	13.73
	Cont	64.9 (10.3)	65.4 (9.8)	64.0	-.9	
Positive Social Self	Exp	60.3 (7.1)	69.5 (6.2)	70.5	+10.2	70.61*
	Cont	63.4 (7.8)	63.3 (7.9)	62.3	-1.1	

Notes

a. The size of the experimental group (Exp) is 55.
   The size of the control group (Cont) is 53.

b. The group means; standard deviations are noted in parentheses.

c. Group means adjusted for pretest scores.

d. The F-statistic has 1 and 105 degrees of freedom for all analyses.

  * $p < .001$

Positive Social Self: This is another "self as perceived in relation to others" category but pertains to "others" in a more general way. It reflects the person's sense of adequacy and worth in his social interaction with other people in general.

Adventure Based Counseling students significantly increase their Positive Social Self score compared to the control group.

TABLE 2 shows the mean scores for all subjects in each group during the 1981-82 study for the "Empirical Scales" of the Tennessee Self Concept Scale. They are described in the manual as being derived from item analyses used to differentiate known diagnostic groups.

General Maladjustment Scale: This scale is composed of 24 items which differentiate psychiatric patients from non-patients but do not differentiate one patient group from another. Thus it serves as a general index of adjustment-maladjustment.

Adventure Based Counseling students become significantly better adjusted than do control group students.

Psychosis scale: This scale is based on 23 items which best differentiate psychotic patients from other groups.

Adventure Based Counseling students significantly improve on the Psychosis scale compared to the control group.

Personality Disorder Scale: The 27 items of this scale are those that differentiated this broad diagnostic category from the other groups. This category pertains to people with basic personality defects and weaknesses in contrast to psychotic states or the various neurotic reactions.

Adventure Based Counseling students significantly improve on this scale compared to the control group.

Neurosis Scale: 27 items which differentiate neurotic patients from other groups.

Adventure Based Counseling students significantly improve on the Neurosis Scale compared to the control group.

Personality Integration Scale: The scale consists of the 25 items that differentiate the Personality Integration Group from other groups. This group was composed of 75 people who, by a variety of criteria, were judged as average or better in terms of level of adjustment or degree of personality integration.

Adventure Based Counseling students showed significant gains on this scale compared to the control group.

The Number of Deviant Signs Score: is the Scales's best index of psychological disturbance. This score alone identifies deviant individuals with about 80 % accuracy.

Adventure Based Counseling students show a significant decrease in deviant signs compared to the control group.

TABLES 3 and 4 illustrate the testing result on the Tennessee Self-Concept Scale during follow-up evaluation completed in 1982-83. Although none of the self-concept scales evidence statistically significant gains for the experimental group, smaller but consistent gains are demonstrated. Thus, positive treatment effects are noted in 13 out of 15 outcomes. If there really were no difference between experimental and control group gains, we should expect roughly a fifty-fifty split; specifically, 7 to 8 analyses favoring the experimental group and 7 to 8 favoring the non-treatment control group. If the subscales were independent, the probability of 13 out of 15 outcomes being in the hypothesized direction is only 0.00412.

There is a remarkable similarity between the treatment effect (difference between ex-

TABLE 2
Tennessee Self Concept Scales:
the "Empirical Scales"
1981–82

Variable	Group[a]	Pretest[b]	Posttest[b]	Posttest[c]	Adjusted Gain	Adj. F-Value[d]
General Maladjust.[e]	Exp	84.6 (8.7)	94.4 (8.4)	95.9	+11.3	31.51*
	Cont	89.1 (11.5)	90.1 (10.5)	88.6	-.5	
Psychosis	Exp	54.2 (7.0)	48.5 (5.0)	48.0	-6.2	20.88*
	Cont	52.5 (6.3)	50.8 (5.4)	51.3	-1.2	
Personality Disorder[e]	Exp	59.1 (8.3)	69.6 (7.2)	71.0	+11.9	69.68*
	Cont	65.5 (12.2)	65.3 (11.0)	62.8	-2.7	
Neurosis[e]	Exp	75.8 (11.1)	86.1 (8.8)	87.3	+11.5	50.92*
	Cont	79.4 (11.6)	79.3 (10.5)	78.2	-1.2	
Personality Integration	Exp	7.0 (3.5)	10.8 (3.2)	11.0	+ 4.0	30.51*
	Cont	7.9 (3.3)	8.5 (3.1)	8.3	+.4	
No. of Deviant Signs	Exp	29.2 (17.6)	12.3 (9.3)	11.1	-18.1	14.13*
	Cont	22.5 (16.2)	17.4 (13.9)	18.6	-5.9	

Notes

a. The size of the experimental group (Exp) is 55.
   The size of the control group (Cont) is 53.

b. Group means; standard deviations are noted in parentheses.

c. Group means adjusted for pretest scores.

d. The F-statistic has 1 and 105 degrees of freedom for all analyses.

e. These scales are inverted, i.e., a positive gain score reflects a beneficial change.

* p<.001

TABLE 3
Tennessee Self-Concept:
The "Positive Scores" (Adventure Based Counseling)

Variable	Group[a]	Pre[b]	Post[b]	Adj Post[c]	Adj RxEffect[d]	F-Value[e]
Total Positive	Exp	323.0 (36.4)	356.5 (28.9)	358.8	+35.2	41.42***
	Cont	329.2 (40.3)	325.9 (47.2)	323.6		
Positive Identity	Exp	115.9 (15.6)	125.7 (11.2)	125.7	+10.2	26.43***
	Cont	115.8 (15.2)	115.5 (15.6)	115.5		
Positive SelfSatis	Exp	104.0 (15.2)	116.0 (12.7)	117.5	+12.3	25.00***
	Cont	108.0 (13.3)	106.7 (18.2)	105.2		
Positive Behavior	Exp	103.1 (11.0)	114.8 (9.2)	115.6	+12.6	44.72***
	Cont	105.4 (16.6)	103.8 (16.3)	103.0		
Positive Physical Self	Exp	66.5 (9.0)	74.7 (6.4)	75.5	+8.1	29.90***
	Cont	69.7 (8.6)	68.3 (9.4)	67.4		
Positive Moral/Ethical Self	Exp	64.8 (8.0)	68.0 (7.2)	67.9	+ 3.1	7.07**
	Cont	64.5 (8.8)	64.7 (10.8)	64.8		
Positive Personal Self	Exp	62.2 (9.5)	71.6 (6.4)	72.2	+8.9	33.34***
	Cont	63.8 (10.4)	63.8 (13.3)	63.3		
Positive Family Self	Exp	65.5 (8.2)	70.1 (7.8)	71.0	+5.5	15.29***
	Cont	67.5 (10.3)	66.3 (11.9)	65.5		
Positive Social Self	Exp	64.0 (7.8)	72.0 (5.6)	71.9	+8.9	60.77***
	Cont	63.6 (9.3)	62.8 (8.6)	63.0		

Notes

a. The size of the experimental group (Exp) is 50. The size of The size of the control group (Cont) is 26.

b. Group means; standard deviations are noted in parentheses.

c. Group means adjusted for pre-test scores.

d. Rx effect = Adj Post (Exp - Adj. Post (Comp).

e. The F-statistic has 1 and 73 degrees of freedom.

*** $p < .001$

** $p < .01$

TABLE 4

TABLE 4
Tennessee Self-Concept Scales
The " Empirical Scales"
(Adventure Based Counseling)

Variable	Group[a]	Pre[b]	Post[b]	Adj Post[c]	Adj Rx Effect[d]	F-Value[e]
General Maladjust	Exp	86.8 (9.3)	96.3 (8.5)	97.4	+10.9f	45.94***
	Cont	89.4 (11.5)	87.6 (13.9)	86.5		
Psychosis	Exp	55.3 (7.8)	49.7 (5.7)	49.9	-3 1	8.67**
	Cont	55.9 (5.7)	53.2 (6.0)	53.0		
Personal Disorder	Exp	67.2 (10.3)	72.2 (8.9)	71.9	+2.6f	4.20*
	Cont	66.6 (11.4)	69.0 (12.5)	69.3		
Neurosis[f]	Exp	80.3 (14.2)	89.1 (9.2)	89.7	+10.5f	24.19***
	Cont	82.7 (14.0)	79.8 (14.3)	79.2		
Personal Integration	Exp	7.8 (3.6)	11.8 (3.4)	12.0	+3.5	28.85***
	Cont	8.2 (3.6)	8.6 (3.5)	8.5		
Number of Deviant Signs	Exp	26.5 (24.3)	12.9 (15.0)	11.7	-13.7	20.02***
	Cont	23.1 (18.7)	24.2 (21.9)	25.4		

Notes

a. The size of the experimental group (Exp) is 50.
   The size of the control group (Cont) is 26.

b. Group means; standard deviations noted in parentheses.

c. Group means adjusted for pre-test scores.

d. Rx Effect = Adj. Post (Exp) - Adj. Post (Comp).

e. The F-statistic has 1 and 73 degrees of freedom.

f. These scales are inverted; i.e., a positive gain reflects a beneficial change.

*** $p < .001$
** $p < .01$
* $p < .05$

perimental and control groups in the 1981–1982 and the 1982–83 data. TABLE 5 shows this consistency.

TABLE 6 shows the mean scores for all subjects in each group during the 1981–82 study for the Piers-Harris Children's Self-Concept Scales. Adventure Based Counseling students show a significant decrease in anxiety compared to the control group. (The scale is inverted, i.e., a positive gain score reflects a beneficial change.)

TABLE 5
Comparison of Two Years' Treatment Effects

	ABC '81–'82	ABC '82–'83
Total Positive	+35.1	+35.2
Positive Identity	+9.0	+10.2
Positive Self-Satisfaction	+13.2	+12.3
Positive Behavior	+13.2	+12.6
Positive Physical Self	+7.7	+8.1
Positive Moral-Ethical Self	+5.5	+3.1
Positive Personal Self	+9.3	+8.9
Positive Family Self	+4.0	+5.5
Positive Social Self	+8.2	+8.9

TABLE 6
Piers-Harris Children's Self-Concept Scales
1981–1982

Variable	Group[a]	Pre-test[b]	Post-test[b]	Adj post[c]	Gain	F-Value[d]
Behavior	Exp	15.0 (3.2)	15.3 (3.6)	15.1	+.1	n.s.
	Cont	13.7 (3.8)	14.1 (3.6)	14.5	+.8	-
Intellect.and School Status	Exp	13.2 (3.6)	14.0 (4.1)	14.0	+.8	n.s.
	Cont	13.0 (3.9)	12.6 (4.5)	12.7	- .3	
Phys. Appearance & Attributes	Exp	7.9 (2.6)	8.3 (3.2)	8.1	+.2	n.s
	Cont	7.2 (3.1)	7.3 (3.3)	7.8	+.6	
Anxiety	Exp	8.8 (2.7)	9.8 (2.7)	9.7	+.9	3.95*
	Cont	8.5 (2.4)	8.6 (2.5)	8.8	+.3	
Popularity	Exp	7.6 (3.0)	8.5 (3.0)	8.5	+.9	n.s.
	Cont	7.5 (2.7)	8.0 (2.5)	8.0	+.5	
Happiness and Satisf.action	Exp	7.2 (1.9)	7.4 (2.1)	7.3	+.1	n.s.
	Cont	6.7 (2.3)	7.1 (1.7)	7.3	+.6	
Total	Exp	59.3 (12.9)	62.3 (15.6)	61.7	+2.4	n.s.
	Cont	56.5 (14.0)	57.9 (13.7)	59.1	+2.6	

Notes

a. The size of the experimental group(Exp) is 50. The size of the control group (Cont) is 27.
b. Group means; standard deviations are noted in parentheses.
c. Group means adjusted for pre-test scores.
d. The F-statistic has 1 and 74 degrees of freedom for all analysis.
* $p > .05$

Student Attitude Inventory

As indicated earlier, the Student Attitude Inventory was also administered to all students. However, because the psychometric properties of this instrument have not been established, the following results should be construed as suggestive rather than conclusive. Analyses of the responses to each test item in the pre- and post-testing showed significant positive movement with students in the experimental group while the control group's responses usually showed no change. Some items that yielded the most dramatic information worth noting are:

Item 9: *I learn*
- □ *A. More in school than I do in any other place.*
- □ *B. More in school than I do in most places.*
- □ *C. Less in school than I do in any other place.*

Nearly 41% of the Adventure Based Counseling students upper grade students indicated learning "less in school than…any other place" at the time of the pre-test. None of the respondents chose that category at the time of the post-test. The comparison group evidenced an 8.1% increase in that category.

Item 12:
- □ *A. I like school.*
- □ *B. I don't like school.*

Just over one-half (53.7%) of the Adventure Based Counseling upper grade students reported liking school at pre-test. Nearly 80% responded positively at post-test. The comparison group, by contrast, showed a small negative change. In the lower grades, both the experimental and control groups indicated more favorable attitudes towards school at pre-test, and both groups registered gains over the year. There was a 14% increase in the Adventure Based Counseling group and a 7% increase in the Comparison group.

Item 14:
You hear students say, "I have a good

teacher." "I have a strict teacher." Think of all the teachers you ever had. Put a check mark against the word that describes them.
- □ *A. Friendly*
- □ *B. Unfriendly*

The upper grade experimental students perceived teachers as friendlier over the course of the year; a more negative change was observed in the comparison group.

Item 18:
The things I learn in school are a lot of junk and will not help me when I get out.
- □ *A. Yes*
- □ *B. No*

The upper grade experimental students showed a more positive attitude toward the value of their education. At pre-test more than 20% of these students ascribe no value to their education; at post test none chose that category. The comparison group displayed slightly greater disaffection over the year.

Item 19:
If I could get my working papers right away, I would get them right away and start working.
- □ *A. Yes*
- □ *B. No*

At pre-test, 63% of the upper grade experimental group of students indicated that if they could, they would get their working papers immediately and start working. At post-test, under 21% made this response. The comparison group showed nearly a 30% increase in this response over the year.

Conclusion

To review, tables 1-6 are for the ABC groups in the towns of Hamilton, Gloucester, and Manchester, Mass. These groups met once per week for the school year and followed the procedures for ABC groups as outlined in Chapter 8, SCHOOLS. The results of the Tennessee Self-Concept Scale and the Piers-Harris Children's Self Concept Scale tests demonstrate movement on the control goal of the ABC program, the improvement of self-concept. More specifically, according to the Tennessee, significant improvements were made in self confidence, identity, self satisfaction, behavior, physical self, moral-ethical self, personal self, family self and social self. The "Empirical Scales" of the Tennessee (they are derived from item analyses used to differentiate known diagnostic groups), show significant improvements in adjustment, psychosis, personality disorder, neurosis, and personality integration scales, and a decrease in deviant signs. The Piers-Harris shows a significant decrease in anxiety. The Student Attitude Inventory showed an increase in attitudes toward learning in school, liking school, teachers, value of education, and desire to stay in school as opposed to starting work.

Appendix B

Activitities Selection Chart
including
The Trust Fall/Spotting Exercise Sequence

Activities Selection Chart

Almost all of the following activities come from either Project Adventure's *Cowstails and Cobras*, *Silver Bullets* (written by Karl Rohnke), and Karl's own newsletter publication *Bag of Tricks*. However, some others come from *The New Games Book*, *More New Games*, *Initiative Games*, *The Cooperative Sports and Games Book*, *100 Ways to Enhance Self-Concept In The Classroom*, and *Values Clarification*.

For ease in reference, the various activities are listed with the appropriate page number from the books in which the activities can be found. An asterisk appears next to certain activities that are more specifically described in the last section. Please note that *Cowtails and Cobras* is out of print, soon to be replaced by *Cowtails and Cobras II*. Though most of the activities will be included in the new publication, the page numbers are not available at this time. The publication details for each of these books is included in the bibliography of *Islands of Healing*.

It is important to note that Trust Fall and Spotting activities are fundamental to all other activities listed. For this reason, we have included a brief section on them following the charts.

The objectives and characteristics for each of these categories are described fully in Chapter 5, **Activities Sequencing.**

Ice Breaker/ Acquaintance Activities

Objective:

To provide opportunties for group members to get to know each other and to begin feeling comfortable with each other through activities, Initiatives and games that are primarily fun, non-threatening and group-based.

Features:

- Fun is a major component.
- Group members interact in a non-threatening manner.
- Success-oriented; tasks can be easily accomplished with minimal amount of frustration.
- Requires minimal verbal interaction and decision-making skills.

Ice Breaker/Acquaintance Activities

Cowstails and Cobras
Add on Tag (103)
Aerobic Tag (100)
Balance Broom (18)
Candle (15)
Carabiner Walk (78)
The Clock (21)
Cobra (12)
Duo Sit (14)
Goldline Joust (103)
Hopping (9)
Impulse (22)
On Belay-Gotcha (82)
Rat Tail (104)
Red Baron Stretch (15)
Ski Pole Slalom (110)
Soccer Frisbee (105)

Bag of Tricks
Frisbee Shootout (5)
Rope Push (15)
Row Boat Stretch (13)
Simplistic Tag (67)
Slow-Motion Push (15)
Triggers Toy (16)

The New Games Book
Catch the Dragon's
  Tail (47)
Fox and Squirrel (59)
Go Tag (53)
Human Pinball (51)
Lap Game (171)
Smaug's Jewels (61)
Standoff (35)

Cooperative Sports and Games Book
Blup Blup Up Up (25)
Frozen Tak (38)
Gesture Name Game (12)
Hop-A-Long (32)
Long Jump (39)
Push 'em Into Balance (40)

Silver Bullets
Balloon Frantic (19)
Boop (49)
Bottoms Up (159)
Circle the Circle (60)
Comet Ball (25)
Double Dutch (156)
Everybody's Up (100)

Fire in the Hole (51)
Frantic (18)
Hoop Relay (61)
Hospital Tag (154)
Mine Field (24)
Moon Ball (31)
Paul's Balls (21)
Physics Phantasy (25)
Popsicle Push-up (166)
Quail Shooter's Delight (63)
Rodeo Throw (59)
Smoke Stack (20)
Tattoo (22)
Texas Big Foot (46)
Toss-A-Name Game (17)
The Turnstile (156)
Two in a Row (156)

------------------------- BY LEVEL -------------------------

Elementary
Blup, Blup, Up, Up
Catch the Dragon's Tail
Comet Ball
Frozen Tag
Gesture Name Game
Long Jump
Mine Field
Physics Phantasy
Rat Tail
Red Baron Stretch
Ski Pole Slalom
Toe Tag

Junior High
Bottom Up
Fox and Squirrel
Hula Hoop Rodeo
Human Pinball
Impulse

Popsicle Push-Up
Rat Tail
Simplistic Tag
Soccer Frisbee
Texas Big Foot

High School
Bottoms Up
Fox and Squirrel
Frisbee Shootout
Hula Hoop Rodeo
Human Pinball
Impulse
Lap Game
On Belay-Gotcha
Popsicle Push-Up
Simplistic Tag
Soccer Frisbee
Texas Big Foot
Toe Tag

All Levels
Add on Tag
Aerobic Tag
Balance Broom
Balloon Frantic
Boop
Bottoms Up
Circle the Circle
Clock
Cobra
Double Dutch
Duo Sit
Everybody's It
Fire In the Hole
Frantic
Go Tag
Goldline Joust
Group Get Up
Group Juggling
Hop-A-Long

Hopping
Hospital Tag
Moon Ball
Name Game Tennis Balls
Paul's Balls
Pin Ball
Push'em into Balance
Quail Shoot
Rope Push
Row Boat Stretch
Slow-Motion Push
Smaug's Jewels
Smoke Stack
Standoff
Tattoo
Triggers Toy
The Turnstile
Two in a Row

De-Inhibitizer Activities

Objective:

To provide a setting wherein group participants are able to take some risks as well as make improvement in commitment and a willingness to appear inept in front of others.

Features:

- Activities involve some emotional and physical risk which may arouse some discomfort and frustration.

- Success and failure are less important than trying and making a good effort.

- Fun activities allow participants to view themselves as more capable and confident in front of others.

- A cooperative and supportive atmosphere tends to encourage participation and increase confidence for all members in the group.

De-Inhibitizer Activities

Cowstails and Cobras
Bump (100)
Dog Shake (12)
Hog Call (87)
Python Pentathlon (20)
Yells (19)

The New Games Book
Bug Tug (121)
Caterpillar (117)
Hagoo (135)
Prui (133)
Skin the Snake (119)

Initiative Games
*Line Ups (27)

Cooperative Games and Sports
Barnyard (26)
Beach Ball Balance (17)
Big Snake (14)
Bump and Team Scoot (51)
Musical Hoops (10)
Sticky Popcorn (20)
Wring the Dishrag (31)

100 Ways to Enhance Self-Concept
Card Game (65)
Guess Who I Am (35)

Silver Bullets
Funny Face (169)
Inch Worm (158)
Samurai (45)

BY LEVEL

Elementary Level
Barnyard
Beach Ball Balance
Big Snake
Bug Tug
Bump and Team Scoot
Card Game
Caterpillar
Dog Shake
Hagoo
Hog Call
Musical Hoops
Skin the Snake
Sticky Popcorn
Wring the Dishrag
Yells

Junior High Level
Skin the Snake

High School Level
Card Game
Dog Shake
Wring the Dishrag
Yells

All
Bump
Funny Face
Guess Who I Am
Hog Call
Inch Worm
*Line Ups
Prui
Python Pentathlon
Samurai

Trust and Empathy Activities

Objective:

To provide an opportunity for group members to trust their physical and emotional safety with others by attempting a graduated series of activities which involve taking some physical and/or emotional risks.

Features:

- Involves group interaction both physically and verbally.

- Generally involves fun, but some fear as well.

- Involves the support and cooperation of group members to care for the safety of others.

- Risk taking occurs at many levels in most of the trust activities.

- The development of trust occurs within the group gradually.

- Trust activities are chosen with the intent of building trust; basic trust activities are initially chosen and can be performed repeatedly to reinforce and insure the safety of group members.

Trust Activities

Cowstails and Cobras
Belaying (29,49)
Blindfold Soccer (104)
Hickory Jump (42)
Trust Drive (42)
*Trust Falls from Perch (27)
Trust Pass (28)
Yurt Circle (21)

Bag of Tricks
Blindfold High Events (16)
Ladder Climb (50)
Life Line (304)
Things You Like To Do (30)
Values Clarification

Cooperative Sports and Games Book
Circle of Friends (42)

Silver Bullets
Blindfold Tube-E-Cide(170)
Compass Walk (176)
Human Camera (177)
Human Ladder (131)
Sherpa Walk (89)
Yeah, But (91)

Unknown Origin
2-Person Trust Fall
3-Person Trust Fall
Airplane
Circle Pass
Elevated Trust Walk
Levitation
Pitch Pole
Rolling Cannonball

BY LEVEL

Elementary
Airplane
Circle of Friends

Junior High
2-Person Trust Fall
3-Person Trust Fall
Blindfold Soccer
Elevated Trust Walk
Hickory Jump
Human Ladder
Ladder Climb
Things you like to do
Trust Dive

High School
2-person Trust Fall
3-Person Trust Fall
Belaying
Blindfold High Events
Blindfold Soccer
Elevated Trust Walk
Hickory Jump
Human Ladder
Ladder Climb
Levitation
Life Line
Pitch Pole
Rolling Cannonball
Sherpa Walk
Things you like to do
Trust Dive
Yeah, But

All Levels
3 Person Trust Fall
Blindfold Compass Walk
   in Groups
Blindfold Compass Walk
   in Pairs
Blindfold Tube-E-Cide
Circle Pass
Circle Pass
Human Camera
Trust Fall from Perch
Trust Pass
Yurt Circle

Communication Activities

Objective:

To provide an opportunity for group members to enhance their ability and skill to communicate thoughts, feelings, and behaviors more appropriately through activities which emphasize listening, verbal, and physical skills in the group decision-making process.

Features:

- Physical activity, verbal interaction and discussion are major components in the sharing of ideas.

- The solving of the problem is the established goal.

- Some frustration is generally evident in the solving of the problem.

- Leadership abilities and skills usually evolve from participants within the group.

- Most activities require at least five members.

Communication Activities

Cowstails and Cobras
* All Aboard (66)
Happy Landings (90)
* Blindfold Polygon (86)
* Tangle (88)
Traffic Jam (87)
Trolley (82)

Bag of Tricks
Rain (81)

The New Games Book
Aura (37)
* Rock-Paper- (109)
   Scissors
Island (127)

Initiative Games
Artist-Clay-Model (14)

Values Clarification
Alligator River (290)
Who's To Blame (374)

**Cooperative Games
and Sports**
Balloon Bucket (53)
Blanketball (53)
Blizzard (27)
Carry On (46)
Partners (12)
Tug of Peace (15)

**100 Ways to Enhance
Self-Concept**
Mirroring (151)
Reflective Listening (75)
Statues (151)

Silver Bullets
The Almost Infinite(131)
   Circle
Body English (35)
Bridge It (127)
Say What (130)
Tusker or Add-On-Tag (42)
The Unholy Alliance (36)
Zig Zag (124)

Unknown Origin
Murder Mystery
Non-Verbal Obstacle
   Course

BY LEVEL

Elementary Level
Alligator River (G-Rated)
Balloon Bucket
Blizzard
Carry On
Happy Landing
Island
Mirroring
Partners
Rain
Statues
Theater Games
Tug of Peace

Junior High Level
The Almost Infinite Circle
Blindfold
Bridge It
Island
Murder Mystery
Sherpa Wald
Who's To Blame

High School Level
Alligator River
Bridge It
Mirroring
Murder Mystery
Rain
Say What
Statues
Two By Four
Who's To Blame

All Levels
Add-On-Tag
All Aboard
Aura
Blanketball
Blindfold Polygon
Body English
Non-Verbal Obstacle
   Course
Reflective Listening
Rock-Paper-Scissors
Sculptor-Model-Clay
T.P.Shuffle
Traffic Jam
Trolley
Tusker
The Unholy Alliance
Wild Woosey
Zig Zag

Decision-Making/ Problem-Solving Activities

Objective:

To provide an opportunity for group members to effectively communicate, cooperate, and compromise with each other through trial-and-error participation in a graduated series of problem-solving activities which range from the more simply solved to the more complex.

Features:

- Physical activity and verbal communication are involved in order to solve stated problems.

- Arousing a higher level of frustration teaches that patience is a virtue.

- Activities demand that group members can demonstrate an ability to listen, cooperate and compromise.

- Leadership roles evolve in the attempt to solve the stated problem or reach the stated goal.

- Trial-and-error approach to learning is most often employed by the group in the problem-solving/decision-making process.

Decision Making/Problem Solving Activities

Cowstails and Cobras
The Amazon (730
The Beam (70)
Board Stretch (75)
Diminishing Load (73)
Electric Fence (70
Emergency (89)
Four Pointer (86)
Hanging Teeter Totter (74)
Infinite Circle (69)

Initiative Run (83)
Jelly Roll (81)
Low Swinging Log (44)
Nitro Crossing (770
Reach for the Sky (680
Stranded (92)
Ten Member Pyramid (81)
Tin Shoe (86)
Vertical Log and Fire (78)
The Wall (71)

Initiative Games
Far Away Island (22)

Silver Bullets
A-Frame (126)
The Diminishing Load
    Problem (138)
Group Juggling (112)
Mohawk Walk (140)
Pick and Choose (77)
Punctured Drum (125)
Ship Wreck (112)
Soft Walk (140)
Spider Web (114)
T. P. Shuffle (110)
T. T. Log (107)
Touch My Can (108)
Two by Four (123)

BY LEVEL

Elementary Level
Far Away Island
Pick and Choose
Ship Wreck.

Junior High Level
A Frame.
Diminishing Load
Group Juggling
Hanging Teeter Totter
Infinite Circle
Nitro Crossing
Oick and Choose
Reach for the Sky
Ship Wreck
Two By Four
The Wall

High School Level
A Frame.
The Amazon
Diminishing Load
Group Juggling
Nitro Crossing
Reach for the Sky
Two By Four
Vertical Log and Tire
The Wall

All Levels
4 Pointer
10 Member Pyramid
The Beam
Board Stretcher
Electric Fence
Emergency
Initiative Run
Jelly Roll
Low Swinging Log
Mohawk Traverse
Pick and Choose
Punctured Drum
Soft Walk.
Spider Web
Stranded
T.P. Shuffle
T.T. Log
Tin Shoe
Touch My Can

Social Responsibility Activities

Objective:

To provide a setting wherein group participants can build upon previous gains in areas of acquaintance, trust, communications, and decision-making, to develop skill in assessing and working effectively with the strengths and weaknesses of individuals in a group.

Features:

- Success in these activities is somewhat dependent upon individuals being able to learn how to support and encourage each other's efforts.

- Activities tend to help participants learn the value of thinking and planning ahead rather than reacting in an impulsive and random manner.

- Activities tend to emphasize that participants in the group communicate and cooperate verbally and physically.

- Activities help participants develop skills in assessing problems and formulating solutions.

- Activities help relate the group to the world "outside" in an empathetic and concerned manner.

- Activities tend to help individuals and the group identify and develop leadership in the group.

Social Responsibility Activities

Cowstails and Cobras
Belaying (29)
Fire Building (118)
First Aid (110)
Initiative Day (124)
Rescue Techniques (111)
Spotting (27)
Winter Safety (112)

Values Clarification
Cave-In Simulation (281)
Fall Out Shelter (287)
"I Urge" Telegrams (264)
Letters to the Editor (262)
Sensitivity Modules (266)
Values in Action (257)

The New Games Book
Siamese Soccer (95)

Unknown Origin
Building A Rope Course
Event
C.P.R.
Community Service
Projects
Environmental Protection
Fundraising Events
Litter Construction

BY LEVEL

Elementary Level
None

Junior High Level
C.P.R.
Cave in Simulation
Fire Building
First Aid

High School Level
Belaying
C.P.R.
Cave-in Simulation
Fire Building
First Aid
Rescue Technique
Sensitivity Modules

All levels
Building Ropes
Community Service
Course Events
Environmental Protection
Fall Out Shelter
Fundraising Events,
"I Urge" Telegrams
Initiative Day
Letters to the Editor
Litter Construction
Projects
Siamese Soccer
Spotting
Values in Action

Personal Responsibility Activities

Objective:

To provide activities and Initiatives of a somewhat more individualistic nature which challenge participants to develop persistence and resistance to frustration in attempting to reach a desired goal.

Features:

- Most activities are "classic" ropes course events that are both the most difficult and trying and the most exciting.

- Activities help group members acknowledge individual and common reactions to fear, stress, and physical limitation.

- Participation in these activities encourages group support for individual efforts.

- Participation helps group members extend the limits of their self-perceived competence and builds self-confidence by successful completion of a difficult task.

- Activities help group members to act on what they have learned about working together, supporting one another, and taking responsibility for one another's safety.

- Many activities require some special equipment and construction and expert advice and training.

Personal Responsibility Activities

Cowstails and Cobras
2 Line Bridge (50)
Balance Beam (52)
Bosun's Chairs (36)
Breathe Easy (91)
Burma Bridge (56)
Commando Crawl (37)
Criss Crotch (46)
Dangle Do (52)
Fidget Ladder (40)
Flea Leap (41)
Giant Swing (53)
High Kitten Crawl (34)
Inclined Log (50)
Log Ladder (45)
Low Swinging Log (44)
Map and Compass (120)
Pamper Pole (58)
Prusiking (115)
Rapelling (60)
Rope Climb (38)
Rope Ladder (134)
Teaching Knots (30)
Tension Traverse (33)
Tire Traverse (75)
Track Walk (23)
Tyrolean Traverse (39)
Wallenda Walk (58)
Zip Wire (63)

The New Games Book
Pina (131)

Values Clarification
Public Interview (139)

Unknown Origin
Commitment Jump
High Criss Cross Rope
Rock Climbing
Tree Climbing

100 Ways to Enhance Self-Concept
Moving In Mindfulness (166)
Public Interview (140)
Self Collage (53)
Spontaneous Movement (168)
Volunteering (207)
Words that Describe Me (195)

BY LEVEL

Elementary
None

Junior High Level
2 Line Bridge
Commando Crawl
High Commitment Jump
Map and Compass
Pamper Pole
Tire Traverse
Wallenda Walk
Zip Wire

High School Level
2 Line Bridge
Commando Crawl
Dangle Do
High Commitment Jump
Map and Compass
Pamper Pole
Tire Traverse
Tyrolean Traverse
Wallenda Walk
Zip Wire

All Levels
Balance Beam
Bosun's Chairs
Breathe Easy
Burma Bridge
Criss Crotch
Fidget Ladder
Flea Leap
Giant Swing
High Criss Cross Ropes
Inclined Log
Low Swinging Log
Pina
Rappelling
Rock Climbing
Rope Ladder
Teaching Knots
Track Walk
Tree Climb

The Trust Fall and
Spotting Exercise Sequence

The Trust Fall sequence and the activity of Spotting are basic material for the psychological and physical well being of individuals, and the emotional development of a group. Though we have tended to refer to it as simply the Trust Fall sequence, it is really part and parcel of the larger issue of spotting, and should be presented as such. The spotting issue is one of the important reality bases of Adventure, for it gives a larger purpose to the trust activities. It is fundamental to Adventure activities as a whole. We recommend that instructors begin this training with a statement to the effect that "If you want to participate in the low and high ropes experiences, you have to pay attention to this initial training."

The sequential approach to Trust Fall activities provides for the gradual development of trust, thereby encouraging greater participation and more profound relationships. The alignment of Trust Fall activities with Spotting concepts provides for a sound, practical relationship that results in a combination of physical and emotional safety.

Please note that following these steps is not necessary for every group, but the concept of moving gradually with your group, especially in counseling situations, is one that we advocate. Decisions of this sort are up to the discretion of the leader.

Step #1: Ice Breaker/Acquaintance
(Here are some sample activities. For additional activities, see p. 273. Selection depends on the needs of the group and time alloted.)
• Warmups and Stretching
• Everybody Up, with the variation of Two-person "get up"
• The Clock
• Add On Tag

• Moonball
• Toe Tag
• Backwards Relay (two teams race each other in a relay, running backwards)

These activities serve to loosen up a group, and get them to touch each other. For many individuals, a simple thing like hand-holding is too much because of either timidity or machismo. That's why the "game" aspect helps you to reach the goal of the group having physical contact without much conscious thought.

Step #2: Deinhibitizer (More sample activities. For additional activities see p. 274.)
• Samurai
• Yells
• Inchworm
• Dogshake
• Lap Game or Circle Sit

These activities ask the group to let go, do something out of the ordinary, and act silly. For example, you can frame Yells by having them imagine that they are lost in the woods. Ask the participants either to go into the center of the group or to sit on the perimeter of the circle. Then get them to scream for help as loud as they can. The debriefing can focus on what an inhibition is, and why it is difficult to let go in front of a group. The same can be said for the yelling that is demanded in the "ritual death" of Samurai Warrior where group members, when "killed" by the gesture of a boffer, must die painfully, dramatically, and loudly (a scream or howl will do).

Step #3: Beginning Trust and Spotting activities
• *Two-Person Mirroring* (one person moves,

the partner duplicates or shadows every move). This can be expanded so that a whole group duplicates the moves of the one person. Unexpected moves should be explained and illustrated in the framing of this activity. This is the beginning point of what Steve Webster (Director of Project Adventure's Ropes Course Construction) calls "Spotter's Knowledge" which is essentially a connection to the climber in terms of concentration, empathy and movement. According to Webster, "Duplicating the movement of the participant forces the spotter to pay attention to what the participant is doing and positions that person to move with any falling action. Spotters need to be able to move in and dampen any motion in a swinging activity, e.g., swinging onto a swinging log, landing on the Seagull Perch, falling off a Rope Swing." Instruction regarding which parts of the body should be protected (the head first, then the chest, stomach and genitals) can be given at this time.

- *Yurt Circle* (the whole group holds hands in a circle, with one person leaning out, the next leaning in, and so forth around the group). It is important to have group balance as a goal, one person not putting too much weight on the persons next to him. Once a balance point is reached, the leader can yell switch, whereby the "outs" will lean in and the "ins" lean out. This exercise can be used to present the concept of group cooperation, getting across the idea at the same time that if one link in the chain breaks, the whole group falls down. This is an important concept in spotting.

- *Rolling* (participants tuck their heads and roll on either one shoulder or the other) is also an important spotting activity, for it teaches individual responsibility relative to the Adventure activities. It is a method of falling that can teach a person to break his fall, rather than fight it and potentially hurt himself. Accompanying this activity is the instruction that one should not fight a fall

too hard. Admit failure, and fall in a safe way, rather than thrash about and try so hard to stay in an activity that the fall is dramatic and out of control.

- *Two-Person Trust Falls* (on the ground) add verbal communication, which is the ground work for spotting (Low Ropes) and belay (High Ropes and Rock Climbing) communication. Besides a physical reassurance by the catcher, who stands behind the faller to remind the faller that the catcher is in fact there and not off somewhere else, there is an exchange of calls between the two. The calls are initiated by the faller and completed the catcher. The sequence goes like this:

Faller: "Are you ready to catch?"
Catcher: "Ready to catch."
Faller: "I'm ready to fall."
Catcher: "Fall away."

The Two-Person Trust Fall leads into the Three-Person Trust Fall, and then follows this sequence:

- *Circle Pass*
- *Levitation*
- *Gauntlet* (this activity is not discussed in any of the literature. The faller walks between two lines of catchers who are lined up facing each other. The catchers should be at the "ready" position. The faller can then surprise group members by falling in their direction at any time. This forces the group to be on their guard, and simulates spotting situations that take place on low cable events such as Tension Traverse, Criss Cross, Wild Woosey, and Mohawk Traverse).
- *Trust Fall from a height*
- *Trust Dive*

According to Webster, it is also important to have "a teaching sequence developed for case spotting." He then quotes the sequence utilized by Stony Acres Outdoor Center, East Stroudsburg, Pennsylvania:

1. Explain concept/meaning of spotting.
2. Demonstrate and explain basic position(s)—stance, arms, hands, and eyes (focus).
3. Practice in controlled, contained context: e.g., Partner Trust Fall, Three Person Trust, Trust Circle, and Two Line Trust Fall (spotters are kneeling).
4. Emphasize relationship of good Spotting to trust.
5. Distinguish between spotting and assisting or helping.
6. Engender pride in becoming a good spotter: Actively promote the attitude and behavior that teasing and joking about not catching someone has no place in Adventure activities.
7. Supervise spotters closely, reminding of proper techniques as needed.
8. Rotate spotters so all have a chance and so all are used to spot appropriate others. (The big people should not end up doing all the spotting.)
9. Two spotters is the minimum number of spotters necessary for any element. Certain elements require more than two. Size, strength, weight, and fatigue also affect minimums. Do not hesitate to require more than the stated minimums in particular situations. Do bear in mind that an overabundance of spotters trying to spot for the same situation can lead to the problem of no one taking her/his job seriously enough because they do not feel their role is important. Make sure that each spotter used really is important to the task at hand. If there are more than enough, then rotate positions and responsibilities.
10. The basic premise in spotting is to offer protection to the individual participating on an activity but it is important to remember that because of unique aspects of ropes course design and the Initiative problems and the variety of terrain that the activities take place on, certain activities may have subtle differences in spotting techniques. These differences should always be carefully explained and looked for.
11. The spotter should be willing to put herself in a potentially risky situation in order to eliminate or minimize injury to another.
12. The spotter should be willing to share in cooperative spotting situations, not trying to do individually what is more easily and safely accomplished by two or more working together.

The psychomotor aspects of Spotting are:

Stance: Balanced, knees flexed to absorb impact, hands up and ready.

Position: Varies with specific elements.

Location relative to participant: Varies with specific elements.

Focus: Eyes constantly on the participant.

Absorbing Force: "Give" with the body, going in the direction of force, or rolling in the direction of force.

If a Low Ropes course is available, and the participants have had adequate training in these events, you should be able to move on to it. Don't hesitate to repeat any or all of the activities at any time. And keep plugging the fact that good spotting is a tangible expression of the Full Value Contract.

Please note that these minimal directions for conducting the Trust Fall/Spotting sequence are not meant as a replacement for more thorough discussions of the individual events that are available in other publications, and for the training received in Project Adventure workshops.

Appendix C
Project Adventure Services and Publications

Services

Project Adventure, Inc., is a national, non-profit corporation dedicated to helping schools, agencies, and others implement Project Adventure programs. Toward that end, the following services are available:

• **Project Adventure Workshops**. Through a network of national certified trainers, Project Adventure conducts workshops for teachers, counselors, youth workers, and other professionals who work with people. These workshops are given in various sections of the country. Separate workshops are given in Challenge Ropes Course Skills, Counseling Skills for an Adventure Based Program, Project Adventure Games and Initiatives, and Interdisciplinary Academic Curriculum.

• **Challenge Ropes Course Construction.** Project Adventure has been designing and constructing ropes courses (series of individual and group challenge elements situated indoors in a gymnasium or outdoors in a grove of trees) for over 15 years. PA Staff can travel to your site and design/construct a course appropriate for your needs and budget.

• **Challenge Ropes Course Source Book.** A catalog service of hard-to-find materials and tools used in the construction of Challenge Ropes Courses. This catalog also contains climbing rope and a variety of items useful to outdoor camping programs.

• **Executive Reach.** Management workshops for business and professional persons. These workshops are designed for increasing efficiency of team members in the workplace. The trust, communication, and risk-taking ability learned in the executive program translate into a more cohesive and productive team at work.

• **Program Accreditation.** The Accreditation process is an outside review of a program by PA staff. Programs that undertake the accreditation process are seeking outside evaluation of their programs with regard to quality and safety. The term accreditation means "formal written confirmation;" these programs are seeking "confirmation" that their programs are within the current standards of safety and risk management. This assurance may be useful for making changes in the program equipment and/or design, and in providing information on program quality to third parties such as administrations, insurance companies, and the public.

Publications

If you would like to obtain additional copies of this book, an order form has been provided on the next page. Project Adventure also publishes several books and pamphlets in related areas. The publications are described below and can be ordered on the same form.

Teaching Through Adventure, *A Practical Approach* suggests ways to use the out-of-doors and the world outside the classroom to broaden and enliven more traditional academic subjects. It gives a brief description of the elements of Adventure Curriculum, describes some examples, and includes a large section on how to develop similar programs in school systems. **$8.50**

Cranking Out Adventure, A Bike Leader's Guide to Trial and Error Touring, is based on seven years of experience with summer bike trips. The book includes such practical information as selection of students, bicycles, routes, and campsites, as well as descriptions of the finer points of "junking" and journal writing. **$4.50**

Going Camping? is a basic guide for teachers taking students camping. This booklet touches on subjects that only a teacher taking students out for the first time can appreciate: ordering the bus, announcing the trip, getting the parents' permission, defining leadership and responsibility. **$3.50**

High Profile. A how-to book on building, belaying, and using indoor ropes course elements. Emphasis is on construction details. Includes climbing walls, rappel areas, tension traverse, trapeze jump, etrier passage, etc. Numerous photographs of construction and participation. **$7.00**

Silver Bullets, A Guide to Initiative Problems, Adventure Games and Trust Activities. This book is our "compleat" guide to all those activities which need few, if any, props. *Silver Bullets* activities (165 in all) have been field-tested, are rated in a humorous way, with many helpful implementation hints. The text is liberally backed up with photos and illustrations. Use to supplement your present program, or to start one. **$14.95**

Bibliography

References

American Heritage Dictionary, 1970, Houghton Mifflin Company, Boston, Massachusetts, p. 1378.

Auden, W.H., 1945, *Collected Poems*, Random House, New York, New York, p. 76.

Bacon, Steven, 1983, *The Conscious Use Of Metaphor In Outward Bound*, Typesmith of Colorado, Denver, Colorado, pp. 5, 10.

Bandura, A., 1977a, *Social Learning Theory*, Prentice-Hall, Englewood Cliffs, New .Jersey.

Bandura, A., 1977b, "Social Learning Theory," *Psychological Review*, Vol. 84, No.2, pp. 191-215.

Bareton, N.L., 1970, "The Architects: Kurt Hahn," *Strive Magazine*, The Abbey Press, London, England, pp. 3-5.

Barich, Bill, Nov.1986, "The Crazy Life," *New Yorker Magazine*, p. 111.

Bettelheim, Bruno, 1950, *Love Is Not Enough*, New York, New York, Avon Books, pp. 51, 225.

Coopersmith, Stanley, 1967, *The Antecedents Of Self Esteem*, W. H. Freeman, Co., San Francisco, California.

Cousins, Norman, 1979, *Anatomy Of An Illness*, Bantam Books, New York, New York.

Csikszentmihayli, Miholyc, 1975, *Beyond Boredom And Anxiety*, San Francisco, 1985, from an article by Mark Havens, 1985, "Adventure Challenge Philosophy," Bradford Woods Papers, Indiana University, p. 22.

Doberman, John, interview in the fall of 1985.

Erikson, Erik, 1950, *Childhood, Youth And Society*, Penguin Books, Limited, London, England, p. 240.

Fitts, William, 1965, 1970, 1971, 1972, "The Tennessee Self Concept Scale," *Counselor Recording and Tests*, Nashville, Tennessee.

Fitts, William, 1970, "Interpersonal Competence: The Wheel Model", *Counselor Recording and Press*, Nashville, Tennessee.

Frankl, Viktor, 1963, *Man's Search for Meaning*, Simon and Schuster, New York, New York.

Garland, Joe, 1978, *The Lone Voyager*, Peter Smith Publishing, Magnolia, Massachusetts.

Glasser, William, 1965, *Reality Therapy*, Harper and Rowe, New York, NY, p. 13.

Harmon, Paul, and Templin, Gary, *Conceptualizing Experiential Education*, a publication of Harmon Associates and Colorado Outward Bound School, Denver, Colorado.

Harris, 1969, *I'm O.K., You're O.K.*, Avon Books, New York, New York, p. 66.

Harris, Bert, interview in the spring of 1986.

Johnson, David W., and Johnson, Frank P., 1982, 1975, *Joining Together* (first edition), Prentice Hall, Englewood Cliffs, New Jersey, p. 410.

Johnson, David W., and Johnson, Frank P., 1987, *Joining Together* (second edition), Prentice Hall, Englewood Cliffs, New Jersey, pp. 390, 394-395.

Lazarus, Arnold, interview in the spring of 1986.

Lazarus, Arnold, 1981, *The Practice of Multimodal Therapy*, Mcgraw-Hill, New York, New York, pp. 4, 33-43, 155-156.

Lentz, Bob, and Smith, Mary, 1976, *Teaching Through Adventure*, Project Adventure, Inc., Hamilton, Mass., pp. 59-66.

Lewin, Kurt, 1944, *Dynamics of Group Action*, Educational Leadership, 1, pp. 195-200.

Lewin, Lippett and White, 1939, "Patterns Of Aggressive Behavior In Experimentally Created Social Climates," *Journal Of Social Psychology*, #10, pp. 271-299.

Marsh, Herbert W. and Richards, Garry E., 1986, "Multidimensional Self-concepts: The Effect of Participation in an Outward Bound Program," *Journal of Personality and Social Psychology, Vol. 50, No. 1.*

Maslow, Abraham, 1962, *Toward A Psychology Of Being*, D. Van Nostrand Co., Princeton, New Jersey.

Medrick, Rick, 1978, *Confronting Passive Behavior Through Outdoor Experience*, Outdoor Leadership Training Seminars, Denver, Colorado.

Miner, Joshua, and Boldt, Joe, 1981, *Outward Bound U.S.A.*, William Morrow and Company, New York City, p. 336.

Mowatt, Farley, 1964, *Never Cry Wolf*, Atlantic Monthly Press, Garden City, New York.

Nussbaum, Gary, interview in the spring of 1987.

Perry, William, interview in 1971.

Perske, Robert, 1972, *The Dignity of Risk of the Mentally Retarded*, National Association for Retarded Children, Arlington, Texas, p. 24.

Quinsland, Larry, K. and Van Ginkel, Ann, 1984, *Association of Experimental Education Journal*.

Rhoades, John, 1972, *"The Problem of Individual Change in Outward Bound: An Application of Change and Transfer Theory,"* unpublished Ed.D. dissertation, U. Of Mass., Amherst, p. 104. This material was taken from *"The Art and Science of Processing Experience,"* a paper by Clifford C. Knapp, Associate Professor of Curriculum and Instruction, Lorado Taft Field Campus, Northern Illinois University, p. 6.

Roethke, Theodore, 1966, *Collected Poems*, Doubleday And Company, Garden City, New York, p. 127.

Rogers, Carl, 1951, *Client-Centered Therapy*, Houghton Mifflin Company, Boston, Massachusetts.

Schweitzer, Claudia, interview in fall of 1985.

Selye, Dr. Hans, March 1978, "On the Real Benefits of Eustress," *Psychology Today*, pp. 60-70.

Sharp, Billy with Claire Cox, 1970, *Choose Success: How to Set and Achieve All Your Goals*, Hawthorne Books, New York, NY.

Shavelson, R. J., and Marsh, H. W., (in press), *On the Structure of Self Concept*. In R. Swarzer, Ed., *Anxiety and Cognition*, Erlham, Hillsdale, New Jersey.

Weber, Richard, 1982, *"The Group: A Cycle from Birth to Death,"* NTL Institute

Woodward, Ted, interview in the fall of 1985.

Important Resource Material

Canfield, Jack, and Wells, Harold C., 1976, *100 Ways to Enhance Self-Concept in the Classroom*, Prentice-Hall, Inc., Englewood Cliffs, New Jersey.

Corey, Gerald, 1985, *Theory and Practice of Group Counseling*, Brooks/Cole Pub. Company, Monterey, California.

Corey, Gerald, and Corey, Marianne Schneider, 1987, *Groups, Process and Practice*, Brooks/Cole Pub. Company, Monterey, California.

Dewey, John, 1938, *Experience and Education*, Macmillan Publishing Co., New York, New York.

Fluegelman, Andrew , 1976, *The New Games Book*, The Headlands Press, Dolphin Books/ Doubleday, Garden City, New York.

Fluegelman, Andrew, 1981, *More New Games*, The Headlands Press, Dolphin Books/Doubleday, Garden City, New York.

Orlick, Terry, 1978, *The Cooperative Sports and Games Book*, Pantheon Books, New York, New York.

Popkin, Michael H., 1983, *Active Parenting*, Active Parenting, Inc., Atlanta, Georgia.

Rohnke, Karl, 1977, *Cowstails and Cobras*, Project Adventure, Inc., P.O. Box 100, Hamilton, Massachusetts 01936. (This book is out of print. Its replacement, *Cowstails and Cobras II*, will be available through Project Adventure, Inc., in 1988.)

Rohnke, Karl, 1984, *Silver Bullets*, Project Adventure, Inc., P.O. Box 100, Hamilton, Massachusetts 01936.

Rohnke, Karl, *Bag Of Tricks*, A Quarterly Newsletter, P.O. Box 77, Hamilton, Massachusetts 01936.

Simon (Sidney B.), Howe (Leland W.), and Kirschenbaum (Howard), 1972, 1978, *Values Clarification*, A and W Publishers, Inc., New York, New York.

Simpson, Benjy, 1978, *Initiative Games*.

Index

Dick Prouty, Jim Schoel and Paul Radcliffe

Dick Prouty is Executive Director of Project Adventure, a position he has held since 1980. Previously he worked for eleven years at Manchester High School (Mass.), teaching Social Studies, directing the Experiential Education program and leading Adventure Based Counseling groups. He was also a Vista Volunteer for two years in New York City. He is a graduate of Brown University (A.B.), Antioch-Putney Graduate School (M.A.T.), and attended The London School of Economics for one year.

Jim Schoel works for Project Adventure in the capacities of program development and training. A founding member of Project Adventure, he taught in an alternative school and led Adventure Based Counseling groups in Gloucester for many years before his return to the Adventure fold. He has also worked for the New York City Urban League Street Academies, and Hurricane Island Outward Bound School. He is a graduate of the University of Washington (B.A.), The Harvard Graduate School of Education (Ed.M.), and spent one year at Union Theological Seminary.

Paul Radcliffe is the Director of Special Programs at Project Adventure and is also involved in program development and training. He is a psychologist with Bachelors and Masters degrees in counseling and psychology from Salem State College. He has also pursued advanced graduate study at Boston University, Northeastern University and the University of Northern Colorado. Prior to joining Project Adventure in 1980, his professional experiences were in teaching, group and individual therapy, and consultation with schools, hospitals and businesses.

To the owner of this book,

      We hope you have found this book helpful. We would like to know as much as possible about your experiences with *Islands of Healing* so that we can take your reaction into consideration for future editions. You can write you comments on this form and mail it to us at Project Adventure, Inc., P.O. Box 100, Hamilton, MA 01936. Many thanks for your help.

1. What did you like most about the book *Islands of Healing*?

2. What did you like least about *Islands of Healing*?

3. If you have an ongoing Adventure program, please describe what effect you think the book will have on your:
• Program design

• Leading

• Briefing/Debriefing

• Other

In the space below (or in a separate letter), please let us know your reaction in general to the book. Were any chapters difficult to understand, or biased toward one point of view, etc.? Do you have any suggestions for future revisions. We'd love to hear from you!